S0-BAM-323

WITHDRAWN

WHAT A YEAR!

BY THE SAME AUTHOR   *Those Rockefeller Brothers*

IN COLLABORATION   *The Private Papers of Senator Vandenberg*

Dear Mr. President

HARPER & BROTHERS, PUBLISHERS, NEW YORK

WHAT A YEAR!

BY JOE ALEX MORRIS

Carl A. Rudisill Library
LENOIR RHYNE COLLEGE

ILLUSTRATED

917.3
M83w

34,825
March 1957

WHAT A YEAR!

Copyright © 1956 by Joe Alex Morris
Printed in the United States of America
All rights in this book are reserved. No part of the book may
be used or reproduced in any manner whatsoever without
written permission except in the case of brief quotations
embodied in critical articles and reviews. For information
address Harper & Brothers, 49 East 33rd Street,
New York 16, N. Y.

FIRST EDITION

B-F

Library of Congress catalog card number: 56–6029

for Clare, who was born that year

acknowledgments

Many of the sources of information used in preparation of this book are mentioned in the text. A basic source obviously has been the daily newspapers and periodicals, and the weekly *Time*, of 1929. Use also has been made of statistical information in *The World Almanac*, *Spalding's Official Guides*, *Historical Statistics of the United States* and official documents published by various governmental departments.

Special thanks are due to my wife for her help and to friends who searched their memories to help fill out the story of 1929; and special mention should be made of two books—*Only Yesterday* by Frederick Lewis Allen, and *The Great Crash, 1929* by Professor John Kenneth Galbraith, whose technical conclusions—as pointed out in the text—have been used as a guide in regard to the stock market operations of 1929. In addition, the accounts of sports events by Paul Gallico of the New York *Daily News*, were an important source of reference.

Other sources of information include:
Middletown, by Robert S. Lynd and Helen Merrell Lynd
Magazine Making, by John Bakeless
Sound and Fury, by Francis Chase, Jr.
Postscript to Yesterday, by Lloyd Morris
Not So Long Ago, by Lloyd Morris
Our Unknown Ex-President, by Eugene Lyons
Chicago, by Dorsha B. Hayes
Detroit, by Arthur Pound
Kings of the Court, by E. C. Potter, Jr.
The Tin Box Parade, by Milton MacKaye

The Last Resorts, by Cleveland Amory
The Great Illusion, by Herbert Asbury
The Tale of Chicago, by Edgar Lee Masters
Since Yesterday, by Frederick Lewis Allen
Beau James, by Gene Fowler
Women Are Here to Stay, by Agnes Rogers
American Mirror, by Halford E. Luccock
The Far Side of Paradise, by Arthur Mizener
Low Man on a Totem Pole, by H. Allen Smith
A. Woollcott, His Life and His World, by Samuel Hopkins Adams
The Big Change, by Frederick Lewis Allen
Man from Abilene, by Kevin McCann
Soldier of Democracy, by Kenneth Davis
The Mark Hellinger Story, by James Bishop
The Aspirin Age, by Isabel Leighton
Call Me Lucky, by Bing Crosby and Pete Martin
Gallico on Sports, by Paul Gallico
Show Biz, by Abel Green and Joe Laurie, Jr.
Vaudeville, by Joe Laurie, Jr.
We Were Interrupted, by Burton Rascoe
The Crack-Up, by F. Scott Fitzgerald
A Library of Popular Music in America, by Sigmund Spaeth
Hollywood, by Leo C. Rosten
Gang Rule in New York, by Craig Thompson and Allen Raymond
Mrs. Astor's Horse, by Stanley Walker
Heywood Broun, by Dale Kramer
The Vicious Circle, by Margaret Case Harriman
The Audion, by Lee De Forest
Autobiography of Lee De Forest
A Conqueror of Space, by Georgette Carneal
Labor Baron, by James Wechsler
The Saturday Review of Literature, 1929
On Active Service in Peace and War, by Henry L. Stimson and
    McGeorge Bundy
A Puritan in Babylon, by William Allen White
The Wasted Land, by Gerald W. Johnson
Adrift on the Land, by Paul Taylor
90 Degrees in the Shade, by Clarence Cason
Forty Acres and Steel Mules, by Henry Clarence Nixon

The Literary Digest, 1929
The Review of Reviews, 1929
Barron's Weekly, 1929
Fortune Magazine
Ol' Rum River, by Ira L. Reeves
America's Sixty Families, by Ferdinand Lundberg
The Saturday Evening Post, 1929
The New Yorker, 1929
Variety, 1929
Collier's Weekly, 1929
Harper's Magazine, 1929
The Atlantic Monthly Magazine, 1929
My America, by Louis Adamic
John L. Lewis, by Cecil Carnes
The Country Gentleman, 1929
Human Geography of the South, by Rupert Vance
Georgia Land Use Problems, by Hartman and Wooten
Pyramids of Power, by Marion L. Ramsey
U. S. Census of Agriculture, 1935
Report of President's Committee on Farm Tenancy
Moody's Manual
Some Southern Mill Workers and Their Villages, by Jennings
    Jefferson Rhyne
Men and Coal, by McAlister Coleman
Filmlexikon, 1948
I Remember Distinctly, by Agnes Rogers
Dry Messiah, by Virginius Dabney
Capital Investments, Brookings Institute
Shares of Upper Income Groups, by Simon Smith Kuznets
The American Mercury
Bernard Baruch, by Carter Field
Bernard Baruch, by William Lindsay White
Bernard M. Baruch, by Harry Irving Shumway
The Night Club Era, by Stanley Walker
Dictionary of American Biography
Encyclopedia of American History, by Richard B. Morris
Abstract of the Fifteenth Census, 1930
The Economic Almanac
Labor Fact Book, Labor Research Association

contents

*Sections of illustrations will be found following
pages 82 and 178*

foreword

This book concerns a year that has come to be regarded as a kind of dividing line in the history of the United States and, for that matter, of a considerable part of the world. It was a year of contrasts—of high achievement and dazzling hopes, of great folly and irresponsibility, of humiliating failure and the smell of fear. But it was more than all that: it was a year of transition. It led out of the roaring, raucous, hell-raising, materialistic and individualistic postwar period and pointed toward an era of tremendous social change. People later would speak of "before 1929" or "after 1929" as Noah's children may have spoken of the days before and after The Flood.

Actually, for Americans busy trying to make a living at the time the transition wasn't so sudden or so clearly defined as it would later seem, in retrospect, to have been. But it was rapid enough and, in the end, it was far-reaching. This book tries to show some of the ways in which we have changed and some of the ways in which we have not changed since 1929. Youngsters who have grown up on easy terms with guided missiles and space ships during the first decade of the Atomic Age may be amused at the crude machines we regarded as mechanical marvels only a little over a quarter-century ago. Oldsters may be reminded of long-forgotten events and say, well, yes—but that isn't exactly the way they remembered it. Nineteen twenty-nine happened to a lot of people in a lot of different ways, but everybody remembers that it happened.

For the most part, the span of a quarter-century between 1929 and 1954 has been used for purposes of comparison, but in some instances other dates have been substituted for various reasons. Statistics, however, are sometimes tricky and cannot always be adjusted to changing conditions. The reader should remember, for example, that the nation's population has increased by forty million since 1929 and that the purchasing power of the dollar has decreased to about half of what it was in 1929. A few brief parts of this book have been written in what might be called semifictional style and are set in special type. The purpose of these sections is to condense the actual experiences of a number of persons into a single episode with several composite characters typical of the period.

The events related in this book occurred, for the most part, in the eleventh year after World War I. This manuscript was completed on the eve of the eleventh year after World War II.

J.A.M.

Guilford, Conn., December, 1955

WHAT A YEAR!

ONE

*. . . . magnificent hope, which, against reason and
knowledge, soars into a heaven of fabulous conviction,
which believes in the miracle and sees it invariably fulfilled.*

—THOMAS WOLFE

JANUARY, 1929

the fabulous year

The First World War was fought in Europe from the summer of 1914 until near the end of 1918, and a decade later, on the eve of the year 1929, the most obvious result of that costly conflict was that two non-European nations were on the way up. The Union of Soviet Socialist Republics, with a new philosophy of world revolution, had grimly survived a series of civil wars, foreign interventions, economic crises and internal conflicts within the ruling Communist party leadership. The United States of America, which before the war was a predominantly agricultural debtor nation, had become a young industrial giant, the world's creditor and a reluctant world power.

It wasn't easy in 1929, the eleventh year after World War I, to foresee what lay ahead—not any easier than it would be in 1956, the eleventh year after World War II, to forecast the future. But a great many Americans were willing to try.

1

2

*Some of the Americans willing to try to guess what lay ahead
could be found at almost any big social gathering in the more
expensive suburbs of a city like New York. They were men who
had to keep their eyes on the ball at the office every working day,
who had to know what was going on everywhere, what was new
today and what would be out of favor tomorrow. And on week
ends they liked to relax , and join in the local social whirl. Take,
for example, the gay crowd that gathered at a large suburban
residence on the last Friday of 1928 for a wedding reception in
honor of a young couple whom we might as well call Mary and
Herbert Browning. Herb was a talented boy from Nebraska who
had attended Princeton and gone into an advertising agency in
New York. And there wasn't much doubt that Mary was as popular
as any girl in the Cloverdale Country Club set, with plenty of
chances to marry since she graduated from Smith College. Actually, they hadn't planned to marry until spring, but Herb had suddenly been offered a big job with an advertising agency in Detroit
and his boss, J. T. Burns, had told him it was too good an opportunity to miss. Herb and Mary talked it over. He had a thousand
dollars in the bank and almost as much more invested in blue-chip
stocks like General Motors and Montgomery Ward, which had
gone up in value since he bought them. Mary was working in a
Fifth Avenue department store for twenty dollars a week, which
wasn't enough to keep her in cigarettes and silk stockings. But she
was fed up with being a career woman and decided she wanted to
go to Detroit with Herb, a decision that was warmly applauded by
her father as well as old J. T. Burns, who took a great interest in
the lives of the young men who worked for him.*

*Even now, in a momentary lull at the reception after Herb and
Mary had cut a slice from the big wedding cake, Old J. T. was
assuring them for the tenth time that their future was bright indeed.*

Anybody, Old J. T. liked to say, anybody who's got his eye on the ball can see that 1929 will be only the threshold of a new era in the United States. An era that doubtless would be even more fabulous than the future already being predicted by some of the country's best thinkers. J. T. had been around for quite a while now and he had seen America move a long way forward since that fellow Woodrow Wilson announced the signing of the armistice—why, that was eleven years ago, my boy!—and there was a lot of high-minded talk about how it was our duty to help spread justice and democracy all over the world. Well, maybe there was something to that. Wilson was a dreamer and things didn't work out for him very well, but plenty had happened to America since 1918—plenty, brother!—and it was only the beginning.

"You'll be an account executive in Detroit, my boy, and the future is wide open. There's no limit to the business horizon in this country. Automobiles? Everybody's got to have one or maybe two. Look at General Motors—going higher every day! Just keep on hitting the ball, my boy."

"Yes, sir. You're right, J. T.," Herb muttered without even listening. He had heard it too often. He knew just what J. T. was going to say next: "My boy, a good advertising man can make people, especially women, buy almost anything. In a few years, everybody will have to have an electric refrigerator. You can convince even a Hottentot housewife that she can't live without one. Everything has been speeded up since the war—airplanes, automobiles, new industrial processes—and now all the benefits are showing up in everyday living, in the kitchen, right here in this living room. Like that six-tube radio over there. Ten years ago nobody would have believed you could hear music or the news over the air—no more than they would have believed you could buy a ticket to fly to Boston in a trimotored Ford airplane. You young people have got the world by the tail, Herb. You can do anything."

Herb nodded, but he wasn't listening. He thought it was about time he got out of his rented morning coat and gray striped trousers and took Mary away from here. He was tired of shaking hands and promising aunts, uncles and former boy friends to take good care of Mary. He was tired of trying to find a nonchalant reply to the pointed remarks of his bachelor friends. And he was especially tired of the young, liberal-minded minister who had discussed with him the theories of Havelock Ellis, unaware to the end that Herb had never read Studies in the Psychology of Sex *and didn't intend to read it.*

Most of the guests, including Old J. T., were now drifting toward the big table loaded with food and a huge bowl of punch, which was mostly champagne that Mary's father's bootlegger had sworn was the real stuff, just arrived from Canada. A bargain at eight dollars a bottle. Mary nodded to Herb and walked toward the stairway, resplendent in a lace veil that had once been worn by her grandmother and a white satin gown that would have shocked grandmother because it dropped in a straight line from her shoulders to just below her knees. Halfway up the stairs, she turned and tossed her bouquet of lilies of the valley to the bridesmaids clustered below.

Herb and his best man, Sam Werner, who was a bond salesman, headed toward the library, where the wedding gifts were on display. Among the silver and chinaware and linens were not a few gadgets that suggested Old J. T. knew what he was talking about. An electric coffee percolator. A toaster that turned over a slice of bread when you opened it. A home movie camera. A set of three cocktail mixers in a leather case. An electric orange squeezer. An electric waffle iron. A little bedside radio. A set of anagrams—they were all the rage. Herb blushed when he saw at the back of the table a little framed sampler that had been made by his aunt: a flower design and the words of the poet, Edgar A. Guest—"It takes a heap o' livin' in a house t' make it home." But outside at the curb

*was the best wedding gift of all, a new five-passenger sedan from
Herb's father. After he and Sam had gone up the back stairs to the
guest room to change their clothes, he pointed out the window to
the new car.*

"Some baby, Herb!" Sam said. "What make?"

*"Oakland. The new model's just out and it must have cost
fourteen hundred buckeroos with those balloon tires and the metal
case for the spare. But she's got sixty-eight horsepower, hydraulic
shock absorbers and a special kind of demountable rim so you
can get a flat off in a hurry."*

*Sam gazed admiringly at the high square top, the leather-
upholstered seats, the fender—on which the spare tire was
mounted in a deep pocket—curving gracefully back to a broad,
rubber-covered running board. Herb already had shed his formal
clothes and was putting on a white shirt with a long-pointed
collar and a blue suit.*

*"You drive Mary and me to the station in the new car," he said
as he fixed the gold collar pin that held his tightly knotted necktie
in place. "Then you drive the Oakland back here and leave it.
Okay?"*

*"Check." Sam began changing his clothes. "You're a lucky guy,
Herb. A beautiful new wife, a beautiful new job and a beautiful
new car. You'll be rich in no time."*

*"How do you get that way? It's you bond salesmen who are
striking it rich." Herb pulled his grenadier blue topcoat from the
closet and picked up a derby, made of flexible felt with a rounded
crown and a flat brim. "I wish I'd had a Wall Street job since I've
been out of college."*

*"Nuts!" Sam shrugged into his shawl-collared camel's hair coat.
"It's not been that good. But everybody says that things are just
getting started—that we're really going to go places in nineteen
twenty-nine."*

"Yeah. I'll say we are!"

3

Herb Browning was by no means alone in his cheerful confidence on the eve of 1929. All over the United States the people —well, at least a great many people—were toasting the prospect of a great year ahead thanks to the modern miracle of mass production and the wonders of scientific progress in the industrial world. And, of course, thanks to aggressive salesmanship. With a population that had increased one-fifth since 1914 and now totaled 121 million, with the value of manufactured products increased more than two and a half times to sixty-eight billion dollars in the same period, it was obvious that the country was at the threshold of something big.

Just take a quick look at the telephone system as a good indication of what had already happened to the country. During the war the total number of phones in the United States had just crawled above the ten million mark. Most of them were wooden boxes that hung on the wall, with a crank to ring Central and a black mouthpiece into which practically everybody shouted at the top of his voice on the theory that if the wires didn't carry his voice maybe the air waves would. By 1929 the number of telephones had doubled and this country had approximately twice as many as could be found in all of the rest of the world. The ordinary telephone was a slender, tubelike instrument about a foot tall, with the mouthpiece at the top, a hook on the side to hold the receiver and a weighted base to hold it all upright on the table, but the French or modern-style telephone was just coming into use. This represented a vast improvement both in design and in communications but unhappily a great many older people still distrusted the instrument and continued to shout lustily into it.[1]

Even more impressive than the telephone was the growth of radio after the First World War. In 1920, radio had been im-

---

[1] By 1954 the number of telephones had soared again, giving the U. S. fifty-two million of the world's ninety-four million telephones. With some exceptions, people no longer shouted into the instrument except maybe when talking on long distance.

portant to ships at sea and of interest to a few amateurs—usually known as radio "nuts"—who understood the Morse code and could build their own sets in the attic. But by 1929, radio was a great industry with annual sales of receiving sets and equipment totaling almost $850 million. Elaborate console model radio sets with seven tubes and built-in superpower magnetic speakers (priced as low as $118) were the most highly prized pieces of furniture in many of the ten million homes equipped to receive broadcasts. National networks had been formed and anybody could tune in on Graham MacNamee's slightly incoherent sports broadcasts or hear Madame Schumann-Heink sing on special occasions. And there were plenty of little independent stations that couldn't afford to hire expensive talent but made a good thing out of playing phonograph records made by famous orchestras, popular singers and comedians. You could get a real laugh out of a record by somebody like the Two Black Crows (Moran and Mack) with their nonsensical conversations about goofer feathers—"the fuzz from peaches"—and other subjects that had once been the stock and trade of something called vaudeville.

"On our farm we found out that white horses eat more than black horses."

"White horses eat more than black horses? That's silly. Why would they?"

"Well, we tried every way to figure it out and we couldn't figure any reason—unless it was because we had *more* white horses than black horses."

But the miracle of science wasn't merely an old vaudeville joke coming over the "air waves." J. L. Baird in England and C. F. Jenkins in America were experimenting with machines on which you could see as well as hear over the air—television would be operating within a decade—and there were new inventions, new discoveries by other scientists almost every day. Although the word "automation" would not really be familiar to the public until a quarter-century later, college professors were gravely debating the problem of what people would do with their leisure time when robot machines had replaced most of the workers or, at least, had made it unnecessary for a man to labor more than a few days a week. The output per man hour in industry had increased enormously since the end of the war. On the government's list of selected industries (with one hundred represented by 1939), output per man hour was up from 45.3 in 1919 to 78.1 in 1929 and the actual physical production in agriculture, manufacturing, mining and the construction business had increased more than 30 per cent.

In Detroit and other Midwestern cities, automobiles were coming off the production lines at a rate approximating five million annually, a record that would not be touched again until twenty-one years later when the six million mark was passed. There were already serious complaints about the traffic problem, especially on Sundays when it sometimes seemed that all of the twenty-three million automobiles in the nation were being taken out simultaneously on pleasure rides. Long lines of automobiles moving at a snail's pace congested the approaches to most American cities on Sundays and holidays, and a "road hog" or a Marmon convertible with a flat tire could tie up traffic for miles on a narrow road. The best engineering brains in the nation were busy solving the traffic problem.[2] The congestion was made to seem even worse because of the inadequate roads, many of which lacked hard surfaces and almost all of which ran through the centers of towns at frequent intervals, creating endless bottlenecks.

For the annual automobile shows in January of 1929 there were no less than forty different American makes and almost three hundred different models, a fantastic array that represented a high point in the industry's competitive history. Most of them—the Whippet, the Erskine, the Moon and the Elcar, for example—were doomed to vanish into oblivion or into mergers within the next few years and there would never be

[2] Twenty-five years later, with some fifty-five million motor vehicles registered in the United States, the best engineering brains were still busy trying to solve the traffic problem.

such a lavish display again in the automobile world.[3] Not a few of the would-be financial titans behind the many automobile companies also were operating on borrowed time and would soon vanish from the industrial scene. In fact, 1929 was the end of one era as well as the beginning of another. The "one-man" company was being outdated. The ordinary people in larger and larger numbers were investing their savings in the big companies and the emphasis was shifting to efficient management in behalf of stockholders. The managerial system was beginning to emerge. General Motors Corporation already had brought under one tent the Chevrolet, Pontiac, Olds, LaSalle and Cadillac factories and stood out in the automobile field, rivaled only by stubborn old Henry Ford, whose delay in shifting from the Model T to the modern power and comfort of the Model A had cost him heavily. Or was supposed to have cost him heavily.

The shift toward broader "executive" management of industry did not mean, of course, that the rich and powerful and colorful figures were disappearing from the world of business. On the contrary, one moderate-sized automobile titan was just shouldering his way to the fore in 1929. Walter P. Chrysler, son of a Kansas railroad locomotive engineer, a one-time apprentice at five cents an hour in the Union Pacific shops and a graduate of the International Correspondence School, had just made a $160 million deal with the Dodge Brothers and was out to challenge the leaders in the automobile industry. He changed the name of the Chrysler Company to the Chrysler Motors Corporation, producing Chryslers, De Sotos, Dodges and the newly introduced (1928) Plymouths.

At the same time, Chrysler announced that in 1929 he would build a new eight-hundred-foot-high skyscraper with sixty-eight floors across the street from New York's Grand Central Station. It would be, he said inaccurately, the tallest in the world with a slender spire rising above mid-Manhattan and a special glass

[3] By 1954, five great corporations—General Motors, Ford, Chrysler, Studebaker-Packard and American—would produce virtually all American automobiles.

case in the ground floor lobby to hold the mechanic's tools which had served young Walter Chrysler well years ago when he was starting his spectacular career. It would have elevators that could rise a thousand feet in sixty seconds and it would be known as the Chrysler Building. *Time* magazine had no difficulty in selecting him as "man of the year" and picturing him— big, bluff and capable-looking—on the cover of its New Year's issue in 1929.

As the new year began, the aviation industry also was trying to build up a boom that had started when a tall, moody boy named Charles Augustus Lindbergh—but known to his friends as Slim and later known to everybody as Lindy—left Long Island one misty morning and flew alone, without a stop, to Paris in a single-engine Ryan monoplane, *The Spirit of St. Louis.* This "stunt" flight by a former airmail pilot who wanted to win a prize of twenty-five thousand dollars was of little technical significance in aviation but, for many reasons, the incredible aura of glory around Lindbergh made a tremendous difference in the development of public confidence in those crazy flying machines and convinced the nation that the Air Age was really here. In 1927, when Lindbergh flew to Paris, civil airways planes carrying mail flew almost six million miles and transported thirty-seven thousand passengers, but by 1929 they were flying five times as many miles annually and carrying almost five times as many passengers.

True, by 1929, commercial aviation wasn't very steady on its feet as compared to a quarter-century later when United States airlines would carry more than thirty million passengers and fly more than fifteen billion passenger miles. It was also true that it took thirty-one hours for an airmail letter (three ounces for twenty-five cents) to get from New York to San Francisco (as compared to about eight hours in 1954), seventeen hours from Dallas to St. Paul and eight hours from Boston to Cleveland— something less than half of the time required by train in most instances. But these schedules couldn't always be counted on, due to various unpredictable difficulties such as the weather and the tricky air currents over the Appalachian Mountains, which became known as a "graveyard" for airplanes.

Many of these difficulties were being overcome, but slowly and sometimes uncomfortably. It was arranged, for example, for air passengers en route from New York to the West to avoid the Appalachians by taking the railroad sleeping cars overnight to Columbus, Ohio. Early next morning they were routed out of bed, transferred by bus to the airport and put aboard a tri-motored Ford—a narrow, silvery bird that rattled and vibrated so violently as to make conversation almost impossible—or perhaps a broad-bellied biplane that was built for greater comfort but soared or dropped like a kite with the changing air currents. In this way, weather, air sickness and mechanical equipment permitting, the modern air-minded traveler might take advantage of the wonders of aviation to arrive in St. Louis somewhat exhausted, often nauseated, and usually hungry but at least several hours ahead of the regular train schedule. If the traveler was a bear for punishment, he could fly on westward the same day to Waynoka, Oklahoma, transfer to a train for an overnight ride to Clovis, New Mexico, and then continue next day by air to Los Angeles—only forty-eight hours out of New York.

4

The acceptance of air travel in 1929—Pan-American was already scheduling overseas flights to the West Indies—was only an example of the many changes that science was bringing about in many fields. Americans were "sold" on science and for good reasons. Americans were in a hurry; the engineering experts were making flying safer and faster every day. Americans wanted more comforts and less drudgery; the electrical engineers were filling the kitchens with labor-saving machines. Americans wanted to make money faster; the new International Business Machine calculators—forerunners of the electronic brain—speeded up business operations by many times. Science had already brought about drastic changes in daily life, and it was difficult indeed to doubt that the scientists could find the answer to any problems that might arise tomorrow.

At the California Institute of Technology, a group of distinguished astronomers was working out plans for a two-hundred-inch telescope that, when erected a dozen years later on Mount Palomar, would extend man's knowledge toward the outer edges of the universe. Sir James Jeans's book, *The Universe Around Us*—Sir James contended that "God is a mathematician; the universe was not created for human beings"—was a best-seller. In England, Alexander Fleming had discovered the miracle of penicillin, although it would be more than a decade before that life-saving drug could be marketed. In America, a bacteriologist who wanted to take a vacation had invented the automobile house trailer, starting a trend that eventually would make seminomads of tens of thousands of Americans who moved from vacation spot to vacation spot or from job to job with their homes in tow.

In Chicago, an ingenious device that forced sand and water taken from the bottom of Lake Michigan through a pipe line and distributed the sand in even layers on the shore was being used to create the famous Lakefront on which parks, hotels and apartment houses would be built in the heart of the city. In Florida, British Major H. O. D. Segrave was putting into shape a long, torpedo-like machine that would set a new automobile speed record of 231.36 miles per hour on the hard-packed sands of Daytona Beach.

Perhaps even more interesting to the imaginative American was what science had done to polar exploration. Commander Richard E. Byrd was leading an expedition in the Antarctic, where he founded Little America, acquainted the general public with the peculiarities of penguins, flew over the South Pole and—most amazing of all—was in direct wireless communication with New York just as if he were in a telephone pay station in Jersey City. This was quite a change from the days when Amundsen or Peary whipped their dog teams through blinding blizzards at forty below zero and vanished into the snowy wastes for months at a time. Snug in a four-man tent after a hot New Year's Eve dinner of pork and beans, bread, peanut butter and applesauce, Byrd rang up the *New York Times*—for which he was special Antarctica correspondent at the time—by wireless and reported that he had washed the dinner dishes, that the dogs were settled down in the snow outside and that, on a twenty-mile trip that day, he had discovered a new harbor that made a big dent in the Bay of Whales.

The unlimited faith of the ordinary people in the infallibility of science successfully met its greatest test, however, in connection with what undoubtedly was to the lay mind the most abstruse of any scientific achievement of 1929. In Germany, a slight, kindly man with sad brown eyes and a halo of iron-gray hair had been working for a quarter of a century on a theory of relativity. He had first expounded the theory in 1905 and, some years later, he had completed formulation of a general theory that—in technical language—included gravitation as determiner of the curvature of a space-time continuum and represented gravitation as a field rather than a force. Outside of scholastic circles, not one person in a hundred thousand could have told you his name until 1929. But in that year Dr. Albert Einstein let it be known that he had found a "key" to the formulation of a unified field theory—that is, a group of equations applicable not only to gravitation but also to electromagnetic and subatomic phenomena.

Nobody could imagine any announcement that would be less likely to increase the pulse beat of the average American. It was estimated inaccurately at the time that there were probably only nine and certainly not more than fifteen highly trained men in the world who could really understand what Dr. Einstein was talking about. Yet, so great was the interest of Americans in science—any kind of science, any kind of sign that man was about to master nature—that the newspapers played up his discovery on a par with, say, the death of Movie Sheik Rudolph Valentino in 1926. That is, they shot the works.

Millions of words were written, most of them for the front

page, about the meaning of Einstein's discovery, although it was obvious that very few of the writers knew the meaning and that still fewer readers were really familiar with the curvature of space. People seemed to be convinced that Einstein had opened one of the last gates to complete knowledge and the fact that he had merely found a "key" to a formula that would not be published until twenty years later was ignored. When an enterprising newspaperman got a photograph of the actual hand-written formula on which the German physicist was working it was promptly slapped on the front page—a design of symbols and figures so strange that the reader might just as well have studied chicken tracks on a white sheet.

It might ordinarily be thought that a little of such "news" would go a long way with the man who paid three cents for his copy of the Cleveland *Press* or two cents for the New York *Daily News*. But, on the contrary, enthusiasm hung on and later when Einstein, draped in a long black coat and a shapeless black hat, arrived in America en route to lecture in California, a mob of reporters and photographers met him on shipboard with one of the zaniest performances in the history of the press. Accompanied by his wife, Einstein came into the lounge of the transatlantic liner *Belgenland* as a diffident, friendly visitor who had no real interest in what all the crowd was doing here but intended to conform to the weird customs of this land that sent a hundred male and female newspaper employees down New York Harbor to meet his ship.

He sat quietly on a big divan that practically engulfed his slight figure. Not so the photographers and reporters, who included many of the big name by-liners of the day. They surrounded him like a menacing wave, shouting questions or asking him to "Look this way, Professor!" Some crowded in behind the divan. Others stood on gilt chairs or tables, and several climbed atop the grand piano in order to see or to be heard. When, merely to get some kind of answers, they had to quiet down enough for questions to be distinguished there was a succession of queries in English and German that touched on the

New York skyline, which he had not had a chance to see yet, the political situation in Washington, the sex situation in Hollywood and the real meaning—in ten words, Professor!—of the theory of relativity. One intense science writer atop the piano read a two-hundred-word hypothetical question concerning the curvature of space, ending with a query as to whether the distinguished visitor agreed. A look of infinite pain crossed Dr. Einstein's face when he heard the translation and he muttered something that sounded like: "Agree? I don't have any idea what he is talking about."

After an hour of such insanity, including a pose for the photographers at the ship's rail, even some of the newsmen were beginning to be embarrassed and to feel sorry for the bewildered-looking little visitor. They need not have wasted their sympathy. At that moment—while photographers shouted instructions and reporters crowded around again—Einstein decided that he had done his duty as a guest in America. He looked slowly around the chattering crowd, not shyly but as if he were seeing some strange creatures in a zoo. He plopped his shapeless hat on his fluffy head and without another word marched away to his stateroom. The crowd silently made way for him. The "interview" was over.

5

The country's genuine interest in Einstein was a kind of exaggerated reflection of confidence in the high priests of science who were leading the nation into a promised land, where mass production, assembly lines, synthetic materials and new sources of power—physicists already knew that the atom could be split, didn't they?—would mean better living and more leisure for everybody tomorrow. This attitude was reflected in the rapid increase in the number of speculators in the stock market. It was estimated that there were more than a million and a half persons "in the market" in 1929, the security of other millions was involved and still other millions were scheming how they could get in. Barbers and shoeshine boys listened carefully to the conversation of their broker customers and invested their savings on tips that Radio Corporation of America or A. T. & T. would climb still higher. Broadway gossip columnists suddenly became financial experts and gave readers "inside information" on stocks that would soon go up ten points. Most stocks did go up ten points and more. Fortunes were made "on paper" every day by men and women who had bought on margin, thus purchasing several times more stocks than they could pay for, and watched the bull market rise, quiver violently for a few days and then rise again. A seat on the Stock Exchange, which had cost three hundred thousand dollars in 1927, was sold for twice that sum in 1929.

The only day-by-day events that really rivaled the stock market in attracting public interest were in the field of sports. The doings of athletic heroes, which a decade before had been chronicled largely in the *Sporting News* or the *Police Gazette*, were now likely to be front page news. College football games, which had once drawn a few thousand undergraduates and loyal alumni, attracted as many as eighty thousand persons to the Yale Bowl on Saturday afternoon or even one hundred thousand to Soldiers Field in Chicago.

The greatest signs of change, however, were in participation sports such as tennis and golf, which was sometimes contemptuously called "cow pasture pool." These sports, particularly golf, had long since ceased to be the recreation of a comparatively few wealthy club members. In 1929, men in white ducks or in plus-four knickerbockers and women in short skirts and eyeshades were scattered over the landscape everywhere in America on every afternoon. On week ends, they became a procession. Robert Tyre Jones was a hero to every one of the millions who sweated and cursed and occasionally cried with joy while knocking a golf ball over the hills, and in the next year Jones would justify that adulation by making a "grand slam" of the world's major golf championships. An intense, nerveless girl named Helen Wills was at the height of a long reign on the tennis courts and Big Bill Tilden, at thirty-six, was still able to come through as national singles champion at Forest Hills. Popular enthusiasm for their triumphs at home and abroad had filled tennis courts with racket-swinging kids in all parts of America—presumably in preparation for the day when science would have reduced the working week to a few days and everybody would have to find new ways of using leisure time.

This obsession of Americans with science, this conviction that the strapping, big-muscled giant of our national economy could indefinitely support a rising stock market was a part of the business community's admirable confidence in what man could do with the future. One might almost say that the big fault of the American in 1929 was timing. To use a golfing term, he was pressing his swing; he was, perhaps, too much in a hurry. He was depending too heavily on mathematical formulas and not enough on human equations.

6

Yet, in 1929, America was regarded as a kind of rock of Gibraltar in the world economy. Much to the regret of most of the citizenry of this country, a large part of the world owed money to the United States and the center of world power inevitably was shifting toward Washington. There was, it is true, little public consciousness of any relationship between economic conditions in Europe and in the United States. Most Americans knew that the "war debts" of European nations to this country were measured in billions of dollars—ten billion dollars, in fact—but there was only mild concern as to whether they would be paid, except in some financial and political circles and in the White House where President Coolidge had summed up policy in a few words: "They hired the money, didn't they?"

What had happened was that at the end of the war Britain and France attempted to make Germany pay for the conflict through reparations but soon decided to settle for enough from Germany to pay their own debts to the United States, plus cer-

tain payments for damages in France. At the same time, the
Germans were busy rebuilding their economy with money that
they got from Americans in various ways such as selling German
municipal bonds. By 1929, there was a kind of ring-around-the-
rosy in which American money was going to the Germans, who
in turn paid the British and the French, who in turn paid the
installments on their debts to the United States.

This seemed to do little for anybody except the Germans,
who had been defeated in 1918 but were probably the most
cheerful people in Europe at the beginning of 1929. Stolid,
respected President Paul von Hindenburg was being cleverly
maneuvered by the devious Franz von Papen, who would eventually lead him into the clutches of Adolf Hitler; but for the
moment the Prussian military hero was staunchly calling for the
"liberation" of Germany from the tyranny of the war victors
and Berliners were in such a gay mood that they consumed no
less than nine million holeless doughnuts at drinking parties to
greet the New Year.

In financial circles, on the other hand, there was great concern about the economic position of Great Britain, one of the
victors in World War I. London endured a cold, bleak New
Year's Eve, discouraged by the steady downward drag of the
nation's trade in the postwar era. No less than 12.2 per cent of
the registered working population was jobless—more idle even
than during the 1926 general strike. There was acute misery in
the Welsh coal fields, where most of the workers' families were
living on a dole of about seven dollars a week and where even
the corner pubs were going out of business. A Christmas Day
appeal by a former international playboy, the Prince of Wales,
had raised a million and a half dollars in relief funds within a
week. The Prince was so impressed by the "ghastly mess" he
saw in the coal fields that he sold his entire stable of horses and
renounced the sport of fox hunting, letting it be known that he
was going to devote himself earnestly to the affairs of the
Crown. But his relief fund campaign soon died out when Prime
Minister Stanley Baldwin was understood to have suggested

that perhaps the heir to the Crown was attracting a bit too much public attention to an unhappy domestic situation. There was little cause for New Year's rejoicing in Britain and the only crowd in London was gathered outside Buckingham Palace to hear the latest official bulletin on the condition of King George V, who was seriously ill.

The outlook in France seemed somewhat better, partly because the iron-handed deflationary methods of Premier Raymond Poincaré had recently stabilized the economy and led to a moderate gain in foreign trade. In Moscow, another iron hand belonging to Joseph V. Stalin was in full control. Disgruntled Russian farmers were being forced into the Communist system of collective farms and Leon Trotsky, the most formidable foe of Stalin, was in exile in the remote town of Alma-Ata, where he was now reported seriously ill of malaria.

There was rejoicing among the common people of Rumania because the Peasant Party of Juliu Maniu had won an overwhelming victory in the parliamentary elections and an era of democratic reform was predicted for the reign of King Michael. The King, who was six years old, stayed home and played with an electric train as the new parliament opened with scenes of enthusiasm. In Rome, Premier Benito Mussolini was forced to economize. It was made known that henceforth Il Duce would send his signed photograph only to the fathers of quadruplets, ending his practice of so honoring the fathers of twins and triplets.

On the other side of the world, President Chiang Kai-shek was in good spirits. He announced that the foes of his government had been crushed, that the flag of Nationalist China had been raised in the long independent province of Manchuria and that all of China was now unified. Tokyo was shocked by the scandal of a burly farmer from Saitama province, who threw himself in the dirt before Emperor Hirohito as that divine descendant of the Sun Goddess Amaterasu Omikami was riding to the opening of Parliament in a golden state coach. The farmer cried out for the Emperor to save the people of

Saitama from floods that were sweeping the province, but the coach didn't stop.

In Nicaragua, the United States Marine Corps announced that it had been pretty successful in restoring peace and order and protecting United States lives and property against the depredations of "bandits" under the leadership of Sandino. The announcement added that the United States forces were now disposed in such a manner as to insure a "free election"—providing the "bandits" didn't try to vote. The statement didn't say so, but it left no doubt in the reader's mind that, despite a considerable loss of lives and the expenditure of large sums from the treasury at Washington, the Marines had not yet captured Sandino, a little man who kept insisting rather plaintively that he was really a revolutionary who wanted Nicaraguans to run their own country.

There wasn't much doing in Washington, D.C., as 1929 began and for the moment Americans generally were taking a tolerant attitude toward affairs in the capital, where, in the opinion of the average citizen, politicians were always bumbling jobs that could have been cleaned up in two days by a cabinet of good, solid businessmen. Calvin Coolidge, whose hand had rested inertly on the helm since 1923, was down in Georgia spending the year-end holidays at the Howard Coffin estate on Little Sapelo Island. No expert marksman, the President had improved his aim somewhat since Thanksgiving when he missed five successive shots at quail. During Christmas week he also missed a deer, but with the help of a crew of beaters who drove the fowls past his position he managed to knock off two wild turkeys and three golden pheasants. He later rode in an oxcart long enough to be photographed for the Sunday newspaper rotogravure sections, donned a ten-gallon hat to attend a rodeo and put on a gay paper dunce cap at the height of the New Year's Eve festivities. So far as the public record shows, he said nothing at all. It was not exactly a typical Coolidge week, but it came close.

On the U.S.S. *Utah,* near the West Indies, President-elect and

Mrs. Herbert Hoover were headed homeward through choppy seas from a good-will tour to Latin America. Wearing white flannels and a blue, double-breasted coat, Mr. Hoover had observed Christmas aboard ship in a cozy atmosphere generated by an electric fireplace that glowed like real red coals. He had taken part in an impromptu party at which a newspaperman dressed as Santa Claus presented him with a tin fish labeled "Congress." An ardent fisherman, Mr. Hoover asked what kind of bait was used to catch such a fish and got a quick reply: "Soft soap, Mr. President." On New Year's Eve, the social season picked up aboard the U.S.S. *Utah* and the Hoovers were amused by a burlesque reception attended by newsmen and others dressed to represent members of the Supreme Court, various military and diplomatic figures and, for a laugh, that pesky little Nicaraguan bandit or revolutionary, Sandino. At a gala dinner, Mr. Hoover indicated his first serious break with Mr. Coolidge, who had been photographed in all kinds of headgear including Indian feathers. Mr. Hoover shied away from wearing a funny hat. Mrs. Hoover, however, insisted that he get into the swing of things and persuaded him at last to don a paper fireman's hat and everybody had a gay time. Although Mr. Hoover wrote a good many years later that he was gravely concerned at the time about the state of the stock market, he was hardly more loquacious on New Year's Eve than Mr. Coolidge. He said: "I wish you all a Happy New Year."

Another political figure, and he seemed almost out of another world, was in the news on New Year's Eve. Alfred E. Smith, who had made the sidewalks of New York and the brown derby famous, was leaving the Governor's mansion at Albany and hundreds of friends gathered at the gates in misty, cold weather to bid him good-by. To some, who asked whether it was true that his unsuccessful race for the presidency against Mr. Hoover had marked the end of his political career, he said scornfully: "Let's put the kibosh on that farewell stuff." To the one, who was succeeding him in Albany, he said: "We've got the home fires burning for you and you'll find this a good place to live."

He waved his brown derby at the crowd and got into the waiting automobile. Inside, he left a tall, broad-shouldered man who wore heavy iron braces on his legs and walked with difficulty as a result of infantile paralysis. Franklin Delano Roosevelt stayed up until midnight, when he took the oath of office twelve hours in advance of his formal inauguration—just in case of emergency.

Down in Mississippi, another governor, a thin-lipped, scrawny man named Theodore G. Bilbo, made a trip to the town of Parchman to look at the body of a Negro convict, Charley Shepherd. Shepherd had raped the daughter of a prison guard, who had mistreated him, and then killed the guard himself when he returned home unexpectedly. Bilbo had called out the National Guard to aid in the search for Shepherd, but when he was caught nobody seemed to think the guardsmen were needed any longer or that it was worth while to spend state money on a trial. A mob of two thousand persons burned Shepherd alive near the town of Drew and a coroner's jury returned a verdict of death "due to unknown causes." Asked whether the state would investigate, Bilbo said that it had "neither the time nor the money" to go into the matter. Shepherd's death brought the Tuskegee Institute's annual "black list" of lynchings up to ten, including four in Mississippi, two in Louisiana, two in Texas, one in Missouri and one in New Mexico. This list was so short that foes of racial discrimination were almost in a mood of self-congratulation. Only two decades earlier, no less than eighty-nine Negroes—in addition to eight whites—had been lynched and the total in 1926 was twenty-three. It would be another two decades before a year passed without a lynching in the United States.

Prohibition enforcement officers in New Jersey raided an abandoned factory near Kenilworth and destroyed an illegal ten-thousand-gallon still, a five-thousand-gallon still, eight thousand gallons of alcohol and fifteen thousand gallons of mash. It was one of the biggest secret distilleries that had yet been found, worth about $150,000 but there was nobody on the premises when the raiders arrived. In Michigan, the mother of ten children was convicted of selling two pints of liquor illegally. It was her fourth law violation and she was sentenced to life imprisonment in the Detroit House of Correction.

"Our only regret," said Dr. Clarence True Wilson, general secretary of the Board of Temperance, Prohibition and Public Morals, "is that the woman was not sentenced to life before her ten children were born."

On Broadway, a new musical comedy *"Hello Daddy!"* opened with Billy Taylor and Lew Fields as its stars. Field's son, Herbert, wrote the book and his daughter, Dorothy, wrote the lyrics. Best quip of the show: "He's a wolf in cheap clothing." J. P. Morgan gave his yacht *Corsair* (upkeep: one hundred thousand dollars a year) to the government of the United States and prepared to launch a new one (cost: three million dollars) at Bath, Maine. In Sarasota, Florida, Circus Owner John Ringling announced that he had bought for four hundred dollars the bathtub in which Jean Paul Marat, French doctor, editor and revolutionary terrorist, was stabbed to death in 1793 by Charlotte Corday.

T W O

... a landscape freed at last ...

Nineteen twenty-nine was a turning point for Americans
. . . for James Cannon, Jr., a determined, tireless man, a skillful and powerful politician, lifelong crusader against sin, father
of the Prohibition Amendment, Methodist Bishop of the Congo,
Cuba and Brazil. He was born November 13, 1864, at Salisbury,
Maryland, as Sherman's march through Georgia pushed the
Civil War toward its end. His father was a merchant; his
mother an ardent temperance worker who died with the White
Ribbon of the Women's Christian Temperance Union across
her breast. At Randolph-Macon College in Virginia, Cannon's
eloquence and scholarship made him an outstanding student
but his classmates remembered him for his tireless, uncompromising struggle against their weakness for strong liquor. At
Princeton Theological Seminary, the only Methodist at that
Presbyterian institution, he was absent on many week ends on
arduous and exhaustive investigations of vice along the Bowery
in New York City. He married Lura Bennett in 1888, became
a circuit riding preacher and, in 1894, the principal of Blackstone Female Institute, a school for young ladies in Nottoway
County, Virginia. But always he kept up the fight against sin
and if there was persistent talk that he bestowed excessive
pedagogical interest on some of his students it may have been

encouraged by his enemies who profited by the sale of alcoholic beverages.

He became head of the Virginia Anti-Saloon League in 1909 and, after three years of bitter attack on "the Knights of the Booze-Bottle" and the drunkards in fashionable society, he forced through the legislature a prohibition law that made Virginia "a landscape freed at last from the pestilence of rum." But it was a close call. A dead-drunk Senator had to be routed out of bed to cast his vote for the dry law, which then carried by 21 to 20. The law did not outlaw various vegetable compounds or other nostrums which then contained from 20 to 40 per cent alcohol and which later registered tremendous sales in Virginia.

Now he was a national figure, a crusader. He worked nineteen hours a day and that wasn't enough to get through all of his work. He couldn't spare ten minutes a day to shave, so he grew a beard. He traveled 150,000 miles a year, but refused to board a train on Sundays, when he went nowhere except by horse and buggy. He was editor of the *Methodist Recorder;* controlled the Baltimore and Richmond *Advocate.* For years he had denounced Sunday newspapers, but when he established a prohibition daily in Richmond it issued a Sunday edition. All of his life he was an avid reader of Sunday comics. During the First World War, he inspected vice conditions "at the front." The Army cleaned up the bottles ahead of him, brought them out again when he had departed. Brigadier General Clarence R. Edwards welcomed him at one post with an outburst of profanity, told him his visit was "underhanded, slimy, treacherous and sneaking."

After the war he was made bishop of part of Texas and Mexico, became chairman of the National Anti-Saloon League's legislative committee which was instrumental in putting the heat on Congress and in gaining passage of the Eighteenth Amendment to make America a "dry" nation. Bishop Cannon was looking for more worlds to conquer. He became a lobbyist at the League of Nations for Article 22, which forbade "such abuse as the slave trade, the arms traffic and the liquor traffic" in mandated territories. At home he had fought the child labor amendment and federal antilynching legislation as invasions of the rights of states, but he now had demon rum on the lam in mandated territories. On a visit to Scotland he crusaded valiantly for prohibition but finally departed to shouts of "go home and stay there" along with "the rest of your cowardly, money-loving hypocritical countrymen." Americans, who insisted on collecting war debts from their former allies, were not popular in Great Britain after the war.

Bishop Cannon had been critical of the Methodist bishops with supervision over distant parts of the world because they didn't always live in the lands to which they were assigned. In 1920 he was made Bishop of Alabama and moved there. The next year he was made Bishop of the Congo, Cuba and Brazil. He moved to Washington, where the Anti-Saloon League needed his services to keep Congress in line, but he later made a trip to the Congo where he nearly died of fever. Safely home again, he devoted himself largely to political affairs and reached the height of his power in 1928 when he led a vicious campaign to defeat Democratic Presidential Nominee Alfred E. Smith in the Southern states. Smith's advocacy of moderate reform in the prohibition laws was enough to win Cannon's enmity, but the campaign branched out from there to play on racial and religious prejudices, particularly prejudice against Catholics and foreigners. "Al Smith wants that kind of dirty people that you find today on the sidewalks of New York." After the triumph of dry forces in the 1928 election, Bishop Cannon was a man to whom congressmen listened attentively and, as one political writer exaggerated it, his "merest wink . . . [could] make a President of the United States jump like a bullfrog."

But 1929 was a turning point for the Bishop of the Congo. Some old stories of his extracurricular activities had come home to roost. They covered a wide range from the Blackstone Female Institute to the lobby of a New York hotel. He was accused of misappropriation of funds which had been entrusted to his care at the college. His lucrative real estate speculations

shocked some of his brethren. He was alleged to have been a
hoarder of flour on which he made a profit in the war. He had
ten different bank accounts. The Hearst newspapers published
charges that he had been extremely friendly with Helen Hawley
McCallum, whom he met in the lobby of a New York hotel
and later described as his secretary. He was revealed by the
bankruptcy of a bucket-shop brokerage house to be an avid
gambler on the stock market. He was prosecuted in the federal
courts on charges of violating the Political Malpractices Act
during the 1928 campaign, when it was alleged that he failed to
account for much of $130,000 in campaign contributions.

All of these things constituted a remarkable bill of particu-
lars against a man who had often spoken harshly of sin and had
once raised a public rumpus in Nashville, Tennessee, because
Sarah Bernhardt was permitted to appear there in *Camille*—an
actress "with unsavory moral ideals" playing "the life of a fallen,
debauched character." But Bishop Cannon was not dismayed.
His wife had died and he had married Mrs. McCallum. He
fought the Department of Justice with bluster and legal technicalities and was acquitted. A woman spectator at the trial
rushed up to kiss him, shouting: "This is a victory for Protes-
tantism!" Her remark seemed to represent the sentiment of
church officials, who declined to bring charges against him or
seek his resignation.

But the end of the Prohibition Era in 1933 also ended the
power of the Bishop of the Congo, Cuba and Brazil. When he
died in 1944, he was almost broke.

*A reformer is a guy who rides through a sewer
in a glass-bottomed boat.*

—MAYOR JAMES J. WALKER of New York

FEBRUARY, 1929

the bootleg days

The skies were clear over Chicago and there was almost a touch of springtime warmth in the sun on the morning of February 14, 1929. Grade school kids skipped along North Clark Street, clutching valentines made of bits of colored paper and laboriously addressed to special friends. When they had gone, the street settled down into a slovenly routine. A few housewives hurried along toward the corner store. Automobiles occasionally bumped down the street. A big truck slowed down and turned into the S. M. C. Cartage Company garage.

The atmosphere was even lazier inside the garage. Two men sat idly in the front office, a dusty room in which no office work obviously had been done for months. There were no records, no typewriter, no books. Even the two inkwells were bone dry. Four other men in the main part of the garage were drinking coffee from heavy mugs. The driver of the truck, in which was concealed a beer vat, pulled on a pair of overalls and began tinkering with his machine. This, at 10:20 A.M., on St. Valentine's Day, was a bootlegging depot of one of the most powerful citizens of Chicago, George (Bugs) Moran, and a few of Moran's employees were standing by to handle an expected cargo of booze.

The Moran mob had been riding high for some months. Given time, Moran might even bring the gang back to the power it had known when it was the O'Banion mob. Dion O'Banion, unfortunately, had been shot to death amid a display of hyacinths and gardenias in his florist shop by three friends who had sold out to O'Banion's chief rival, Scarface Al Capone, the most notorious of modern hoodlums. O'Banion was succeeded as leader of the North Side gang by one Hymie Weiss, who was succeeded by "Schemer" Drucci, who was succeeded by Moran, but for a long time the Moran crowd had played in bad luck while the Capone mob flourished. Lately things had been looking up again. A few months earlier, a Capone lieutenant, Tony Lombardo, had been knocked off in a flurry of bullets at the busy corner of Madison and Dearborn streets. Scarface himself was said to be worried and to be hiding out. And only a couple of weeks earlier Moran had engineered the hijacking of a shipment of Canadian whisky to Capone—or at least he was credited with being the engineer.

At 10:30 A.M. on St. Valentine's Day, the S. M. C. Cartage Company ceased to be a bootlegging depot. A dark blue automobile of the type used by police slid to a stop in front of the door and five men, three of them wearing police uniforms, got out carrying submachine guns—known to gangsters as "typewriters"—and shotguns. This caused no great excitement in the garage because raids were commonplace and cops could be bribed. The newcomers motioned the two idlers in the "office" toward the main part of the garage with the four coffee drinkers and the truck driver; then ordered all seven to line up facing the north wall of whitewashed brick. Suddenly, there was terror in the garage; there was something wrong about these cops. James Clark, Moran's brother-in-law and first lieutenant, looked at them closely as he moved over to the brick wall with a gun barrel poking him in the back.

"Put your noses against that wall."

Clark sputtered: "Say, what is this, a . . ."

"Okay. Let 'em have it!"

A roar echoed hollowly in the big garage and seven men crumpled in front of the red-splashed wall. Approximately a hundred bullets had been about evenly divided among them. One who crawled a few feet on the floor had his head ripped open by another volley.

The three men in uniform took the hot guns from their two companions in plain clothes. The latter raised their hands above their heads and walked out to the street, closely followed by the uniformed men with guns. All of them got into the dark blue automobile and drove rapidly away. "Another bootlegger raid," muttered Mrs. Alphonsine Morin, who watched the car roll down the street. When the real police arrived at the garage a bit later, the only living things they found were a big police dog plunging on its leash and a boy named Frank Gusenberg who had twenty bullets in his body and didn't say much before he died a few hours later.

The Chicago police were quick to blame the massacre on the underlings of Capone, who was sunning himself on a secluded Florida beach on Valentine's Day. Apparently the only living person who questioned their judgment was Assistant U.S. Prohibition Administrator Fred D. Silloway, who had a standing feud with the Chicago police because they seldom did anything to help enforce the federal prohibition laws. He said he believed the assassins were real city policemen getting revenge on bootleggers who had failed to pay them promised bribes.

2

The St. Valentine's Day massacre was a brutal example of the efficient technique developed by gangsters during the Prohibition Era, which dated from 12:01 A.M., January 17, 1920, when the Eighteenth Amendment to the Constitution and the Prohibition Act, better known as the Volstead Act, became effective. None of the murderers was caught by police but presumably two of them were "bumped off" three months later when Moran mobsters shot down two Capone men and, according to police, were prevented from killing Scarface Al himself only by an accident. That Capone was frightened seemed evident shortly afterward when he was arrested in Philadelphia and sentenced to a year in jail for carrying a .38 caliber revolver. Police said he apparently wanted to be in jail where his enemies couldn't shoot at him. "I've been trying to retire," he said. "I'm tired of murders and shootings."

By 1929 violence had become an almost daily occurrence in the multibillion-dollar bootlegging industry and sudden death was not uncommon either for dealers in illicit alcohol or for their customers. In nine years, prohibition enforcement agents had spent two hundred thousand dollars and had killed 159 persons "in self defense," according to the official record, to enforce the Eighteenth Amendment. They had also killed not a few bystanders by accident or mistake. Bad liquor had killed no less than 1,565 consumers in the past year. The bootlegging wars had killed many others, but nobody knew just how many because quite a few victims had been encased in cement and dropped into the ocean by rival mobsters.

Summed up in a few sentences, such statistics give the impression that the United States in 1929 was a land terrorized by brutal thugs and by hardly less civilized government officers who roamed the countryside in fast automobiles and raced along the coasts in powerful speedboats, usually shooting wildly at each other and anybody who happened to get in the way. On the basis of news reports, many Europeans were inclined to regard America as hardly safer than in the days of red Indian massacres.

This was a distorted impression. The American scene was not lacking in serious blemishes, but by 1929 the people generally had made certain necessary adjustments to life under the Eighteenth Amendment. Saloons were operating quietly and almost openly in some cities, liquor was sold freely in night clubs and speakeasy restaurants, distilleries ran day and night with only slight efforts at disguise and railroads transported huge cargoes of liquor and beer labeled as olive oil or heavy machinery. The ordinary citizen's only contact with the violence behind the façade of this vast, illicit industry was a bootlegger's telephone number and the newspaper accounts of raids, killings and corruption. Almost a decade of living under the Volstead Act had conditioned a large part of the population to bribery of public officials, to law violation and to drinking liquor that was generally inferior if not actually poisonous. By 1929 the pattern was established. Some ten thousand dry agents, Coast Guardsmen, snoopers and ax-men (to break down speakeasy doors and break up bar equipment) were making seventy-five thousand arrests a year at a cost of twenty million dollars to the taxpayers. But anybody who wanted a drink could get it without serious risk, except in a few states. The federal law applied to the manufacturer, seller or smuggler but not to the buyer of liquor; and prohibition was merely an inconvenience to most American drinkers. Nor did this situation seem likely to change soon.

This does not mean that the obvious dangers of the Prohibition Era—the astounding spread of highly profitable racketeering and mobster rule, the breakdown of respect for law and constituted authority, the growth of political cynicism—were ignored. On the contrary, the journalists, the preachers, the sociologists and even the politicians of the day devoted themselves assiduously to exposing and discussing these dangers from a number of radically different viewpoints. Not a Sunday passed that pastors failed to thunder warnings to their flocks against what was popularly called "making whoopee!"—a word that apparently was invented by Rudyard Kipling but revived in 1929 by a Broadway columnist named Walter Winchell to denote gay drinking parties. Most preachers wanted better dry law enforcement.

From another viewpoint, some journalists and politicians were demanding modification or repeal of the Eighteenth Amendment on the grounds that it was responsible for the spread of lawlessness. The states of Rhode Island and Connecticut had never approved the Eighteenth Amendment; the states of Maryland, Montana, Nevada and New York either refused to enact prohibition enforcement laws or repealed them by 1929. Ex-Governor Alfred E. Smith of New York, titular head of the

Democratic party, drank only an occasional glass of champagne
but he did not hesitate to sit at a banquet table where whisky
bottles were openly displayed. New York City's Mayor James J.
Walker was a regular patron of night clubs where liquor was
dispensed and a regular consumer of whatever spirits were
available. One afternoon a rumor circulated that Walker had
been shot and reporters rushed to his office, only to find that the
rumor was false. "Shot?" Walker cried in reply to their questions. "Why at this hour I'm not even half-shot!" New York
Police Commissioner Grover Whalen denounced as "buck passing" the suggestion from Washington that his men should close
down the city's speakeasies.

The Association Against the Prohibition Amendment issued a
list of its board of directors, including such prominent industrialists and financiers as Newcomb Carlton, president of Western Union; John J. Raskob, a vice-president of Du Pont; and
General W. W. Atterbury, president of the Pennsylvania
Railroad.

These developments were signs of ferment, but realists
did not regard them as meaning a quick end to prohibition
For the time being, at least, the country was caught in a strange
three-cornered web of circumstance that seemed to leave it as
helpless as a fly in the spider's trap. On one corner of the web
was the Anti-Saloon League and its affiliates. They had a dry
law and were so happy about it that General Superintendent
Francis Scott McBride blandly announced after an inspection
tour that enforcement "was never so good as it is now." On
another corner were the illicit liquor makers, the smugglers, the
mobsters, the hired killers, the bootleggers and the corrupt
public officials. They were flooding the country with liquor at
a huge profit to themselves and were even happier than the
Anti-Saloon League.

On the third corner of the web were the politicians who
could "vote dry and drink wet" and most of them did. Congress
was certain to support any Anti-Saloon League proposal within
reason and 70 per cent of its members were officially "dry."

When it came to personal preferences in beverages, however, there was good reason to believe that the percentage changed rather drastically. Representative M. Alfred Michaelson of Illinois, who had voted for stiffer penalties for Volstead Act violators, was indicted after his six trunks sprang a leak in Florida while he was en route home from Panama. He was cleared when his brother-in-law claimed the trunks. Representative E. E. Denison of Illinois, who supported all prohibition measures for fourteen years, was indicted when dry agents found in his room in the House Office Building a trunk containing twenty-four bottles of whisky and gin. Denison said they weren't his. On the steps of the Senate Office Building, police arrested George Lyons Cassidy with a pint of whisky hidden under his coat. They charged he was the "Man in the Green Hat," a bootlegger who three years before had escaped after dropping and breaking a brief case filled with bottles of liquor in the House Office Building. On the floor of the Senate, Smith Wildman Brookhart of Iowa, an ardent dry, told how he and a score of other senators had attended a "booze party" given by prominent Wall Street figures at a Washington hotel. "In the reception room," he recalled, "someone lifted up a curtain on a bookcase and underneath was a rack of beautiful silver hip flasks and the word went around to help yourself." The Senator said he didn't take one, but that other senators would have to answer for themselves. None confessed.

None of these disclosures changed the conviction of politicians that it was smart to vote dry while drinking wet. And the ordinary citizen felt more or less helpless to do anything about prohibition: he fatalistically took a chance almost every time he took a drink. If you wanted to look first at the worst side of prohibition, taking a drink was a kind of ritual that required a degree of courage in some parts of America. In sections of the Middle West, which H. L. Mencken liked to deride as the Bible Belt, there was strong sentiment in favor of prohibition and bottled whisky was both scarce and very expensive. Under such circumstances, the ordinary citizen often could afford only a clear type of moonshine made in little backwoods stills, delivered in jugs or fruit jars and usually called White Mule because it had a powerful kick. Since few moonshiners could wait for the stuff to age, this liquor was usually mixed with ginger ale or canned grape fruit juice to make it moderately potable. But if no mixer was available, it could be taken straight with some difficulty.

The experienced drinker kept the fruit jar tighly closed until he was ready to drink. Then he held his breath while he unscrewed the lid and quickly lifted the jar to his lips, gulped the clear liquid, replaced the lid and screwed it tightly into place again. Only then did he attempt to breathe. Frequently this was difficult. For a few moments he coughed and shuddered violently. Slowly, his breathing began again, his eyes opened and the strained, anxious expression on his face was replaced by an equally strained and anxious smile. He wiped the fusel oil from his lips and, if it was then possible for him to speak, said: "Boy, that's got a kick—and how!"

White Mule drinkers were not typical of America. They represented an extreme wing, largely composed of younger people who didn't know any better or older drinkers who could not afford anything better. Moonshine when properly aged could be good liquor and, in any event, it could quickly produce the desired effect in those imbibers who were merely determined to become intoxicated. Unhappily, the fact that there was a law against intoxicants seemed to cause a considerable proportion of the population to regard it as their duty to get themselves "crocked" at regular intervals. It was "the thing to do" and the result was often violent nausea, millions of Sunday morning hangovers and irreparable damage to hundreds of thousands of stomachs.

The result might also be sudden death. Throughout the Prohibition Era there was a remarkable willingness on the part of otherwise normal citizens to risk injury or death in behalf of drunkenness. One of the most dangerous potions was Jamaica ginger, which could be legally sold in drug stores as a medicine and which was almost pure alcohol. Throughout the Midwest, the use of "jake" was fairly common in the early 1920's and, despite the fact that literally thousands of users were paralyzed, it seemed to be sold more widely than ever about 1929. The concoction particularly affected the leg and hand muscles and the victim often walked with difficulty for months or, if he continued to use the stuff, might be permanently crippled.

Other and even more lethal liquids also were consumed, according to accounts that appeared rather regularly in the press. One cheap but apparently popular drink among bums was canned heat, made by melting down the solidified alcohol that was sold in cans for use under chafing dishes. It was frequently fatal. Rubbing alcohol was occasionally consumed and some down-and-outers managed to get drunk in the winter time by guzzling alcohol or antifreeze mixtures from the radiators of automobiles parked on the street. In the spring of 1929, a prisoner in the Hampden County jail at Springfield, Massachusetts, told the district court that he had been happily intoxicated for six months on denatured alcohol used for shellac in the prison workshop.

At some time or another, someone drank almost every liquid that contained alcohol, including vanilla extract, for the specific purpose of getting drunk. In an authoritative account of the drinking habits of the time, Herbert Asbury wrote in *The Great Illusion* that farm hands sometimes drank a vile beverage drawn from the bottom of a silo, where silage had rotted and fermented. He also listed various regional drinks such as: Maryland's Panther Whisky, heavy with esters and fusel oil; Virginia's White Lightning, which was "dangerous"; Philadelphia's Soda Pop Moon, which contained isopropyl alcohol, a deadly poison; Jackass Brandy from Virginia, which was made of peaches and caused internal bleeding; Indiana's Goat Whisky, which sold for a dollar a pint; Ohio's Straitsville Stuff, manufactured in stills hidden underground in the coal mines; Kansas City's Sweet Whisky, a distillation of alcohol combined with nitric and sulfuric acids that soon destroyed the kidneys; Chicago's Yack Yack Bourbon, which contained iodine and burnt sugar; and California's American Whisky, which was manufactured in Mexico from "potatoes, rotten cactus and whatever else was available."

All of these, of course, were the worst of the Prohibition Era beverages and were carefully avoided by citizens who could afford anything else. In a slightly higher economic echelon, there was much potable liquor to be had and in the best circles there was even a small amount of imported whisky, gin and rum, although not anything like as much as believed by those who paid fancy prices for something "right off the boat." With rare exceptions, the good liquor was cut and mixed with alcohol by the bootlegging syndicates and in most cases the real or faked labels of famous foreign brands covered a brew that was produced in New Jersey or Pennsylvania or Illinois.

3

There were many sources for liquor in America. For example, the government permitted a number of distilleries, breweries and wineries to operate at various times during the prohibition period on the ground that a certain amount of whisky, rum and wine were required for industrial, medicinal and religious purposes. Much of this production seeped into illegal channels. Whisky was often stolen or illegally removed from storehouses —fifty thousand gallons vanished suddenly in 1929—and replaced by barrels of colored water. And records in the same year showed that about one hundred thousand doctors issued eleven million prescriptions for more than a million and a half gallons of whisky necessary to the health of their patients.

Another source—perhaps the greatest source, according to Mrs. Mabel Walker Willebrandt, Assistant Attorney General in charge of prohibition prosecutions—was the ninety million gallons of alcohol produced annually for industrial purposes. This was almost twice as much industrial alcohol as the country had required prior to prohibition and the experts could only guess how much of it was being used illegally. The guesses ranged from fifteen million up to thirty million gallons.

Industrial alcohol, by addition of various ingredients during manufacture, was made unfit to drink and often poisonous. But illegal plants were set up to "cook" out the poisons, after which it was used to cut real whisky, providing the bootlegger had any real whisky. Lacking real whisky, he could start from scratch and produce almost any type. If he wanted Scotch, he used alcohol, water, coloring, glycerin, fusel oil and a little creosote to give it that imported "smoky" flavor. Such a mixture in bottles bearing the faked label of a famous British firm could bring ten dollars when properly marketed. If it was wrapped in burlap bags caked with salt water and held until the day after newspapers reported a Coast Guard clash with smuggling ships off New York Harbor, the price soared.

Intoxicating beverages in one form or another—applejack known as Jersey Lightning, Maryland rye, Kentucky bourbon— were produced all over the country in backwoods stills large enough to supply a few families and in huge distilleries disguised as soap or chemical factories. The big bootlegging syndicates of the Prohibition Era specialized in plants for "cooking" alcohol and Colonel Ira L. Reeves, who was prohibition administrator for New Jersey, later told how he raided a place in New Jersey called the Bone Yard.

We came to an iron fence on the left side of [a country] road, and to a break in the fence, which was rapidly being closed by a short, stocky man trying ot swing a heavy iron gate. We made a sudden swerve to the left [with our automobile], struck the partially closed gate a glancing blow, knocking down the man. We followed a side road, which apparently led to a large building with a tall factory chimney among the trees, about 100 yards from the main road.

We passed through another gate. There were a number of lights within the building as we approached but the moment we stopped the car all lights went out. We resorted to our flashlights and gained entrance by breaking down the door. What we saw would have delighted Al Capone. While not the largest, it was one of the most complete "alky" re-cooking plants I ever saw. It was as spick and span as the generator room of a public service lighting plant—tools all clean and in order; brass polished and every detail showing evidence of the most careful attention. We found hundreds of empty five-gallon cans and about one hundred such cans filled with alcohol which was presumed to be "cleaned" and ready to be shipped. We got 14,000 gallons of "uncleaned" industrial alcohol partially treated.

Then we made a most important discovery, which accounted for the name Bone Yard. One half of the building was partitioned off for use as the "re-cooking" still. The other half was a rendering plant where dead animals were disposed of. The terrible stench incident to such a plant made it possible to run the "alky" plant without detection by the sense of smell. In the battle for smell supremacy, the rendering plant won.

Stills, cooking plants and breweries were often ingeniously hidden in barns, old churches and underground caverns, but few of them were as sanitary as the Bone Yard. One plant raided by Reeves was in an old cow barn with a hayloft overhead. "Floating around on top of the ale in the vats were all sorts of refuse and filth—straw, hay seed, mice, bugs, flies and other things not calculated to add to the potability of the ale. I found floating in one vat a large dead rat, almost as big as a fair-sized rabbit." In the barn were no less than half a million faked labels of ale manufactured by a famous Canadian brewing company. After several years of experience, Reeves estimated that not more than 2 per cent of the alcoholic beverages sold by bootleggers as imported stuff was genuine.

A vast quantity of real foreign liquor was brought illegally across the United States's eighteen-thousand-mile borders, but almost all of it was cut before being sold to Americans. The Canadian and Mexican borders offered fairly easy passage for smugglers and by 1929 there were fleets of foreign ships bringing liquor regularly from the West Indies and elsewhere. These ships anchored in "Rum Row"—far enough off the coast to be technically beyond the jurisdiction of the U.S. Coast Guard but not too far for fast smuggling boats to pick up a cargo that could be landed under cover of darkness or with the connivance of federal agents and police. There were "Rum Rows" along the Atlantic and Pacific coasts and in the Gulf of Mexico, and the ships were presumed to be safe from search or seizure as long as they remained twelve miles from shore. There was constant smuggling across the Detroit River from Canada despite the fact that in 1929 there were more than a hundred armed government boats on guard in that Great Lakes area.

In the beginning, the Coast Guard was far from enthusiastic about the war against the rum runners but, later, under pressure from Washington, they tightened up patrols, clamped down on men who were taking bribes and on many occasions exchanged fire with speedboats carrying liquor to shore. Several such encounters occurred practically in New York Harbor and on one occasion in view of tens of thousands of persons on the beach at Coney Island. The crowd cheered the rum runner, which had a comfortable lead as the boats roared past.

The most noteworthy encounter at sea, however, occurred in the Gulf of Mexico where the Canadian schooner *I'm Alone*, with twenty-eight hundred cases of liquor aboard, was sighted off the Louisiana coast by the Coast Guard cutter *Walcott*. Captain John Randall, the Canadian skipper, reckoned that he was outside the twelve-mile limit. The *Walcott's* skipper did his own reckoning and decided that the *I'm Alone* was only 10.8 miles off shore and was therefore subject to search. When the Canadian vessel ignored the *Walcott's* signals, the cutter opened fire, calling on other Coast Guard boats for assistance. The *I'm Alone* outran the *Walcott's* "hot pursuit" but later was caught by another Coast Guard cutter, the *Dexter,* and sunk by gunfire—some two hundred miles off the coast. One crewman was killed and the others were put in irons and landed at New Orleans.

This brought a vigorous protest from Canada and led to some interesting remarks in the Canadian Parliament. William D. Euler, Minister of National Revenue, disclosed that he had personally made a trip on a rum runner crossing the Detroit River to the United States and indicated his belief that the American officials weren't really much interested in stopping the illegal traffic. Canadian officials, he said, always notified the American customs officials by telephone when a boatload of liquor cleared from the Canadian side of the river. But recently the U.S. customs officials had suggested that such notification be made by letter, which would arrive long after the cargo was landed and obviously could have no purpose other than to show for the record how much liquor was being transported.

Riding in the smuggling boat on a daylight trip, Euler asked the skipper: "Do you often cross in the daytime?"

"Oh, sure. It just happens that the U.S. customs men aren't there when we get across."

There were many instances in which prohibition agents "shook down" bootleggers instead of arresting them, in which smuggling boats landed under police protection on the coast and in which crooked judges and politicians took pay-offs from mobsters, distillers and brewers. The elaborate organization behind bootlegging was illustrated by a raid in October of 1929 on a twenty-room New Jersey mansion, once the country home of Oscar Hammerstein, famous Broadway producer. The house was richly furnished with oriental rugs and expensive divans and tables, but on the roof was a searchlight for flashing signals to rum boats at sea and under the house were tunnels where boatloads of liquor could be stored. In a cottage on the grounds was a radio station for communication with ships and around the estate were trenches and concrete machine-gun emplacements, presumably to ward off a possible raid by rival gangsters. The books of the syndicate showed expenses for 140 employees, 10 speedboats, 50 trucks, 6 oceangoing liquor ships and a fund of hundreds of thousands of dollars for "protection." Thirty-two persons were arrested and many cases of liquor seized, but the most notorious of the gangsters captured was later released for lack of evidence and it seemed unlikely that the raid had disturbed the men at the top of the syndicate.

"The prohibition service," Prohibition Administrator Reeves

said later, "proved to be a training school for bootleggers. While in the service, they naturally learn all the ropes of the underworld as well as the government's methods in attempting to apprehend and convict violators. . . . Naturally, when leaving the service of the prohibition forces, they are sought after by those engaged in the illicit business." And he added that "the price and quality of bootleg liquor have always been considered a barometer of the degree of effectiveness being attained [by enforcement officers]. The price now [1930] is lower and the quality better than at any time since prohibition went into effect, thus definitely proving that the degree of enforcement has about reached zero. As an example: Gin is cheaper in the national capital now than it was before the days of prohibition."

4

"I'll pour you another drink, Harry. Here, hand me your glass."

"Thanks, Fred. Nice party you and Mary Ann got going here. Little quiet for Saturday night but lots of fun. Most fun we've had since we moved to Denver. Say! what kind of poison you putting in these glasses?"

"That's tiger milk, Harry. Guaranteed to turn a flat tire into the life of the party."

"Hm-m. Doesn't have much taste. How do you make it?"

"Easiest thing in the world. You get a half gallon of alcohol and mix it with a half gallon of distilled water—you got to be sure to use distilled water. Then you put in some lemon peel and some orange peel—cut up the peel of about three of each—and let it sit for eighteen hours. Then serve with fruit juice and ice."

"I think it's just plain grapefruit juice!"

"No, Ellen. It's just that the peel kills the taste of the alcohol. I got hep to that talking with a fellow in the store next to me on Champa Street. A guy who really knows his groceries when it comes to mixing a brew. How do you like it, Jerry?"

"Seems okay, Fred. But back in Omaha we always made home

brew. You can buy the malt and the yeast anywhere and if you follow the directions—"

"It's sure to explode all over the house! Anyway, it smells the place up positively."

"Aw, have a heart, Marge. It's not so bad; not the way I make it. Let me tell you how to keep it from blowing up. You just—"

"Say, Jerry, we're making wine. Had a keg of grape juice sent over last week from the delicatessen store. Fellow who sold it to me said it would be 25 per cent alcohol in a month. He's going to send a service man around once a week to check on how it's doing. And I'm here to tell you it's doing something already! The head of the keg bulged out and Patricia was afraid it would spray all over the clothes closet. But the service man came over and fixed it up with a gooseneck tube."

"Banana oil! Why horse around with wine? The easiest thing is to spike a bottle of near beer with alcohol. . . . Yes, thanks, Fred, I'll have another one as long as you're on your feet."

"We made some good bathtub gin last winter. Very simple: alcohol, oil of juniper, glycerin and water. Stir and serve. More wallop than this stuff, Fred. Two drinks and you do like they say in that song—Faw Down and Go Boom."

"This home brew we made in Omaha had a real kick—"

"Oh, don't be a pill, Jerry! Come on and dance. There's Rudy Vallee on the radio and he's going to sing 'My Time Is Your Time.'"

"What did you say you call this stuff, Fred?"

"Tiger milk, Harry."

"Oh, yeah. I'm here to tell you that it's smooth. Got a kick, too, eh, Ellen?"

"I think it's just plain grapefruit juice!"

"It sneaks up on you."

"You said a mouthful, Fred."

"I still think it's just plain— Oh, Fred! I'm sorry I knocked *over my glass. Let me get a rag to wipe it up before it ruins the carpet."*

"Hey, does anybody know the words to 'The Foggy, Foggy Dew'? I want to sing tenor."

"Now, sugar! Take that lampshade off your head—you'll ruin it and it doesn't add anything to your S.A."

"Well, don't get all hot and bothered about it. After all, I've only had a couple of drinks."

"Applesauce!"

"Yes, thanks, Fred. I'll have one more. What did you say you call this?"

"Tiger milk—and it's all tiger."

"I'll carry the melody—you sing bass."

"Fred, what I wanted to tell you was how we mixed this home brew back in Omaha. First you get some—"

5

For those Americans who did not concoct their own brews at home there were plenty of places—known as speakeasies, gin mills, whoopee parlors and even by the old-fashioned name of blind pigs—where a drink could be purchased across the bar or from under the counter. The pattern varied, of course, in different parts of the country, depending on local traditions and the attitude of local officials toward the Volstead Act. In staunch "dry" states such as Kansas, Nebraska and New Mexico, a stranger might have trouble finding a saloon and eventually end up in a dark alley buying a pint from a man who took precautions against being seen by the constabulary. But in large "wet" cities such as San Francisco and Chicago and especially New York, the best way for a stranger to find a drink was to ask the first cop he met on the street for directions to the nearest speakeasy. It was seldom more than a block away.

Despite a new federal law called the Five and Ten that provided stiff penalties of five years in prison and a ten-thousand-dollar fine for sale or smuggling of liquor, the police announced that they had counted no fewer than thirty-two thousand speakeasies in New York City in 1929. Congressman W. I. Sirovich estimated that there were approximately a hundred thousand places in New York City where illegal beverages could be purchased in some form and the best guess in Chicago was that the number of speakeasies there topped ten thousand. In Washington, where the Prohibition Bureau had boasted of a "clean-up" of saloons, a couple of reporters made a quick tour of the national capital and bought liquor in forty-nine different establishments.

There were, of course, many raids on speakeasies and many arrests, but not nearly enough to cause serious inconvenience. One prohibition agent, checking over statistics for several years, concluded that bootlegging was a much safer—and more profitable—racket than robbery because less than one-half of one per cent of the dealers in illicit liquor were ever arrested. The number bumped off by rival bootlegging gangs, however, may have run a little higher. Practically all speakeasies paid some kind of protection money—known as "ice"—to police, prohibition agents and politicians, as well as to racketeers who otherwise would have shot up the joint. Such payments ranged from a few dollars to hundreds of dollars a month and the recipients ranged from the cop on the beat to such characters as Jimmy Hines, powerful Tammany Hall politician and pal of gangsters Larry Fay and Dutch Schultz.

Speakeasies varied from holes-in-the-wall where for a dime you could buy a shot of "smoke"—usually dangerous alcohol—to beer joints hidden behind stationery stores and to plush restaurants off Park Avenue hidden behind costly political protection. Many modest speakeasies set up a shallow phony "salesroom" on the street front, usually featuring some obscure product that no passer-by would think of buying. The windows would be filled with a display of heavy machinery—say, a hydraulic jack or the piston of a railroad locomotive. Across the front would be a neat sign: "STUNK & FELDINGHOUSE, INC." and about six feet behind the windows would be an office desk and a wall with a door in the middle. Nobody ever sat at the desk, but a great many customers entered and disappeared through the door in the wall to the back room where a regular saloon was in operation.

There also were countless restaurants where the food was good and moderately priced—perhaps a dollar and a half for a good Italian meal—and where you could get a cocktail served in a teacup for seventy-five cents and a bottle of wine for another dollar. By 1929 there were still "clubs" where it was necessary to present a card to the doorman who inspected new arrivals through a peephole in the door, but experience had shown that such precautions didn't stop federal agents who brought their own axes. Many speakeasy-restaurants operated more or less openly in the cities, although they might refuse to serve liquor to customers they suspected as informers.

All of these illicit businesses—the dives, the farmhouses where wine was sold in the kitchen, the false-front saloons, the good and the mediocre restaurants that served liquor—were seemingly a permanent part of the American scene in 1929, but the finest flowers of the Prohibition Era were the night club and the clip joint. At times, it was difficult to distinguish between night clubs and clip joints but, in general, the latter was a dive where suckers with a pocketful of cash were overcharged for bad whisky, tossed out by strong-arm bouncers if they protested and rolled by prostitutes if they had any cash left, which was unlikely. Detroit, Chicago and Philadelphia were pioneer cities in the clip joint business, and New York wasn't far behind.

A little experience helped drinkers in distinguishing between night clubs and clip joints. In 1929, two young newspapermen who had just arrived in New York from Colorado collected their Friday afternoon pay checks and set out to find a drink. A taxi-cab driver took them to a Greenwich Village club with a peephole in the door and told them to inform the doorman that "Sam sent us." They were admitted to a bar where they sat at a table and were promptly joined by two unattached young women. Everybody had a few drinks and, a couple of hours later, a large, exceedingly tough-looking waiter put on the table a bill that totaled more than the reporters' combined pay checks.

FAIRBANKS

Sells only the best and at lower prices.

All our merchandise is analyzed and tested by a registered chemist and is sold with a positive guarantee of your money back if not entirely satisfied in every way.

Phone Your Orders:

Open: 9 A.M. to Midnite

Free Offer

FREE with every purchase of $2.00, ½ pint of MOUNT VERNON.

With each purchase of $4.50 or over, we give you FREE one bottle of GIN or a bottle of BACARDI.

With every $10.00 purchase one bottle of SCOTCH or a full pint of any brand RYE or any Cordial.

Open: 9:00 A.M. to Midnite

CALL—

Fairbanks

Prompt Delivery Service

PRICE LIST

GINS

Booths High & Dry	$ .75	3 for $2.00
Piccadilly	1.00	3 for 2.50
Holloways	1.00	3 for 2.75
Gilbey's	1.00	3 for 2.75
White Satin	1.25	3 for 3.25

Imported GINS

Gilbey's Frosted	$2.00	3 for $5.00
Holstkamp (Jugs)	$2.00	3 for 5.00

RYE

Golden Wedding	pt. $1.75	3 for $4.50
Lincoln Inn	1.75	3 for 4.50
Four Aces	1.75	3 for 4.50
William Penn	1.75	3 for 4.50
Old Dougherty	1.75	3 for 4.50
Chicken Cock (Canned)	2.00	3 for 5.00
7 Yr.-Old Canadian	3.00	3 for 8.00
Irish Whiskey	qt. 4.00	2 for 7.00

PRICE LIST

BOURBON WHISKEY

Indian Hill	pt. $1.75	3 for $4.50
Old Log Cabin	1.75	3 for 4.50
Old Crow	1.75	3 for 4.50
Genuine Bourbon	3.00	3 for 8.00

ALCOHOL

U.S.P. Pure Grain, 190 Proof

Quart	$1.50
Gallon	5.50
Sealed 5 gal. Tins	24.00

BACARDI

Bacardi (Oro)	qt. $1.50	3 for $4.00
Bacardi 1873	qt. 2.00	3 for 5.50
Bacardi (Gal.)		6.00
Jamaica Rum	3.00	2 for 5.00

COGNAC

Hennessy*** - Martel - Bisquit Dubouche
Specially priced at $4.00 qt.

PRICE LIST

Domestic SCOTCH

		Quart
Johnny Walker	$2.50	3 for $6.50
Vat 69	2.50	3 for 6.50
Usher's Green Stripe	2.50	3 for 6.50
Teacher's Highland Cream	2.50	3 for 6.50
Black and White	2.50	3 for 6.50
Peter Dawson	2.50	3 for 6.50

SCOTCH (High Grade)

		Quart
McCallums Perfection	$4.50	2 for $8.00
Chivas Regal	5.00	2 for 9.00
Buchanan's Oval	5.00	2 for 9.00
Lawson's Liqueurs	6.00	2 for 10.00
John Dunbar	40 oz. 6.00	2 for 11.00

CORDIALS

Marie Brizard   P. Garnier
Following Brands Always on Hand:
Creme de Menthe — Creme de Cacao
Apricot — Mandarin — Blackberry
Cerise
Especially priced at $3.00 qt.
Benedictine — Chartreuse —Cointreau
Especially priced at $4.00
Italian and French Vermouth $3.00

A New York City bootlegger's card of prices.

At the same time two more tough characters took up stations near the table. Hiding their terror, the reporters ordered two more drinks and one of them went to the washroom, where he telephoned his office and explained his plight to an assistant city editor. "Just sit tight at that table and have another drink," he was advised. Twenty minutes later the doorman admitted a uniformed policeman who looked around and barked: "I'm looking for a couple of crooks named Smith and Jones. You there! What's your names?" The reporters admitted to the names. "Okay, you two," the cop growled. "You're wanted at the station. Come along." They went as rapidly as possible, leaving the check on the table. Outside, the cop marched them to the corner and told them to head for home. "Good thing your boss is a friend of the lieutenant," he said. "Otherwise you'd got hell beat out of you. What kind a reporters are you anyway—too dumb to know when you're in a clip joint?"

The night club, on the other hand, was a spot where the clipping of the sheep was carried on in a more subtle manner, with gaiety, friendliness and sometimes even with elegance. Belle Livingston converted an old brownstone mansion into a plush drinking spot, with lights kept low and cushions on the floor for cutomers who were bold enough to believe they could get to their feet again after absorbing bootleg whisky. Gilda Gray, the ageless Queen of the Shimmy, packed the younger generation into the Piccadilly Rendezvous with her version of the hula-hula but the place eventually went broke because it was monopolized by Yale, Harvard and Princeton boys who brought their own liquor and paid only a cover charge or for a few bottles of ginger ale at $1.50 a pint. The slang word "heel" may have originated with the Piccadilly waiters, who applied it to the college boys—meaning a tightwad or one who saved money by wearing rubber heels on his shoes.

There were plenty of night clubs to choose from. Customers happily handed out big tips and paid a dollar or more for a thimbleful of bootleg bourbon in order to sit uncomfortably at crowded tables and hear Broadway's melancholy Helen Morgan, perched atop a piano, singing:

> Some day he'll come along,
> The man I love. . . .

And, as the night wore on toward dawn, not a few of the revelers were accustomed to piling into taxicabs and dashing up to Harlem to put the finishing touches on the evening at the Cotton Club or another of half a dozen well-known Negro night spots.

Perhaps the best-known if not the most elegant of the New York night clubs were connected with the name of Mary Louise Guinan, a broad and brassy blonde from Waco, Texas, with a penetrating voice and a gift for mixing politicians, society figures, gamblers, gunmen and businessmen from the Midwest. Miss Guinan, usually known as Texas, was sponsored by notorious gangsters, protected by well-known politicians and admired by many of the less conservative members of New York society, who followed her from one to another of half a dozen different night clubs during the late 1920's. Her first venture in 1922, when she was in her early forties, was sponsored by Mobster Larry Fay, who wore gaudy, London-tailored costumes over his bulletproof vest. Her later Texas Guinan clubs were said to have been financed by Gambler Arnold Rothstein, who, like Fay, died of bullet wounds.

A typical Texas Guinan Club was a big, rather barren room filled with small tables and a bandstand adjacent to a dance floor hardly larger than a billiard table. The smoke was thick, the music was loud and the pony chorus of girls—young, pretty and lightly clad—had so little room in which to maneuver that they were practically in the laps of ringside customers. Miss Guinan, once a singer of sorts, wore glittering sequin-covered gowns and often blew a police whistle in her role as mistress of ceremonies and greeter of customers. She approached both jobs with such remarkable candor that several of her more penetrating remarks have been preserved for posterity. "Hello, sucker!" was her familiar greeting. And her technique in introducing a performer was to demand: "Give this little girl a great big hand, folks!"—a command that later generations of night clubbers and radio listeners would hear to the point of nausea. Miss Guinan also was credited with first describing a free spender from the Middle West as "a big butter-and-egg man."

When Chester P. Mills was prohibition administrator for New York, he made many attempts to secure evidence of violation of the Volstead Act that would put Miss Guinan in jail. Her clubs frequently were raided and sometimes closed but she always contended in court that she was merely a hired entertainer who had no idea that liquor was being served. The government was never able to prove otherwise to a jury.

One of Miss Guinan's trials in April of 1929 was played to standing room only. Crowds jammed the corridors of the Federal Building and let out a roar of approval when the verdict of "not guilty" was announced. That night, clad in a bright red dress, she entered her club behind a brass band and was given a standing ovation by the customers. "She kissed everybody in sight," *Time* magazine recorded.

The smoky air was thick with vindictive joy. Harry Thaw, onetime maniac, hysterical with delight, jigged up and down at his table until Miss Guinan led him out on the floor to introduce him. She read congratulatory messages from such friends as Manhattan's Congressman Fiorello La Guardia [later mayor of New York City], Henry Zittel of *Zit's* [theatrical weekly], Billy Walsh and Moe Levy, nightclub "boys" now in a New Jersey jail.

Miss Guinan then reached a kind of peak as a shining example of American scofflawism during the Prohibition Era when she sang:

> I was carried down to court accused of selling liquor.
> I got a hand upon the stand that made the lawyers snicker.
> Judge Thomas said, "Tex, do you sell booze?"
> I said, "Please don't be silly;
> I swear to you my cellar's filled
> With chocolate and vanilly."

Nobody could accuse Miss Guinan of being snobbish. Many sophisticated persons of the social and artistic world visited her clubs. But the mass of customers was made up of out-of-town businessmen on a spree in the big city, junior executives entertaining customers on an expense account, drunks with plenty of cash and climbers who wanted to get their names in the gossip columns. And of course the racketeers. Miss Guinan nevertheless had set the pace for development of what became known as café society in New York and she helped speed the demise of the kind of stiff-neck society that had made it possible for Ward McAllister to win a place in snob history by selecting four hundred persons as the only Americans worth knowing socially. At Texas Guinan's the younger generation of New York's best families were on first-name terms with mobsters, arms-around-the-neck with Broadwayites and willing to pay well for the favor of a doorman who carried a blackjack.

They would never go back to the old ways or the old ideas. After the end of prohibition in 1933, not a few rum runners and speakeasy owners turned legal and converted their establishments into plush restaurants that became centers for the swirl of café society life in New York. Even the grandchildren of some of Texas Guinan's customers would find it necessary in 1956 to have a speaking acquaintance with a few aging Prohibition Era rum runners if they expected to get a good table at some of the best clubs.

6

"Prohibition!" snorted a fat and talkative businessman in a *Saturday Evening Post* short story by Booth Tarkington in 1929.

Unless that law is changed before [my little daughter] grows up, nobody can tell what's liable to happen to her and all these other innocent little children playing here, happy and healthy in the sunshine today. . . .

"You see the danger, don't you? If Prohibition lasts till they grow up, what's the exact proportion of 'em 'll die from poisoned liquor? And of those that don't die, what's the exact proportion 'll have their health shattered? How many of 'em 'll have their eyes ruined by wood alcohol? You see why I hate to have my little Helen get to be even six years old: she'll be just one year nearer the brink! . . . But I've got to let her take her chance, don't I?"

"Why, no," I said. "It seems to me that it'd be fairly simple to avoid it . . . if she didn't drink. . . ."

He stared at me. "Why, my soul, man! Just look at these young people of sixteen and upward all around us. You know what prohibition has done to them, don't you? You don't suppose they know how to get good liquor, do you? You don't suppose they bother about getting good, reliable bootleggers or having the stuff analyzed? For that matter, how many of 'em could afford it? Most of these parents here don't give their children very liberal allowances, so how is a boy or girl of sixteen or seventeen or eighteen going to be able to show any caution, even if they felt like it. . . . Poor little Helen. . . . It's a terrible thing to look forward to. . . ."

Author Tarkington, of course, was satirizing parents who worried about their children in the mornings but set a horrible example in the evening by getting blotto drunk at neighborhood parties where the younger generation couldn't miss seeing their elders weaving wildly around the house, singing ribald songs and driving their automobiles through the hedges. His character's conversation, nevertheless, was not too greatly exaggerated. Despite the fact that the prohibitionists had scored a great victory in the 1928 presidential and congressional elections, public concern about prohibition in general and public resentment against many dry agents in particular were being increased every day. There had been criminals and crime, racketeers and rackets long before the Prohibition Era. Nobody could blame the drys for having invented gangsterism or political corruption. But prohibition had made it possible for crime to pay as never before in modern times; it had created a climate in which the gunman and the rum runner were romantic, adventurous figures.

Even more disastrous, it had led millions of Americans to break the law or to sympathize with lawbreakers because they regarded the Eighteenth Amendment as an infringement on their rights—and because they wanted a drink. They were hostile toward the "dry snooper" who was pictured by such noted cartoonists as Rollin Kirby and Daniel Fitzpatrick as a funereal figure with blue nose and pig eyes, with a black stove-pipe hat, a long black coat and white cotton gloves. Crowds that witnessed raids on speakeasies often threatened or interfered with prohibition agents and on some occasions created so much confusion that bystanders were able to make off with bottles or even barrels of liquor that had been—temporarily—confiscated.

The public was often incensed by the tactics of the dry agents. At one time, agents stood at the gangplank of ocean liners and patted passengers, including some women, on the hips or legs as they came ashore to see whether they were carrying liquor flasks. On Biscayne Bay, at Miami, a Coast Guard picket boat vainly chasing a suspected rum boat fired some two hundred pistol and machine-gun bullets that crashed wildly into an occupied houseboat, a business establishment on Flagler Street, two residences and a post against which a night watchman was leaning. In New York Harbor, the yacht *Restless*, with its owner, Broker Stuyvesant Fish and his family aboard, was fired on near the Statue of Liberty by a U.S. patrol boat, which then put an agent aboard for a thorough search of the ship. No liquor was found.

In Kane County, Illinois, four deputy sheriffs acting on the tip of a snooper who was paid five dollars, broke into the home of Joseph De King in Aurora after throwing mustard bombs at the windows. De King was knocked unconscious. Mrs. De King was at the telephone screaming for help when a deputy fired a shotgun loaded with slugs, wounding her fatally. The De Kings' twelve-year-old son shot a deputy in the leg with a revolver but was overpowered. One gallon of homemade wine was found in the cellar. In Minnesota, Henry Virkula was returning to his candy store at Big Falls after a trip across the Canadian border when two men leaped into the road with a big "Stop" sign. Virkula braked but the car didn't stop until it had passed the two customs agents, one of whom shot the candy store owner in the back of the neck, killing him. No liquor was found in the car.

All of these things and many other incidents gave the wets

ammunition for their attacks on the Eighteenth Amendment. "The prohibitionists, when they were lobbying their panacea through Congress and the state legislatures, were perfectly willing to make terms with any sort of lawlessness in order to get what they wanted," H. L. Mencken wrote in the *American Mercury* in 1929.

This alliance with corruption has been succeeded, since Prohibition got upon the law-books, by an alliance with other and even worse varieties of crime. There seems, indeed, to be no limit to the complaisance of the Prohibitionists in this direction. They are not only willing to condone the most barbaric kinds of assault and the most atrocious kinds of murder; they seem actually eager to promote such crimes. . . . Worse, they encourage by shrewd and deliberate devices every known sort of fraud and false pretense, so that in communities where they are in power neighbor is ranged against neighbor, the immemorial decencies are abandoned and life becomes almost intolerable. And yet all this wholesale aiding and abetting of crime is carried on in the name of Law Enforcement.

To most readers, even readers of the *American Mercury*, Mencken's words may have seemed a bit harsh as doubtless he intended them to be. There was no question that a great many thinking people were worried or alarmed by conditions in the ninth year of the prohibition era. In the nation's wettest city, for example, Mayor James J. Walker had a few words to say about conditions that had come to his attention. The honest workers of New York going to their jobs at dawn, he said, often encountered tipsy revelers in evening clothes staggering away from night clubs. This, Mr. Walker remarked indignantly, was likely to give the workers a bad impression of society and might open the road to Bolshevism. To correct this grave situation, the New York Mayor added, he believed that the tipsy revelers should go home at 3 A.M.

THREE

...nor dashed a thousand kim....

Nineteen twenty-nine was a pivotal year for Americans
. . . for James J. Hines, a sturdy man with steel-blue eyes, a
cap of short white hair and cheeks that were reddened by sun
and wind on the fairways of expensive golf clubs. Son of a New
York City blacksmith whose political connections kept him busy
shoeing the horses of firemen and police, Hines became a
smith at the age of fifteen and the captain of an election district before he was old enough to vote. He "got out the vote"
and if there was fighting to be done on election day he was
among the best with his fists—good enough to be arrested twice
around the turn of the century for street brawling. He could
and did see that ballot boxes were stuffed in behalf of the
Democratic candidate when necessary. He never hesitated to
take off his leather apron and hurry to the police station or the
magistrate's court to aid a friend or a loyal party worker. He
knew the importance of distributing a ton of coal or a basket of
groceries to cold and hungry families when Thanksgiving rolled
around. He knew when to fight for control of the party organization in his district and when to join the opposition if he
couldn't lick them. He knew how to build a gang of strong-arm
roughnecks and how to lead them against rival gangs and, in
1910, he personally punched his chief rival off a wagon which
he had mounted to make a political speech.

By 1912 he was in full control of the Eleventh Assembly District and was chief clerk of the Board of Aldermen at five thousand dollars a year. He sold his smithy, went into the trucking business, closed out his bank accounts and thereafter never deposited a penny anywhere in his own name. The migration of Negroes to Harlem during the World War overflowed into the Eleventh District and, to hold power, Hines had to spread his largesse. He needed more money. He leased the top floor of his political club for crap games and poker, a concession that was run by the notorious gambler and underworld banker, Arnold Rothstein. He was moving up in Tammany Hall now and he became involved in a deal by which political influence was used to get glucose—under wartime controls—released by the government for a beer-making company in which he had become interested. The deal netted him a share of the profits estimated at forty-six thousand dollars a day, until the promotors quarreled and the supply of glucose was cut off.

In a rough and rowdy campaign of vote buying and ballot box stuffing, Hines tangled with Tammany Boss Charles F. Murphy and gained control of the Thirteenth District as well as the Eleventh in 1921, making good use of "goon squads" supplied by some of his friends who were just beginning to realize the possibility of rum running and other rackets developing in the Prohibition Era. By now Hines's name, seldom mentioned in the newspapers, was known throughout the underworld and he controlled or strongly influenced an important minority of votes in the Tammany Hall executive committee. As election day drew near, his henchmen might pass out at least a thousand dollars a day in crisp dollar bills to a long line of callers at the Monongahela Democratic Club with instructions on how to vote. "It's relief," Hines told reporters. "There are a lot of poor people in this district."

But there was more to Hines's power than dollar bills. He had been aided by the underworld when he was fighting for power. Now the underworld demanded its pay-off. In one way or another, Hines was of service to or associated with almost every racketeer and gunman who flourished during the Twenties—Owen Madden, a gangster who pushed racketeering into the coal, laundry, night club and prize fighting businesses; William Vincent Dwyer, perhaps the most notorious rum runner of the times; Frank Costello, who played the field and would be the leading character a quarter-century later in Kefauver Committee investigation of crime; Lucky Luciano, head of narcotics, liquor and prostitution rackets and later a deportee to Italy; and a number of others. He was doing fine in 1929 when he became associated with Arthur Flegenheimer, better known as Dutch Schultz, a quick-tempered beer peddler and policy game racketeer with a penchant for ready gunfire.

Schultz in 1928 had been a bartender in a speakeasy in the Bronx but he took over when his boss and partner was bumped off by Legs Diamond's gunmen. He hired a squad of gunmen and branched out into retailing needle beer, driving competitors out of the area by threats or murderous beatings. His income from beer alone in 1929 was estimated at $131,000 and he would soon make millions from the policy or "numbers" gambling games and from industrial rackets. Meantime, he had Hines on his payroll, probably for thousands a week. Hines's power in political affairs increased steadily. His name was whispered as the man who could get things done, the man with influence in the courts. He was investigated by able prosecutors but they could pin nothing on him. And behind Hines stood the gangsters. "These gangsters owed their success to politics," Craig Thompson and Allen Raymond wrote later in *Gang Rule in New York*. "There was Hines, a man whose nod made judges and prosecutors out of clubhouse lawyers. . . . Yet, he was only a paid hireling of a thug named Arthur Flegenheimer, [who] wanted the use of Hines' power. And Hines . . . sold because the bargain brought him the money and the strength to maintain that political machine on which his own power rested."

He maintained it for almost another decade. Late one night in Newark, two gunmen found Schultz in a bar and restaurant and shot him fatally. Three Schultz bodyguards also were killed. The dying gang leader raved for several hours in a hospital, saying wildly that "John" had shot him in a quarrel over a million dollars, talking about his childhood, calling for his mother and, at one point, uttering an amazing but meaningless sentence: "A boy has never wept, nor dashed a thousand kim."

But it wasn't just Schultz who went down. He took Hines with him, although two years passed before District Attorney Thomas E. Dewey could get an indictment of the Tammany potentate. On the testimony of former Schultz employees, he was convicted and sentenced to prison. If he knew who had "dashed a thousand kim" he never admitted it.

It's been years since there's been either a head or a tail to the Democratic Party.

—WILL ROGERS, 1929

MARCH, 1929

the political scene

Low, rain-filled clouds hung over the capital of the United States at midday on March 4 when two men wearing silk top hats, cutaway coats and gray pin-stripe trousers climbed into an automobile at the White House and started a solemn drive down Pennsylvania Avenue. Except for the fact that inauguration of a new Chief of State required a ceremonial trip to the capitol, neither President Calvin Coolidge nor President-elect Herbert Clark Hoover would have chosen to motor along Pennsylvania Avenue. Nor would anybody else. It was a drab street, pockmarked with old and grimy buildings—grocery stores, cheap hotels, an old market, souvenir shops, a burlesque theater, lunchrooms, a Chinese laundry, a fortune teller's establishment, a gasoline station and the building in which the Leong Tong made its headquarters.

Nor had the spreading activities of the United States government done anything to improve the beauty of the capital's proudest avenue. In the Mall, which Major Pierre Charles L'Enfant had planned in 1800 as a glorious garden alongside the avenue, there was a scramble of federal buildings thrown up hurriedly during World War I as temporary offices. There were junk heaps and powerhouses with unsightly black smokestacks scarring the center of the nation's capital. In 1929, Washington had become a city of more than half a million—it would be eight hundred thousand by the 1950's—but it had suffered severe growing pains. The magnificent plans of L'Enfant had been all but forgotten for almost a century, since old Andrew Jackson arbitrarily had the Treasury Building constructed at a point where it blocked the sweep of Pennsylvania Avenue from Capitol Hill to the White House. By Civil War times, the city was a scraggly mess with railroad tracks twisting across the Mall. Then there had been a period of cleaning up and planting trees; after the turn of the century the old railroad station, where President Garfield was assassinated, was torn down but Washington's central area remained an architectural hodge-podge.

Almost the only encouraging sights that greeted Mr. Coolidge and Mr. Hoover that March morning were the partly completed Department of Commerce Building—massive walls stretching a thousand feet along Fourteenth Street—and slabs of New England granite, Tennessee marble and Indiana limestone piled up on the Mall in preparation for construction of the six-million-dollar Bureau of Internal Revenue Building. These were the first steps in an ambitious, $275-million program of construction that was close to the hearts of both men. Mr. Coolidge had pushed the program because he had discovered that it would be cheaper to build new federal offices than to continue renting them haphazardly. Mr. Hoover, who had presided over the Department of Commerce in an inadequate yellow brick building at Nineteenth Street, was enthusiastic about the plan because he felt it was about time Washington began to live up to its place in history.

Under the plan, which had been approved in 1926, the city returned to the basic principles of L'Enfant. The Mall would be cleared and a ramshackle area between the capitol and the handsome new Union Station would be torn down. A glistening, white marble building would be constructed near the capitol for the Supreme Court, which for seventy years had met in a tiny chamber in the capitol. But, most important, the government had acquired twenty-three blocks in a great triangle be-

tween Fourteenth Street, Pennsylvania Avenue and the Mall
(then B Street, but now Constitution Avenue) and here would
be erected six great buildings housing the departments of Labor
and Justice, the Internal Revenue offices, the Interstate Commerce Commission, the Department of Commerce, the Archives
and the independent offices. Within a few years the whole face
of Washington would be radically changed and the United
States would have one of the most impressive capitals in the
world.

But on the dreary March day in 1929 this work had hardly
started and the only impressive thing about Pennsylvania
Avenue was the throng that cheered the retiring and incoming
Presidents and a fat, strong-voiced boy at the corner of Tenth
Street who cried: "Oh, you Herbie!" as Mr. Hoover sedately
lifted his silk topper in greeting. Mr. Coolidge, the crowd noted,
doffed his hat oftener and more gaily than his successor, and
perhaps with good reason. He was shedding the burden of office
at a time when "Coolidge Prosperity" was untarnished. He had
lived up to the campaign slogan of "Keep cool with Coolidge."
He had watched the country's business graph rise to unparalleled heights, except for agriculture, and he had done nothing
to disturb the great Wall Street boom. He had soothed Republican congressmen—virtually put them to sleep, some said—with
occasional White House breakfasts of sausage, buckwheat cakes
and Vermont maple syrup. He had, despite tight inner tensions,
earned a reputation as "Silent Cal" and as a sly jokester. He had
taken a nap regularly every afternoon, he had more or less
suppressed his disdain for the popular Mr. Hoover and he had
finally announced that he did "not choose to run" for re-election
in 1928. A lot of people thought that Mr. Coolidge might have
been persuaded to run and that he was even a mite disappointed when the Grand Old Party so readily took him at his
word and turned to Mr. Hoover, but if so he never acknowledged it. In all, Mr. Coolidge had been one of the nation's least
exciting Presidents at a time of unusually exciting growth.
"Give this country four more years of this Unparalleled Pros-

perity," Humorist Will Rogers wrote in the *Saturday Evening Post*, "and the people will get so tired of having everything they want that it'll be a pleasure to get poor again."

Mr. Hoover, on the other hand, was just picking up the burden or—as he intimated much later—it might be said that he was just about to pick up the tab for the banquet that had been enjoyed by his predecessor. An entertaining companion and storyteller among a few friends, the new President seldom gave a public impression of great happiness and he often seemed painfully ill at ease. He had not distinguished himself in his campaign against Democratic nominee Alfred E. Smith, who had risen from the New York slums to be recognized as an able and honest Governor of New York, a remarkable orator and an advocate of moderate reform in the prohibition laws. Mr. Hoover, a poor Quaker farm boy from Iowa who had gained international recognition as an engineer and considerable wealth through investments abroad, stepped lightly around the controversy over prohibition, which he called "a great social and economic experiment, noble in motive," and kept his campaign speeches on a high ethical level. But the whispering campaign against Smith—a Catholic, a slum product, a "wet" and a Tammany Hall politician—was one of the most vicious in many decades. Nor was it always whispers. Mrs. Mabel Walker Willebrandt, Assistant U.S. Attorney General, made an appeal to two thousand Methodist pastors to rally church members behind Mr. Hoover as a friend of prohibition, and later said that the appeal was specifically ordered by the Republican National Committee and James Francis Burke, who was Mr. Hoover's chief political adviser. Such tactics were no favor to Mr. Hoover. Nor was his luster increased over the long run by the ease with which the nation's cartoonists pictured him as a kind of round-faced, rumple-haired kewpie doll in high stiff collar and business clothes.

Yet, at the age of fifty-four, Mr. Hoover was regarded by the people generally as one of the most promising statesmen to take the presidential oath in a long time. He had won universal acclaim for his handling of relief work after World War I. He had, after some early troubles, made a reputation for efficiency and enterprise as the Secretary of Commerce. He had a grasp not only of domestic problems but of the great issues confronting the world eleven years after the war. He was able and respected, and if he was not, perhaps, an experienced political leader there were plenty of experts around—including several friends among newspaper correspondents—to offer advice.

The rain fell steadily on the thousands that had gathered at the capitol to see Mr. Hoover sworn in by Chief Justice William Howard Taft, who asked the President-elect to "preserve, maintain and protect" the Constitution when he should have said "preserve, protect and defend." Wind-driven spray drifted across the outdoor platform and dripped from the new President's hair as he began his rapidly spoken address. "The whole world," he said, "is at peace. . . . Surely civilization is old enough, surely mankind is mature enough so that we ought in our own lifetime to find a way to permanent peace." He spoke of business conditions, of increasing crime, of a special session of Congress to enact farm relief and tariff changes and of prohibition, the enforcement of which, he said, would be studied by a national commission to be named soon. "I have no fears for the future of our country. It is bright with hope." He finished in a steady rain and returned to the White House, while Mr. and Mrs. Coolidge hurried across the plaza to the Union Station and caught the first train back to Massachusetts.

2

One reason for the public's high regard for Mr. Hoover was his reputation as a Big Administrator and a high-level Efficiency Expert, and efficiency was admired above almost everything in the bustling, confident world of 1929. Technological advances and new business methods after World War I had led to all kinds of things that made everyday life better and easier for millions of Americans. Now Mr. Hoover would have a chance to get some engineering efficiency into government where, as everyone knew, it was badly needed. The people were inclined to picture the new President as prepared to make a scientific approach to whatever problems might confront the nation and they were inclined to believe that, since he was not trained as a politician, Mr. Hoover would soon put an end to the familiar political shenanigans that caused so much trouble in Washington. The noted cartoonist, Herbert Johnson, pictured the new President at the teacher's desk in "America's New School of Government" with the pupils—labeled as Business, Finance, Labor, Science and Industry—studying their lessons industriously and happily except for a dopey-looking bad boy who was identified as "Party Politics." This dunce had to be dragged to the classroom by Uncle Sam, who said hopefully to Teacher Hoover: "Maybe you can keep him out of mischief." The public believed Mr. Hoover knew the answers to such problems, knew how to bring government up to date; and, in a way, the public was right. By 1954, Mr. Hoover would be known as America's greatest living expert on governmental efficiency; but not exactly because he showed up well in 1929 as a St. George among the political dragons.

Once in the White House, the President lost no time in introducing a note of efficiency. He had a telephone installed on his desk. All previous Presidents had gone to an adjoining room on the rare occasions when they used the telephone, but now Mr. Hoover could be in instantaneous touch with his cabinet officers and other executives. He put in a system of buzzers, with various buzz signals to summon various secretaries. He removed an old green student's lamp, several ornate paperweights and a jar of smelling salts from the presidential desk. He closed the White House stables at a saving of fifteen thousand dollars a year. He retired the White House yacht at what was called a saving of three hundred thousand dollars. He donned black sweater and gray flannels and gathered at 7 A.M. with distinguished politicians and officials in the White House backyard to play "bull-in-the-ring"—tossing a heavy medicine ball around a circle for exercise. Mr. Hoover got his weight down from 198 to 185 in this manner but not without casualties. Mr. Justice Harlan Fiske Stone of the United States Supreme Court tossed the ball so vigorously that the presidential wind was knocked out of the presidential stomach on one occasion. Ambassador to Belgium Hugh Gibson caught the ball in his face and had a red mark on his nose for a week. Newspaper correspondent William Hard slipped, sprained his ankle and was on crutches for several days.

Mr. Hoover also fished, carried stones and built dams—and urged his guests to do the same—at his week-end retreat on the Rapidan River in the Shenandoah National Park. "Some of us thought Herbert Hoover was an impersonal, cold sort of person, with a great brain that seemed a little icy," remarked the Jacksonville (Florida) *Journal.* "But now our President has been revealed as a man who knows play as well as work. . . . Herb acquires and retains that human touch—by building dams."

The Hoover break with old-fashioned ways was completed with the establishment of a secretariat. Whereas other Presidents had had one secretary, Mr. Hoover had five—James Francis Burke, political strategist, a dapper little Philadelphia lawyer with a penchant for wing collars, English walking shoes and a Malacca stick; George Akerson, a two-hundred-pound former newspaperman who handled appointments; Walter H. Newton, former congressman from Minnesota who dealt with patronage problems; E. French Strother, former editor of the *World's Work* who researched presidential speeches; and Lawrence Richey, who once had been a boy detective with the William J. Burns Agency and a long-time personal investigator for Mr. Hoover. Except for Burke, who was general counsel for the National Republican Committee and served at the White House without pay, the secretaries received ten thousand dollars a year and a great deal of publicity. At the spring dinner of the Gridiron Club, the Washington newspaper correspondents burlesqued the secretariat in a skit that showed them running about wildly in an effort to appear busy. The correspondents also pictured the administration as "water-cooled, dry-batteried and using no oil," with Mr. Hoover presiding in iron-handed fashion over a cabinet of ten robots, all of whom were made up to look like pale shadows of the Chief Executive.

With remarkable prescience, the correspondents reminded the robot cabinet that every administration has to have a "goat" and asked who it would be this time. All ten robots shouted: "Who but Hoover?" and then sang:

> Be content to be just echoes
> If he plays a one-man game,
> Then when trouble comes a-knocking
> Just let Herbert take the blame.
> When a target they hunt, he'll be there out in front
> Who but Hoover will get all the blame?

"With only one secretary on the job," remarked an anonymous Washington correspondent writing in the *American Mercury*, "it used to be a relatively simple matter to make contact with the President. But surrounded as he is now by this elaborate cordon, the boys [in Congress] are at a loss as to which secretary to shine up to. . . . All this is hard on the politicians, but it gives the Super-Administrator himself a great out." Another critic, commenting on the secretariat, snapped out the opinion that it showed Mr. Hoover "is a man who makes big jobs out of little ones."

All of this merely emphasized that Mr. Hoover—or the Chief, as he was known to the White House staff—was in favor of catching up with the times. The burden of the presidency was becoming greater every year and in the future there would be more rather than fewer secretaries and the executive offices, which were enlarged in 1929, would be expanded again and again in the next twenty-five years. It is difficult to imagine what ridicule would have been heaped upon Mr. Hoover if—like his successors—he had gone so far as to appoint an "assistant President" or to employ a staff of experienced writers to prepare his speeches or to make use of advertising experts in planning his campaigns. But then the White House, like many other treasured American institutions, was never the same again after 1929.

Mr. Hoover began his administration with an elaborate plan for closer and more regular contact with newspaper reporters—an idea that he soon abandoned. But there was a great deal more informality around the White House than in Coolidge's day. Mrs. Lou Henry Hoover was an energetic, friendly First Lady with a good sense of humor and the Hoover grandchildren, Herbert 3rd and Peggy Ann, frequently romped noisily around the house. Mrs. Hoover was a national leader in the Girl Scouts and didn't think it beneath her dignity to sit on the floor while meeting with a troop of girls. Her Girl Scout name was "Buffalo."

There were sometimes some amusing incidents at the White House because, in addition to the President, there were two other Hoovers working there. The President's naval aide was Lieutenant Commander Gilbert C. Hoover (no relation) and the White House major domo was Ike Hoover, who had been around for years. It was inevitable that Ike Hoover sometimes got messages intended for the President and vice versa. One day Ike Hoover telephoned an order to the grocery store and talked to a new order clerk.

"This," he said, "is Hoover at the White House."

"Sure, dearie," the new girl replied brightly, "and this is Queen Marie of Rumania."

3

As President, Mr. Hoover presided honestly, efficiently and energetically over the affairs of a government that was rather blindly near the end of an era of unfettered freedom for private enterprise. By modern standards, it was not a very big governmental operation. When Mr. Hoover took office there were less than 600,000 federal employees or about one-fourth as many as would be on the payroll in 1954. There were about 215,000 men in the Army and Navy combined and the lowest pay for a private was twenty-four dollars a month, but by 1954 (after the Korean War) the number of men and women in the two services would be more than ten times as great and the lowest basic pay would be more than three times as high. The United States Air Force didn't even exist as a separate service in 1929, but a quarter-century later it would have a strength of approximately a million men and women. Thus in a period of twenty-five years the peacetime armed forces of the nation were increased fifteenfold.

What such changes in government—especially the growth of defense spending—meant to the average American is best illustrated by the change in income tax rates over approximately the same period. In 1929, the rate of normal tax on the first $7,500 of net income was 1½ per cent, with exemptions of $1,500 for a single person and $3,500 for a married person or the head of a family. For those in the higher brackets, the rate mounted to 5 per cent at $12,000 plus a surtax that was graduated up to 20 per cent on $100,000. Thus a married man earning $7,500 a year in 1929 could not possibly pay more than $60 in income tax and, after making authorized deductions, probably would pay considerably less or nothing at all. The man with an income of $100,000 might, but probably would not, pay up to $16,000.

By the 1950's there had been some changes made. The exemptions had been cut by more than 60 per cent to a flat $600 per taxpayer plus the same amount for each dependent. The tax rate, including surtax, for practically all wage earners was just above 20 per cent or about fourteen times the rate on modest incomes in 1929, and the surtax rate had been boosted to 87 per cent in the upper brackets.[1] If deductions other than for himself and his wife were disregarded, the married man with a salary of $7,500 in 1954 could theoretically pay a maximum tax about twenty-eight times as large as his maximum payment of $60 on the same salary in 1929; and the man with an income of $100,000 might find his taxes quadrupled to more than $67,000.

Mr. Hoover managed to run the government in 1929 on less

[1] Taxes were reduced slightly in 1955.

than four billion dollars and his tax collectors managed to bring in a little more than four billion. The national debt was whittled down that year to less than seventeen billion dollars. A quarter-century later the Department of Defense alone would be spending ten times as much annually as the entire government budget for 1929, and over-all government expenditures would be in the neighborhood of seventy billion dollars. So vast was the growth of government expense in this period that by 1954 the national debt would be increased sixteenfold to $275 billion and the budgetary *deficit* would be about as large as the *entire budget* for Mr. Hoover's first year in office. In the same period the per capita cost of government to Americans increased fourteenfold to about $440 a year.

But such statistics give only the vaguest idea of the change in government from a physical as well as a philosophical viewpoint. In 1929, there was no Social Security Administration, no Tennessee Valley Authority, no National Labor Relations Board, no Securities and Exchange Commission, no Rural Electrification Administration, no Atomic Energy Commission—to mention just a few. Nor was there a "cold war" to keep world powers in a state of nervous emergency.

Mr. Hoover's chief link with the past, with the Coolidge administration, was Andrew W. Mellon, small, white-haired, aristocratic-looking Pittsburgh financier and industrialist who was often described in Wall Street as the "greatest Secretary of Treasury since Alexander Hamilton." This description was not always greeted with enthusiasm in other quarters and the Democratic leader of the House of Representatives, John Nance Garner, once regarded as a rather radical Texan, demanded a congressional investigation of some two billion dollars in Treasury tax refunds and secret credits to large corporations, including more than a million refunded to what was once the Mellon-controlled Aluminum Company of America. Mellon said he was obeying the law, which he defended. He wasn't investigated.

In the Vice-President's chair was a former Kansas jockey, Charles Curtis, who had served the party well in the Senate. Packed off to London as ambassador was a colorful Chicago banker, former Vice-President Charles G. Dawes, who had once attempted to "reform" the rules of the Senate but had finally acknowledged that nobody could do anything about regulating that august body. Asked by a reporter whether he would wear silken knee breeches at the Court of St. James's, Dawes fingered his florid, hand-sewn necktie, took his famous underslung pipe out of his mouth and asked: "Do you want a diplomatic answer or do you want the answer your question deserves?"

The reporter suggested that Dawes be himself. "Okay," said the new ambassador. "You can go plump to hell and mind your own business." On state occasions in London, he wore formal evening clothes.

Henry L. Stimson resigned as Governor General of the Philippines and returned to Washington as Secretary of State but otherwise the new cabinet was regarded as merely average: Secretary of War James W. Good, who would soon be succeeded by Patrick J. Hurley, a handsome war hero from Oklahoma; Secretary of Navy Charles Francis Adams of Boston, a noted amateur yachtsman and descendant of two Presidents; Attorney General William Mitchell, Postmaster General Walter F. Brown, Secretary of Interior Ray Lyman Wilbur, Secretary of Agriculture Arthur M. Hyde, Secretary of Commerce Robert Patterson Lamont and Secretary of Labor James J. Davis.

Not all of the political figures active in 1929 were as hard-working, as self-effacing or as respectable as those who gathered closely around the Chief; nor were they all Republicans. There were some who were rascals, some who would be thrown out of office and some who would go to jail. It was a commentary on the times that the year's Pulitzer Prize for newspaper cartoonists was won by Rollin Kirby's ironic drawing of several portly Old Guard Republicans, clad in prison stripes, holding up their hands in horror at the political scandals that were swirling anew around New York's odoriferous Tammany Hall.

In Washington, the last of the notorious Teapot Dome oil bribery case figures—Harry Sinclair and Albert Fall—were sentenced to imprisonment. Oilman Sinclair got ninety days in a common jail in the District of Columbia for contempt of the Senate because he refused to answer questions about the 1924 sell-out of government oil reserves. He was given number 10520 and assigned to work in the jail pharmacy because he had once been a pharmacist's assistant. "I've been made a victim," he said later, "of a political campaign to elect honest Democrats by proving how dishonest the Republicans were."

Albert B. Fall, former Secretary of Interior under President Harding and the first convicted cabinet felon in United States history, was sentenced in District of Columbia Supreme Court to a year in prison following a sensational trial on charges of taking a hundred-thousand-dollar bribe from Oilman Edward L. Doheny. Fall was seriously ill but refused to have his case postponed. Carried into court in a wheelchair, he contended that the bribe was a loan and the tears rolling down his cheeks won such sympathy from the spectators that the verdict of guilty was greeted with angry cries of protest. It was a strange, emotional ending in a case that had involved one of the most outrageous betrayals of public trust in the nation's history. The wife of one of the jurors who found Fall guilty was so upset that she pursued her husband into a near-by park, where the jury was being photographed, and screamed at him: "You miserable rat!"

In Louisiana, a pudgy, strong-voiced Democrat of thirty-five, Governor Huey P. (Kingfish) Long faced impeachment charges after ten months in office. A "red neck" poor boy from the pine woods town of Winnfield, Long had clawed his way into political power by promising the farmers a great many things—roads, free hospitals, free textbooks—that were long overdue in Louisiana. Once in the driver's seat, he made good on many of his promises by increasing taxes on business, by cowing the legislature and by ruthlessly setting up a dictatorial regime. Long was an amazing combination of spellbinding orator, able executive, unscrupulous demagogue, flashy dresser and hell-raising playboy.

Nineteen charges were brought against him, including bribery of legislators, using the militia to loot private property, carrying concealed weapons, demolishing the Executive Mansion and disposing of its furniture, acting in a frisky manner with a woman on a settee and subornation of murder. In a sworn affidavit, a former prize fighter and Long bodyguard, Harry A. (Battling) Bozeman, said:

> Huey P. Long . . . said to me: "Battling Bozeman, I am the Kaiser of this state. When I crack my whip whoever dares to disobey, I'll fire 'em." The Governor had been drinking. He says: "Battling Bozeman, I am going to call an extra session of the Legislature. This J. Y. Sanders, Jr., [leader of the opposition] is going to disapprove of all my measures and I want to do away with this——." I says: "Governor, what do you mean?" He says: "I mean for you to kill the ——, leave him in the ditch where nobody will know how or when he got there. I'm governor and if you were to be found out I would give you a full pardon and many gold dollars."

Replying to these charges, Long said that the Standard Oil Company and others were trying to frame him because he had proposed a five-cents-a-barrel tax on all refined oil and gasoline. He said his foes were spending huge sums to buy his downfall. But Long didn't take any chances on the impeachment charges going to a vote. His men rigged the electric voting machine in the legislature so that red lights, which meant a vote for adjournment, flashed on regardless of which buttons the legislators pushed. There was a small riot on the floor, with members fighting and cursing each other. Then the session broke up. Long made a speaking tour to rally support in the farming country, cracked down in every possible way on his foes and a couple of weeks later persuaded the state senate to drop the charges.

This victory for the red-headed Governor was more important than generaly realized at the time. Long posed as a coarse, loud-mouthed backwoodsman, but he turned into one of the cleverest and most dangerous political figures in America. In a time of economic distress, he advocated a Share-the-Wealth plan that made him popular in various Southern states. He became a member of the United States Senate, where he often purposely acted the role of clown but steadily built himself up as an undisciplined power in national affairs. In 1934, he "invaded" Arkansas and directed a Democratic primary election campaign that resulted in a stunning defeat for the party leaders in Washington, including James A. Farley who was then at the height of his patronage power. With the White House as his announced goal, Long was only at the threshold of his career in 1935 when he met a slight, dark-haired man with a political grudge in the halls of the magnificent new state capitol at Baton Rouge and was shot fatally a split second before his bodyguards poured a chattering volley of bullets into the assassin.

Some other Democrats also were having their troubles in 1929. In Oklahoma, Governor Henry S. Johnston was impeached for "general incompetence," convicted and removed from office —the second governor of that state to be ousted in six years. In New Jersey, Democratic Boss Frank Hague's power was challenged in a bitter battle with a Reform-Fusion group seeking to end the iron-handed reign of the Mayor of Jersey City. Hague, a Democratic national committeeman, had been charged with municipal graft and corruption and was the object of a legislative investigation. But the Mayor's North Jersey machine was too much for the reformers who succeeded only in reducing his usual seven-to-one majority to three to two. Thus reassured as to the people's high regard for their leader, the Hague cohorts wrecked the Reform party's headquarters and stoned its leader when he ventured into the street.

James J. Walker of New York City, popularly known as "the late Mayor Walker" because of his inability to arrive anywhere on time, was preparing to win re-election as the candidate of a battered but still avaricious Tammany Hall. But he would find it inconvenient to complete the term because of a legislative investigation that disclosed a broad streak of corruption in his administration, prompting Walker to resign hurriedly and depart for Europe. In Chicago, a Boston-born politican named

William Hale Thompson was the mayor and front man for a political network that may have included a record number of gangster overlords, lawbreakers and racketeers, but "Big Bill" was not a man to dodge the issues of the day. He campaigned like a pre-Revolutionary patriot on a "hate-the-British" platform and publicly offered to punch the King of England on the nose. Democrat Tom Pendergast was quietly and firmly in control of Kansas City and a large chunk of Missouri—so firmly in control that he would boast that he could have a Chinaman elected to the United States Senate if he chose. One of his protégés was Jackson County Presiding Judge Harry S Truman, who was later chosen by Pendergast to run for the United States Senate. He was elected easily and did well in Washington. In Pennsylvania, Joseph R. Grundy, who raised more than half a million dollars to help elect Mr. Hoover, had the situation in hand for Republicanism.

It was not, however, the political bosses—good or bad—who were always in the public eye during 1929. Sometimes the scene of action shifted to the drawing rooms of Washington society, where the fate of nations and of political parties seemed to be overshadowed by the question of whether a buxom matron from Kansas would sit above or below the salt at state dinners.

4

Washington, D.C.

Missoula Thursday Club
Missoula, Montana

DEAR MADAM CHAIRMAN & MEMBERS:

Well, girls, I promised when Harold and I left for our nation's capital to serve under The Great Engineer that I would write you all about it and I would have written weeks and weeks ago except that there has been so much excitement here and little me right in the midst of it all, seeing all the famous people and having the time of my life. Some of the goings on here would slay you, girls! honestly, just slay you!

But I want to make this an orderly report, so I guess I better tell you what's going on in Washington by putting the most important things first, like I did in my reports when I was recording secretary of The Club. Well, really one of the most important things in our government today as I see it in my jaunts around the city—the White House, the Capitol and various social engagements—is the way they're treating Mrs. Gann. That's Dolly Gann, the sister of Vice-President Curtis. Her name is Gann because she's married to Edward Everett Gann, one of the nicest little men you ever saw. I ran into him on the street only last Friday and would have stopped to talk but he seemed to be in a hurry, going to his law office, I imagine. You really should meet him sometime.

Well, I've given this whole situation the "once over" and I think I can tell you some things that will make your hair turn. You see, the Vice-President is a widower and lives in a twelve-room suite at the Mayflower Hotel—it's ritzy, and how!—but he gets a cut rate from the hotel. Mrs. Gann acts as his hostess. She's a very handsome woman with red hair and kind of robust. But some of the old pills in society here don't seem to like her. The first thing that happens is that the Senate Ladies Luncheon Club, which is the wives of all the senators, elected Mrs. George Moses from New Hampshire as president last February, although ordinarily they elect the wife of the Vice-President. Well, Dolly may have been miffed—I forgot to say that we all call Mrs. Gann Dolly—but she didn't say anything. Then on Inauguration Day, she and Mrs. Dawes went together to the Senate gallery and do you know there wasn't any seat reserved for Dolly—not even when she was hostess for her brother who was taking the oath right there! If it hadn't been for Mr. Herbert Hoover, Jr., who got right up and gave his seat to Dolly, I don't know what would have happened. As for Mr. Gann, I don't have any idea where he sat or if he even got in.

Believe you me, Dolly was fit to be tied. The next day Mr. Curtis

*just sat down and notified Mr. Kellogg—he's the Secretary of
State who's kept on working until Mr. Stimson got here from the
Philippines—that Dolly was his hostess and entitled to the rank
and privileges of the wife of the Vice-President. Mr. Curtis has
been around Washington a long time and really knows his groceries when it comes to things like protocol—that's what they call
manners here—and you would have thought that would have
ended the whole business. But Mr. Kellogg hemmed and hawed
and finally said well, Dolly could like it or lump it but she ranked
below the wives of the Chief Justice, the Speaker of the House, the
Secretary of State and all foreign ambassadors or ministers.*

*Before saying what happened next, I guess I ought to explain
that our Society here in Washington is pretty stiff-necked. The
most stiff-necked are called Cave Dwellers because their families
have been around for just ages. But then there are also Society
People like Mrs. Edward B. McLean, who owns the Hope
Diamond and whose husband publishes the Washington* Post, *and
Mrs. Nicholas Longworth, who used to be Alice Roosevelt and
married the Speaker of the House in a White House ceremony.
Well, on Easter morning, Mrs. McLean gave a big breakfast party
at her famous estate called Friendship. Just everybody was there,
including Mr. Curtis and Dolly and Mr. Gann. But when Dolly
and Mr. Curtis went up to the head table there was a place for him
but none for Dolly. Mr. Curtis got red in the face and huffed and
puffed, but in the end Dolly went to sit with her husband at a little
corner table.*

*Next day everybody in Society was gassing like mad about it!
And Mr. Curtis told the newspaper boys that Mr. Kellogg ought
to reverse his protocol ruling. "Fat chance!" I said to myself when
I heard of that. But then the President and Mrs. Hoover invited
Dolly and Mr. Gann to the White House for dinner and
Mr. Hoover himself escorted Dolly into the state dining room.
Of course, there weren't any other wives there but it showed how*

*he felt about it. Really, he's the sweetest man and so is Lou Henry
—that's what we call Mrs. Hoover. She's very democratic.*

*Well, by this time, Mr. Stimson had taken over from
Mr. Kellogg and he said that his department didn't want to be
mixed up in such affairs and that the Washington diplomats could
seat Dolly wherever they pleased, so the ambassadors all had a
meeting and voted to accept Dolly as the Vice-President's hostess
and then Ambassador Carlos Davila—he's from Chile—gave a
dinner and Dolly wore a silver lace dress and sat at the head of the
table next to Mr. Davila. Mr. Gann sat down at the foot of the
table but they could look at each other from time to time. It was
a real triumph and just shows to go you that you have to know
your stuff to get along in this town.*

*Of course, some people are never satisfied and there's been a
kind of feud between Dolly and Alice Longworth ever since and
they say that Mr. Hoover is going to have to arrange separate
dinners this year for the Vice-President and the Speaker—just to
avoid getting the two women in the White House at the same time.*

*The newspapers keep telling all about the whole thing and the
other day I thought it was real sweet of a man out in Kansas—
fellow named William Allen White who lives in some little town
out there—to write a piece in his paper defending Dolly. This is
what he said: "Kansas hereby tells the whole world that there will
be a real ruckus if Washington don't do right by our Doll. Unless
she is borne to dinner triumphant on the shoulders of Mrs. Nick
Longworth and seated in the center of the table as a centerpiece
with a silver candelabra in both hands and fed her soup with a
long-handled spoon by the wife of the Secretary of State, Kansas
won't be responsible for what her presidential electors do in 1932.
Verbum sap!" I cut it out of the newspaper and sent it to Dolly
because I thought she'd like to be cheered up, even if only by a •
hick from Kansas.*

Well this report is too long and I'll sign off now. We've been just

*terribly busy since we got here. I've been to the White House
three times and, while I haven't actually seen the President or
Lou Henry, there are some wonderful gentlemen there who show
you all the famous rooms. We get out in Society a good deal and
last week went to a wonderful Montana party given by our Congressman and saw lots of people from Missoula. Harold works
hard and of course his responsibilities are heavier now that he's in
the government but only last week one of the Assistant Directors of
the Government Printing Office told him that in a few more
months he might be moved from the night shift to the day shift.
As Harold was saying only today, once you get hep to how things
are done in Washington it's a lot better than running a linotype on
a newspaper in Montana.*

With oodles of love to all,

GRACE H.

5

The attitude of the average American toward public servants
was examined in a unique manner in 1929 by Professor Leonard
White of the University of Chicago, who published his findings
in an exhaustive report on *The Prestige Value of Public Employment.* White was concerned that most Americans held a
low opinion of elected officials and that the best minds in almost
all communities avoided politics like the plague. Examining the
reasons behind this situation, he tried out a "word association"
test on many citizens in all walks of life and got some interesting results. He would select a subject at random and then ask
him to blurt out his immediate reaction to certain key words.

"Alderman," snapped the Professor to one citizen.

"Grafter," was the prompt reply. Another replied "big cheese"
and a third said "crook" without a moment's hesitation. When
the key word was "City Hall" some of the replies were: politics,
graft and corruption.

There wasn't much that went on in Washington during 1929
to raise the prestige of officeholders in the eyes of the public.

The game of politics was played with greater enthusiasm than ever and with no holds barred. A man of high ideals and with deep sympathy for humanity, Mr. Hoover realized perhaps better than anyone else that 1929 was a time of change and that there were great opportunities for his administration to point the way toward a brighter, stronger America. He had his head and not a few filing cases full of plans for all kinds of improvements in such varied fields as agriculture, flood control, elimination of waste in manufacture and distribution, child welfare, stimulation of home construction, banking practices, the rights of labor and economic planning toward the abolition of poverty. He believed that these and many other forward steps could be achieved not by government compulsion but by free and voluntary co-operation.

Unfortunately, the President's engineering blueprints failed to make allowance for the stress and strain of politics. Not only was Mr. Hoover an inept politician but he believed that it was beneath the dignity of the President to fight back in the rough-and-tumble political style of the day. And to add to his difficulties, his lieutenants in Congress with few exceptions were particularly weak and his luck was generally bad.

The Democratic strategists were quick to see the chinks in the President's armor and, instead of sitting back quietly during the first year of the new administration as was usual in political warfare, they went into action immediately. National Chairman John J. Raskob, a Wall Street financier, raised several million dollars among his wealthy acquaintances to clear up the 1928 campaign deficit of a million and a half dollars and to finance the new attack, which proved to be a remarkable political innovation and set a pattern for future campaigns by both major parties. Hired for twenty-five thousand dollars a year to quarterback the attack was Charles Michelson, veteran political correspondent of the New York *World*, a slight man with baleful eyes and graying hair parted in the middle. Michelson set up offices and a staff in the National Press building and conducted a day-by-day study of every administration move. And day-by-day,

Michelson turned out expertly written partisan ammunition for use by the National Committee or by Democratic congressmen in criticism of the President or in an effort to widen the strife that had already appeared within Republican ranks. Although later the Republicans would call Michelson a "smear artist" and claim that he distorted much that Mr. Hoover did or said, the fact is that the President had some serious political difficulties with the Republican-controlled Congress almost from the beginning and that he was wide-open to the kind of counterattack the Democrats launched.

Although Mr. Hoover often was inaccurately accused of not having much sense of humor, there was a joke circulated in Washington that probably gave the best short version of his relations with Congress. The scene of this imaginary conversation was the White House where the President was talking to an adviser about the frustrations of dealing with certain obstreperous congressmen.

"There ought to be a law," Mr. Hoover was supposed to have said, "that would give the President the right to hang two men every year without being required to give any reason or explanation."

"Yes," the adviser replied, his thoughts on a number of rebellious Republican senators. "But I doubt that two would be enough."

"I see your point," replied the President, "but I could easily get word to twenty or thirty others that they were being seriously considered for the honor."

It is unlikely that the problem ever seemed that simple to Mr. Hoover, but it must have been a temptation at times to think so. He had been elected by a landslide in which he carried forty states and received 444 of 531 electoral votes. Republican governors had been elected in twenty-eight states and Democratic governors in only five. Yet the President was never able to make really effective use of this great political power. His prestige was with the people rather than the party politicians. Mr. Coolidge was supposed to have referred to him bitingly as "the

John L. Lewis as he appeared in the 1920's when engaged in a bitter and often violent struggle for control of the United Mine Workers. (United Press)

A scene during the 1929 Gastonia, N.C., textile strikes, which resulted in violence and bloodshed and attracted nation-wide attention to working conditions in many Southern mills. (Wide World)

George Herman (Babe) Ruth wa[s]
past his prime in 1929 but he sti[ll]
combined in his murderous swin[g]
the grace of a ballet dancer and th[e]
power of a Paul Bunyan slicin[g]
down a pine tree with a single blo[w]
This picture was probably taken i[n]
the late 1920's. (United Press)

Bobby Jones, in the golfing costume of the day, was plagued
by bad luck and was almost
struck by lightning in 1929,
when this picture was taken, but
he came back the next year to
win golf's "grand slam." (Wide
World)

Albie Booth, pictured here in 1930, was a fleet, elusive runner on his way to gridiron stardom in 1929, when he set a record of twelve touchdowns in a single season for Yale and beat Harvard, 3–0, with a drop kick. (Wide World)

There was quite an argument in 1929 over whether it was proper for women tennis stars to abandon their traditional white stockings in tournament play. Helen Wills Moody, pictured here in 1930, was a leader of the bare-legged faction and an easy winner both in the fashion arena and on the tennis courts. (Wide World)

Dazed and holding his head, Roy Riegels of the University of California sits on the ground after his sixty-four-yard "wrong way" run in the 1929 Rose Bowl game against Georgia Tech, which won the game, 8–7. (Wide World)

Primo Carnera of Italy got into the heavyweight boxing picture in 1929, not so much the basis of his skill as a pugilist as on t basis of his huge size and a big ballyhoo ca paign. When he later came to America, pho graphs such as this, with acrobatic dan Mary Lee on his shoulder, helped build him as a drawing card. (Wide World)

Huey Long was Governor of Louisiana in 1929 and just starting his climb to national prominence. Here he talks about his intention of becoming President during an interview with reporters when he was at the height of his political power. (Wide World)

President Coolidge and President-elect Hoover, shown on their way to Mr. Hoover's inauguration, were both Republicans but they didn't always see eye to eye, as inadvertently suggested by this photograph. (United Press)

Retiring Governor Alfred E. Smith of New York and his successor, Franklin D. Roosevelt, wave their silk hats at the inaugural parade in 1929 at Albany. Their political friendship soon began to cool when Mr. Roosevelt failed to appreciate his predecessor's advice on how to be successful as Governor. (Wide World)

Fred Allen, a reformed librarian and an unsuccessful juggler, was making a reputation as a wise-cracking comedian in Broadway musicals in 1929. He is shown here at a somewhat later date. (NBC photo)

Graham McNamee of the Nationa Broadcasting Company was per haps the best-known radio an nouncer of the 1920's. His broad casts of sports events carried a fee ing of excitement into living roon across the nation even on occasion when McNamee gave a garble version of what was going on in th field of battle. (NBC photo)

The original crooner, Rudy Vallee, was a success almost from the day he left Yale and took his Connecticut Yankee band to Lon-don. In 1929, he developed one of the first big variety network shows on radio. (NBC photo)

he "Amos 'n' Andy" network show was launched in 1929 and almost
pped. But once it had caught on nothing could stop it. (Culver)

Frenchman with a winning smile
a stiff straw hat invaded Amer-
in 1929 for a whirl at Broad-
y and Hollywood. Here Maurice
evalier, who quickly sang his
y into public favor, is shown in a
pleasant mood during the film-
in 1929 of *Paramount on Parade*
h Evelyn Brent, who wears a
vie version of a 1929 under-
nent known as "step-ins."
lver)

Clara Bow became the epitome of sex appeal as a motion picture star in the late 1920's. She had "It"—a quality of difficult to define but presumably shared with Helen Troy, Lillian Russell and Marilyn Monroe. Here the "It" emotes in a movie. (Culver)

An early photo of Bing Crosby, who gave up a brief career of hell-raising in 1929 and was soon making a million dollars a year on radio and in the movies. (CBS photo)

Mr. and Mrs. John Barrymore (Dolores Costello), of Hollywood's brightest stars, during one of the ca moments of Barrymore's career in the late 19 (United Press)

Everybody was watching the stock market ticker in 1929, including Edward G. Robinson in this scene from a play called *Kibitzer*. (Culver)

One of the teenage perils of prohibition was drinking out of a flask—nobody ever knew for sure what was in it. Here Joseph Lee and Millicent Green illustrate the rite in a scene from the play *Street Scene,* the Pulitzer Prize winner that was still running in 1929. (Culver)

Several newcomers to Broadway made a hit in *The Little Show* of 1929, including torch singer Libby Holman, shown here with actor Clifton Webb. (Culver)

One of the products of the Prohibition Era was trio of speakeasy night club entertainers, Clayto Jackson & Durante, who were in a Ziegfeld show 1929. Here Jimmy Durante turns his "schnozzol toward Ruby Keeler, a graduate of the Texas Guin night club dancers and the bride of singer Al Jolso (Culver)

An outstanding success of the 1929 theatrical season was *Journey's End*, a British play about the war that had ended eleven years earlier. There were no women in the cast. (Culver)

Animal Crackers, featuring the zany antics of the Marx Brothers, had a long run that lasted into 1929. Here Groucho makes a proposal to Margaret Dumont. (Culver)

Comedy singer Eddie Cantor had a busy year in the theater, from which he planned to retire; in Wall Street, where he played the market; and in a book in which he told how he lost his shirt in Wall Street. He had to get back to work in the theater and, later, on the radio as shown here. (NBC photo)

A glamour girl of society's younger set in 1929 was Miss Barbara Hutton, shown here in a photograph taken in the previous year. (United Press)

The son of the former President of the United States was married to Flore Trumbull, daughter of the Governor of Massachusetts, in 1929—Mr. and M John Coolidge and their wedding party. (Wide World)

The latest fashion for the business girl in 1929—a "fetching little tailormade ensemble of mannish material and cut to wear with a tucking shirt." (Wide World)

heatrical version of the latest styles e this coat and hat worn in 1929 actress Irene Bordoni. (Culver)

Weiman, writer, demonstrates proper length for skirts in 1929 e actress Gertrude Lawrence on. (Wide World)

The king and queen of the Jazz Age, Scott and Zelda Fitzgerald with their daughter in Paris during the middle 1920's. (Brown Brothers)

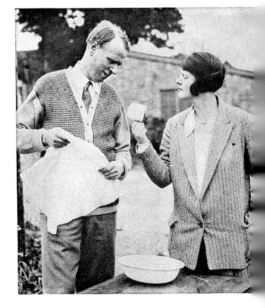

Sinclair Lewis published *Dodsworth* in 1929, soon after his marriage to a noted newspaper correspondent, Dorothy Thompson. Here they are on the first day of their honeymoon in the English countryside, which they toured in an automobile trailer. Mrs. Lewis is critical of her husband's dishwashing abilities. (Wide World)

rnest Hemingway was one of a large umber of American literary figures ho preferred the French Riviera in 929. This photo was taken two years arlier.

Alexander Woollcott was a top-notch reporter for the *New York Times* before he became dramatic critic and essayist. Here, in the 1930's, he looks at a book in which some of his newspaper and magazine articles were collected. (Wide World)

It took determination and a certain athletic skill to clamber into a rumble seat such as is shown on this 1929 Oldsmobile. (General Motors photo)

Here is a famous automobile racing driver, Barney Oldfield, in the 1 Cadillac sport phaeton which he drove from Los Angeles to Detroit in the t remarkable time of five days. He said he never would have made it so quic except for the new Duplex-Mechanical four-wheel brakes on the car. (Gen Motors photo)

bright boy" and the Republican Old Guard was rightly doubtful that he could be counted on to "play the game." And Congress, scenting trouble, worried by falling farm prices and by
rising clamor over prohibition, was in a rambunctious mood
that might have frustrated a President with far greater political
skill than Mr. Hoover.

Congress in 1929 established no impressive legislative record,
but it kicked up some beautiful political rumpuses, especially in
the Senate. The House of Representatives, under the firm hand
of Speaker Nicholas Longworth, was a less newsworthy battlefield although it provided a good hunting ground for feature
writers because of half a dozen women among its membership.
Among them were Ruth Bryan Owen of Florida, daughter of
the famed orator and easily the most beautiful legislator in
Washington, and Ruth Hanna McCormick of Illinois, who
prompted one reporter to say that he had never seen "a woman
who had more sex appeal on the platform and less off." A third
Ruth was Mrs. Ruth Baker Pratt of New York, one of the
wealthiest members of the House and a veteran of the political
wars. There was also a "widow's row" occupied by women
who had succeeded their late husbands in the House and
by one—Katherine Langley—whose husband, a former congressman from Kentucky, was in the federal penitentiary at
Atlanta.

The Senate had no women members but it was more talkative
and more likely to change its mind than the House. Most of the
old orators, the famous debaters who had shouted across the
cherry-red desks and had taken snuff from the little wall boxes
that were still freshly filled each morning, were gone or going.
But there were still some who could hold the attention of the
gallery—the hoarse, leonine William E. Borah of Idaho, thunderous Joseph T. Robinson of Arkansas, gentle, ironic George
W. Norris of Nebraska, sharp-tongued Thaddeus H. Caraway
of Arkansas, old, white-combed Carter Glass of Virginia, aggressive Thomas J. Walsh of Montana, and pedantic Hiram
Johnson of California.

In this body, the best Mr. Hoover could get as Senate Leader was a big, cigar-chewing, oleaginous man from Indiana, James E. Watson, who looked and sometimes acted like a nineteenth-century statesman but whom the Baltimore *Sun* correspondent Frank Kent described as "a blithering blatherskite, the most blatant bluff any state has sent to Washington in years . . . a fraud and a faker." Watson, who once had to deny charges that he was a leader in the Indiana Ku-Klux Klan, had fought Mr. Hoover in the preconvention campaign of 1928 but now, like most of the Old Guard, he declared himself an ardent supporter of the President and began a bumbling term as Majority Leader in what was often called "the greatest deliberative body on earth."

The two problems placed before Congress when Mr. Hoover summoned a special session soon after his inauguration were farm relief legislation and adjustments in the tariff for the benefit of agricultural producers. In the last speech of his presidential campaign, Mr. Hoover had proposed a farm relief plan involving tariff revision and creation of a Federal Farm Board with adequate working capital ($500 million) to reorganize marketing procedure and to aid co-operatives in handling surplus crops. But by the time Congress got to work on the plan, the farmers believed that these proposals were too conservative. They were suffering from low prices and overproduction and they believed that the best solution was the so-called Export Debenture Plan, a complicated scheme designed to aid disposal of surpluses by allowing exporters of farm produce a bounty equal to one-half of the tariff rate on the same commodity.

Not a few Midwestern and Western senators, led by Smith Wildman Brookhart of Iowa, attacked the President's conservative approach to the problem. In the end, Mr. Hoover got his way, but it was no political victory. A few days later, Minnesota's Governor Theodore C. Christianson called on the President to inform him that the farmers were unhappy and would make trouble at the polls unless the proposed tariff revisions were more to their liking. Agricultural prices were low and Mr. Hoover's popularity rating in the farm country was showing signs of weakness.

6

The hottest and longest congressional controversy of 1929 revolved around tariff revision. Tariff legislation always cuts across party lines because an increase in duties to protect the product of one part of the country from foreign competition usually means that other parts of the country will have to pay higher prices for that product. Mr. Hoover originally had asked for limited changes favoring the depressed farming areas. The legislation was introduced by two Westerners, Senator Reed Smoot of Utah, and Representative Willis C. Hawley of Oregon, but by the time it had been worked over and revised in secret committee sessions many observers remarked that it seemed to bear the heavy imprint of Joseph R. Grundy, president of the Pennsylvania Manufacturers Association and a potent lobbyist for Eastern industrialists. Midwestern congressmen began to mutter that instead of aiding the farmers by raising duties on agricultural products, the bill primarily aided the manufacturers by raising the prices that farmers had to pay for almost everything they needed.

This development—coming on the heels of discontent over the farm relief program—was an opportunity too good for the Democrats to miss. In the House, Minority Leader Garner bitterly denounced Speaker Longworth's dictatorial methods in rushing enactment of the bill under the familiar "gag" rule. A dozen Republican congressmen rebelled against the party leadership and voted with the Democrats. Representative Mary T. Norton of New Jersey, widened the Democratic attack by declaring that the bill would require women to pay from 10 to 75 per cent more for "everything that goes to make a woman comfortable"—silk, fine toilet soap, shoes and perfumes. When Smoot described Mrs. Norton's attack as a "false tale," she replied: "Senator Smoot must consider the women of the country devoid of intelligence. Paid lobbyists are not my friends and advisers in my work in Congress. Can Senator Smoot say as much?"

By this time the Democratic National Committee's publicity "mill" had begun to hit its stride under the direction of Michelson and the political statements, cleverly designed to make newspaper headlines, came thick and fast. In the Senate, Pat Harrison of Mississippi, took up the attack: "No band of pirates ever looted a victim better than these distinguished gentlemen [the authors of the bill] . . . seek to rob the American people. The Senator from Utah . . . wants to keep us from smoking cigarettes, he wants to keep us from smoking pipes. No wonder he bows his head in shame." More and more the Democrats ignored the merits or lack of merit of the legislation in order to press home to the public the idea that the legislation was rigged in favor of the big manufacturers.

"The working man may worry because his shoes will cost a dollar or two more," Representative James V. McClintic of Oklahoma said with heavy sarcasm, "but truffles for his *pâté de foie gras* are on the free list. His sugar bill goes up as does his milk bill and his meat bill, but he can get Gobelin tapestries for his humble home duty free."

The Democrats were given aid and comfort by a group of Midwestern and Western Republican senators who opposed the bill or parts of it. Senator Borah of Idaho, denouncing the higher protectionist rates for industry, pointed out that the United States Steel Company earnings were the highest in the history of the company, that Bethlehem Steel had a gain of 160 per cent in earnings the first six months of 1929, that Republic Iron and Steel Company showed increased earnings of 208 per cent and Youngstown Sheet and Tube Company earnings increased 145 per cent. Senator Norris of Nebraska revived the farm relief Export Debenture Plan as an amendment to the tariff bill and it was approved, 42 to 34, despite the frantic opposition of the Republican leadership. Senator Watson, floundering as Majority Leader, made a radio appeal to the public to have faith in the administration's determination to enact a fair and equitable tariff measure and then departed, exhausted, for a rest in Florida on his doctor's orders. President Hoover permitted the issuance of a couple of White House statements reflecting the hope of the Chief Executive that Congress would get down to business and speed up enactment of the bill, but to no avail. Senator Harrison, irked by the long hours that the Senate was being held in session, demanded that his colleagues quit work on Saturday afternoons so he could take in a baseball game.

The tariff legislation was now in a hopeless muddle—no bill would be passed until 1930—but the Democrats had made a pretty good crop of political hay at a time when the administration should have been reaping the fruits of the 1928 Hoover landslide. It is generally accepted that the political debacle that overtook the Republicans during the Hoover administration stemmed from the Wall Street crash in late October, and no doubt that is historically correct. But throughout the summer of 1929 when the Stock Exchange quotations rose higher every day the seeds of discontent were being planted as the Democrats took up the role of friend of the farmer and belabored the administration as the "friend of big business." Even the staunchly Republican New York *Herald Tribune* was moved later in the year to say uneasily that "it should be realized that the Republican party is fundamentally the party uniting the western farmer with the eastern industrialist. This primary function seems to have been forgotten and in the interest of the party it should be revived." And the *New York Times* added that the manufacturers got about what they wanted from Congress but "the farmers got nothing. The western Republicans feel that they were treated as poor relations." Even when, late in the year, the administration cut taxes by $160 million the Democrats were quick to claim that it was mainly for benefit of large corporations, which received $100 million of the reduction. The Democratic line that would eventually flower into biting attacks on "the economic royalists" was beginning to take shape and the Republican party's long and comfortable grip on the voters of the great American Middle West would not be the same again for two decades.

Having stalled the administration's tariff program, the Democratic strategists had no intention of abandoning the initiative in the political field. Senator Harrison got ponderously to his feet at his front-row desk one day and interrupted debate with a charge that Republican Senator Hiram Bingham of Connecticut had hired as an aide on tariff matters one Charles L. Eyanson, ten-thousand-dollar-a-year assistant to the president of the Connecticut Manufacturers Association. Eyanson had been put on the federal payroll, he added, and had been attending secret hearings of the Senate Finance Committee on tariff legislation.

In no time at all, cries of outrage echoed across the Senate chamber, the problem of tariff revision was all but forgotten and the Great Lobby Hunt was on. Actually, the Bingham-Eyanson case was merely a kind of curtain-raiser for the Great Hunt, which centered in the coming weeks around one William B. Shearer, who claimed he got a twenty-five-thousand-dollar "jackpot" from the big steel and shipbuilding companies to wreck the 1929 Naval Disarmament Conference at Geneva. But Shearer, whose activities will be discussed in a later chapter, was not typical of the Washington lobbyists who were the main quarry of a Senate special investigating committee. There had, of course, been lobbyists in Washington since government began and there would be even more lobbyists in Washington after 1929 despite the fact that Congress would require them to register and identify their clients. (About one thousand were registered in 1954.) But, following a long and frustrating struggle over the tariff bill, the Senate Democrats and not a few Republican insurgents were in a mood for political hell-raising and it is doubtful that lobbyists were ever dished up in greater numbers or in more style than in the next few months.

Bingham angrily denied that he had been unduly influenced by the Connecticut Manufacturers Association or that he was wrong in hiring Eyanson. On the contrary, he said, he was uninformed on tariff problems and had been justified in asking the Association to send him an expert on the subject. The committee questioned him rather savagely—a tall, white-haired former Yale professor, Bingham was too handsome and too pedantic to be popular with his colleagues—and he eventually agreed that he had probably "made a mistake." Then he made the error of attacking the committee in a speech from the floor of the Senate, refused to apologize and sat in pale silence as his colleagues adopted, by a vote of 54 to 22, a motion of censure against him—an exceedingly rare action that would not be repeated until 1954 when the Senate censured Senator Joseph R. McCarthy of Wisconsin.

Meanwhile, the committee listened to a parade of lobbyists and alleged lobbyists and employers of lobbyists who made headline news for the nation's press almost every day. Many of these the senators pictured as avaricious fakers who falsely claimed that, for a good salary, they could "influence" legislators. Or as "suckers" misled into paying lobbyists for doing nothing. Often the committee wandered far afield to take up purely political matters or to pursue personal grudges.

A star witness was Joseph Grundy, wealthy manufacturer and powerful political potentate in Pennsylvania. He gruffly advised the committee that he had raised three-quarters of a million dollars for the Coolidge campaign in 1924 and almost a million for the campaigns in 1928 and that the contributing manufacturers expected a return on their investment. He shed a tear for the vanished old-time lobbyists who "really knew the tariff" problem and said he was in favor of setting up a school that would teach the art of tariff lobbying. He added, in a formal statement, that some states such as Arizona, South Dakota, Idaho, Mississippi and Montana didn't contribute much toward the national upkeep but the senators from those states were most vocal against the tariff bill. "It was a great mistake," he added, "to give each state two senators."

"When it comes to the interests of Pennsylvania," asked Senator Thaddeus H. Caraway of Arkansas, "the people of Idaho ought not to say anything?"

Grundy: "They ought to talk darned small."

Senator Thomas J. Walsh of Montana: "How would you silence Borah [of Idaho] and myself?"

Grundy: "Your own intelligence would suggest silence on such matters [as the tariff]."

Senator John J. Blaine of Wisconsin: "You think Pennsylvania would be better off if it seceded from the Union?"

Grundy: "In the Civil War we contributed more than any other state to keep the Union together."

Caraway: "You contributed more people who stole everything they could get their hands on than any other five states. They even stole the library out of the Supreme Court."

Such exchanges did nothing to woo the Western states' farmers back into a happy alliance with the Eastern Republican leaders, but the investigating committee's tactics were so frankly political and often so reckless that the sympathy of the public sometimes turned toward its intended victims. "The injustices perpetrated by George III before the American Revolution," said Professor William Starr Myers of Princeton University, "were no worse than some that have been perpetrated by senatorial investigating committees. . . . They seek not facts but to put somebody in a hole."

Undismayed, the committee turned up Lobbyist Herbert C. Lakin, who had been busy in behalf of the Cuban sugar industry. He had written letters to his employers indicating that his "influence" extended to advisers of the President and that Mr. Hoover "seems to be genuinely interested in our cause." Under questioning, Lakin acknowledged that he might have been stretching things a bit in order to impress his employers and that his remarks about the President might have been "injudicious." But at least the committee's blunderbuss firing had begun to rattle around the White House and, even if there were no hits on the target, it was the White House that the Democrats had been aiming at all the time.

7

The extent to which the Democratic attacks and the maneuvers of Republican insurgents in Congress damaged Mr. Hoover's leadership—if it was damaged—is not easy to estimate because of still greater woes that were to befall his administration. But the *New York Times,* perhaps more hopefully than confidently, did not take a discouraging view of the situation in which the President found himself. Politicians who had once sneered at Mr. Hoover's lack of adroitness, it said, do so no longer because he has "become a fairly good politician."

It is possible that the Senate as a whole may instictively feel a certain opposition to him [the *Times* said]. This is partly on account of his personality, partly on account of his methods. He represents promptness and energy and efficiency. . . . The Senate moves very slowly, wastes a lot of time and would rather debate than act. . . . A certain amount of dislike and even friction is sure to result. . . . But no senator is "out" for the President's scalp. Thus far he has never been attacked in the Senate so fiercely as were most of his predecessors in the Presidency.

It is possible, of course, that Mr. Hoover would have been able to gain control of the political situation and assert his leadership if there had been no economic collapse. But, in retrospect, the *Times* editorial seems unduly optimistic and fails to take into consideration the chaotic divisions within the Republican party, especially in the Senate, at a time when business was booming to unprecedented levels.

The Old Guard Republican senators, such at Watson, George Moses of New Hampshire and David A. Reed of Pennsylvania, were fighting grimly to maintain their control of the party machinery, but they were harassed more and more vigorously by the insurgent or so-called Progressive Republicans such as

Borah, Norris and Gerald Nye of South Dakota. Nor could they always be sure that Mr. Hoover would be in their corner on political matters. In New Jersey, the regular Republican organization wanted former Senator Joseph S. Frelinghuysen appointed to the Senate seat left vacant when Walter E. Edge became Ambassador to France. But the President wanted Dwight W. Morrow, who had served ably as Ambassador to Mexico, and it was Morrow whom the Governor of New Jersey appointed.

In Pennsylvania, William S. Vare was accused of having stolen the senatorial election by spending almost eight hundred thousand dollars to win the Republican nomination. Republican insurgents joined Senate Democrats in voting 58 to 22 to refuse to seat him. Senator Nye then further angered the Old Guard by publicly warning Governor John S. Fisher of Pennsylvania against filling the vacant seat by appointing anyone connected with "the Mellon-Grundy-Fisher machine. . . . We cannot damn one ill-smelling Pennsylvania machine without damning the other." Fisher had little choice but to defy his critics and he promptly appointed Lobbyist Grundy to represent Pennsylvania in the Senate. The appointment stuck, too, although Grundy had to sit, rosy-cheeked and smiling, on the Senate Floor for three hours while his appointment was denounced as "corrupt" and "an insult to decency." "I feel," he said later, "like a cat in a strange garret."

Such battles and recriminations racked the Republican party and whatever M. Hoover may have done or tried to do to restore harmony or to get even a working agreement was not obvious to the public. On the contrary, even his best friends sometimes seemed to add to his woes every time they tried to rush to his defense. Secretary of the Navy Charles Francis Adams went back home to Boston to speak at a Republican banquet. "I know nothing of politics," he began, with the understatement of the year. "But I might give you a little gossip. There are two sides in Washington—a very brilliant administration side and a legislative side that is a little foggy, to use a nautical term. . . . About a dozen men [in the Senate] call themselves Republicans but owe no real allegiance to our party. . . . If the President had nine lives, he might devote five of them to these men but he wouldn't win their votes. But he emerges as a great figure out of this fog. He skillfully avoids the shoals and rocks." Adams ended with reference to "an obscure conference committee" of senators and representatives who would probably decide the fate of the tariff bill.

The Democrats had a field day with the speech in the Senate trying to figure out just which Republican members were "foggy" and which were "obscure" but they were interrupted once by two of Secretary Adams' villains—Brookhart and Borah. Had not Adams himself once been a "distinguished insurgent" in Massachusetts, asked Brookhart. Borah was quickly on his feet.

"He was not distinguished," asserted the Senator from Idaho.

With Republican feathers so thoroughly ruffled, the only soothing remark that occurred to Democratic goader Pat Harrison was that, after all, Mr. Hoover was "as negative a quantity as we have ever had" in the White House.

In the course of the summer, Borah, Brookhart and Senator Lynn J. Frazier of North Dakota—all former Hoover enthusiasts —broke openly with the administration. Freshman Senator Arthur H. Vandenberg of Michigan disrupted the party leaders' plans by forcing through a measure for congressional reapportionment that was particularly obnoxious to some of the Southern states. The President "fired" Dr. Hubert Work, who had done about as much as anybody to get him nominated in 1928, from the Republican National Committee. The reasons for this break were never very clear, but Claudius H. Huston of Chattanooga, Tennessee, was then named National Chairman in line with Mr. Hoover's hope of building up the party in the Southern states.

At a strategy dinner of Republican leaders in New York,

James Francis Burke, counsel of the National Committee, stirred up trouble anew by calling the Senate insurgents "pigmies and obstructionists, who should not be re-elected." At the same meeting it was announced by Senator Moses that Otto H. Kahn, international banker, had agreed to act as treasurer of the Republican Senatorial Campaign Committee for the 1930 election. This appointment caused such wild glee among the Democrats and such anger among the Republican Progressives that Kahn declined to serve, but Moses was still good for one more blunder. A few days later, angered by collapse of the tariff legislation, he told a meeting of New England manufacturers that the Republican insurgents in the Senate were "sons of the wild jackasses." And to this Reed of Pennsylvania, added that they were "worse than Communists."

For months thereafter the "sons of the wild jackasses" harried the Old Guard leaders bitterly and enthusiastically. And they were joined by still another group of Republicans, known as the Young Turks—about a score of junior members who had decided it was time to get rid of the Watson-Moses leadership and install a more enlightened directorate. By the end of the year, a large chunk of the Republican victory of 1928 had been dissipated by intraparty feuding, by depressed farm prices and by the Democrats' able political exploitation of these difficulties. If the farmers—conservatives in most respects—had not lost confidence in Mr. Hoover's conservative engineering approach to the problems of government, they had at least begun to wonder whether their own difficulties called for some more drastic solution. It would not be long before wonder turned to conviction, opening the way not just for Democratic victory in the 1930 congressional elections but for a decade of intense sociopolitical upheaval that would erase permanently many of the Old Guard's cherished concepts of the role of government in a democracy.

"The old parties have continued to mouth the old phrases and flaunt the old slogans," remarked Philosopher John Dewey of Columbia University, on his seventieth birthday in October of 1929. "But behind the scenes they have surrendered abjectly to Big Business interests and become their errand boys." Professor Dewey proposed to found a new league for independent political action. This was doubtless a constructive idea, but too late. They didn't know it yet, but time had just about caught up with "the errand boys."

...*it was borrowed time anyhow....*

Nineteen twenty-nine was a restless year for Americans ... for F. Scott Fitzgerald, who had worn out the Twenties and was already beginning to look back on the Jazz Age with nostalgia. As a handsome, almost pretty boy in St. Paul he had dreamed of fame and glory on the football field at Princeton and when the coach threw him off the squad after one day's practice, he still had the dream of fame and glory. If not with a football, then with a typewriter. He clung tightly to the dream of fame and glory and, once he had fallen in love, of riches.

They came with incredible swiftness. By the time the Jazz Age was in full flower he was famous and glorified as its most illustrious historian. He was married and was horribly, romantically and jealously in love. And he was beginning to make "more money than he had dreamed of, simply for telling people that he felt as they did, that something had to be done with all the nervous energy stored up and unexpended in the War." He was a little surprised that he had, as was often pointed out later, actually established the Jazz Age in the public mind by unconsciously being a part of it. The success of *This Side of Paradise* had made the Fitzgeralds—Scott and Zelda—sophisticated characters in the era of Flaming Youth and, although they had felt naïve and uninformed at first in New York, they immediately began trying to live up to their reputation.

They spent money freely and were seen with the right people at the right speakeasies. They were young and handsome—Scott with tousled yellow hair and a scarf twisted around his throat, Zelda with reddish-golden hair, a sun-tanned complexion and little makeup. They seemed not to have a care in the world, and probably didn't. If they arrived two hours late for dinner they were charmingly apologetic and would drink happily and gaily until late in the night when, exhausted, they might drop off to sleep on a divan. Refreshed, they might keep going indefinitely—riding on the tops of taxicabs, leaping fully clothed into a fountain on Fifth Avenue, weeping because they were so happy and had everything they wanted and knew they couldn't ever be so happy again. Scott was quick to get into a fight. Zelda danced on the dinner table. "This was the generation whose girls dramatized themselves as flappers," Scott would recall later, "the generation that corrupted its elders and eventually overreached itself less through lack of morals than through lack of taste. May one offer in exhibit the year 1922! That was the peak of the younger generation, for though the Jazz Age continued, it became less and less an affair of youth. The sequel was like a children's party taken over by the elders. . . . By 1923 their elders, tired of watching the carnival with ill-concealed envy, had discovered that young liquor will take the place of young blood, and with a whoop the orgy began. . . . A whole race going hedonistic, deciding on pleasure."

Scott worked—*The Beautiful and Damned* in 1922 and *The Great Gatsby* in 1925 plus scores of short stories for the slick magazines—but the Fitzgeralds were still restlessly searching for something, running faster and faster and stretching out their arms farther and farther, trying to miss nothing. They bought a secondhand Marmon automobile (Zelda promptly wrecked it on a fireplug), moved to a country house, threw drunken week-end parties, flirted, quarreled, spent money, went into debt, wrote a play called *The Vegetable* (which flopped), drove automobiles into ponds for the fun of it and became a kind of legend of the unrestrained Twenties. Except that there wasn't anything legendary about it. It was just that later people couldn't quite believe that it had really happened that way. "It was borrowed time anyhow—the whole upper tenth of a nation living with the insouciance of grand ducs and the casualness of chorus girls."

Still searching, trying to find solid footing somewhere, they went to Europe, where Zelda momentarily fell in love with a French aviator and Scott was thrown in jail for fighting six taxicab drivers and a policeman. They drank too much too often, wandered from France to Rome to Capri to France, more frustrated and more in debt at every step. The Riviera was overrun with Americans spending the paper profits they had won on the stock market; for a time it seemed that all of New York's leading literary figures had deserted the Hotel Algonquin and moved to the Cap d'Antibes. One night a group gave a farewell party for a couple who were leaving for Paris and after a number of toasts had been drunk Zelda announced that the departing guests should have gifts as well as honeyed words. She took off her black lace panties and tossed them toward the male guest of honor. He announced he would perform a heroic act in return, and promptly dived off the terrace into the Mediterranean. There were a few moments of wild confusion and by the time the hero was back on dry land the party observed that Alexander Woollcott, not to be outdone, had stripped to the skin, donned a straw hat, and was walking sedately toward the hotel lobby, puffing on a cigarette. He entered, got his key and retired to his room.

There were many other escapades and practical jokes, in which Scott often collaborated with Charles MacArthur and Donald Ogden Stewart. They wrote four-letter words on the walls of Grace Moore's villa. They raided a small restaurant, kidnaped the proprietor and waiters and threatened to throw them off a cliff. But something was wrong. Their search was wearing out. Zelda was often moody; once hurt herself plunging headlong down a flight of stairs when Isadora Duncan rather openly invited Scott to her house to spend the night. Scott was frustrated, unable to work effectively. And both were occasionally so drunk that some of their acquaintances began to avoid them. Scott impulsively and for no reason kicked a box of flowers out of the hands of an old woman peddler while his friends looked on in horror. Zelda once lay down in front of their automobile and insisted that Scott run over her. The search was no longer worth the effort. "We grew up," Zelda said, "founding our dreams on the infinite promise of American advertising. I still believe that one can learn to play the piano by mail and that mud will give you a perfect complexion."

Back in New York it was no better. The city was "bloated, glutted, stupid with cake and circuses" in 1929 and a new expression "Oh, yeah?" summed up for Scott all the enthusiasm that anybody could muster. "My barber retired on a half-million bet in the market and I was conscious that the headwaiters who bowed me, or failed to bow me, to my table were far, far wealthier than I. This was no fun." They fled again to Europe and cheap hotels and then to North Africa, where they heard that the stock market had collapsed. They didn't care. The search was almost over now for Zelda. She would soon be in a sanatorium—and die there in a tragic fire. Scott stumbled on. Some would say that *Tender Is the Night* and *The Last Tycoon,* which he never finished, were the books that made his reputation secure, but he died believing he had failed. "All is lost save memory. . . . I can only cry out that I have lost my splendid mirage. Come back, come back, O glittering and white!"

CHICAGO, 1929—*A questionnaire circulated among 700 ministers and theological students (none Catholic) showed that 53 per cent of the ministers believe in "a real hell" and 60 per cent believe the devil exists as a real being.*

CHAMPAIGN, ILLINOIS, 1929—*J. Bruce Haney fell asleep and was disqualified after rocking for 280 hours and 30 minutes in the Rocking Chair Derby.*

PHILADELPHIA, 1929—*Scarface Al Capone, America's most notorious gangster overlord and now a prisoner at Eastern Penitentiary has subscribed to "Country Life" Magazine.*

APRIL, 1929

the human comedy

There is a natural tendency on the part of historians and others to attach a special name to any decade that marks a drastic change in our way of life, that stands out as a period to be remembered either with a little shudder of horror or with a wistful smile of happiness. At the end of the nineteenth century, the Gay Nineties were a welcome change from the stern mood of Victorianism and the very words evoke a picture of elaborately dressed and carefree women, of gallant gentlemen wearing top hats and sideburns, of glistening carriages and lively champagne parties, of laughter and the click of croquet balls on the lawn. It is, in retrospect, a happy picture that leaves no room for the humdrum life of the 1890's, the sweatshops, the saloon brawls, the outdoor privies, the coal-dust-covered trains, the twelve-hour working day and the muddy streets that were considerably more familiar to most Americans than top hats or

Carl A. Rudisill Library
LENOIR RHYNE COLLEGE

champagne. We insist upon thinking of the 1890's as a gay and gallant decade. They were a time of change; a reference point in history.

So were the Roaring Twenties. Not everybody, of course, was roaring any more than everybody was gay in the Gay Nineties. But the Twenties were full of action and robust growth and excitement and a tendency to carry everything to extremes. The First World War had been fought in a spirit of high idealism to "make the world safe for democracy." It was followed by a period of deep disillusionment because the world wasn't remade overnight in a better mold. But youthful America made a determined, reckless break with the past. The result was the Emancipation of Women, the Jazz Age, Flaming Youth, Flappers, the Golden Era of Sports, the Glamorization of Gangsters, the Red Hot Baby in Short Skirts, the Big Nonstop Business Boom, "Yes, We Have No Bananas," Necking in Automobiles, Marathon Dances, the Greenwich Village Art Movement, the Miracle of Radio and the Great Emphasis on Sex. It was a long way from the stiffly corseted and heavily petticoated woman of 1919, with skirts concealing her ankles, to the flat-chested, short-haired, lipsticked, baby-faced woman of 1929, who had "It," smoked in public, drank in speakeasies, wore her skirt above her knees, drove an automobile at fifty miles an hour and remarked in mixed company that all women should have premarital sex experience. It was a long way, but America made it in a decade that roared to its climax in 1929.

Certain reservations should be made about 1929, especially in regard to Sex. There had been a far-reaching revolution in morals and manners and some of the changes that had occurred were here to stay. For instance, women were not going to give up their hard-earned place in business and public affairs. Some two thousand self-supporting women were present in 1929 at the meeting of the National Federation of Business and Professional Women's Clubs on Mackinac Island, Michigan, where Mrs. Eva Hunt Dockery of Boise, Idaho, won loud applause by predicting that in the next ten years there would be a woman in the cabinet, twenty-five women in Congress, and five women governors. She was right about the cabinet minister and very close to the mark on her other predictions.

On the other hand, by 1929 some of the steam had gone out of the revolt against the old ways. Perhaps a pinch of salt should have been prescribed to go with H. L. Mencken's remark that "more women are self-supporting and independent than ever before and more women, I suspect, wish they were dead." But there is not much doubt that the new morality and the new sex freedom were more talked about than practiced. While much of the talk was true, the old traditions were not generally discarded. Adultery remained as a sound basis for a divorce action, despite the popularity of Bertrand Russell's lectures throughout the nation on "free love." College boys and girls were still expelled for unbecoming conduct, despite the fact that Judge Ben Lindsey of Denver had gained national recognition as an advocate of "companionate marriage." As one writer of the day pointed out, the whole subject of sexual promiscuity had been confused by "a liberal share of buncome" that had been printed in the newspapers and magazines. And in 1929 there were signs that a reaction had set in; that soon the loud and persistent talk about freedom of the sexes would be just a little old-fashioned.

Yet this trend was no more than a ripple on the surface as the Twenties roared toward their climax. Money was easy to make —on paper—and excitement was easy to find. It was a day of extravagant promotion, of zany fads, of mixed social values and free spending. It was, Westbrook Pegler noted, An Era of Wonderful Nonsense. Anything, they said, could happen, and usually did.

2

One of the things that happened at the end of the Roaring Twenties was a speed-up of all forms of communication. Better automobiles, better roads, airplanes, radio and wireless transmission of photographs had become a part of the postwar mass production civilization of the United States. Distances were shortened. People who had spent half a lifetime within a fifty-mile radius of their birthplaces in Midwestern towns now thought little of dashing halfway across the continent to New York on a business trip or of driving two thousand miles through the Rocky Mountains on a vacation. Flights across the Atlantic Ocean were becoming so common that twenty-two-year-old Arthur Schreiber was able to "stowaway" on the French monoplane *Yellow Bird,* which took off from Old Orchard Beach, Maine, for Paris. Due to headwinds and the extra weight of the stowaway, the *Yellow Bird* was forced to land in Spain. What happened in London or Bombay or Tokyo in the morning was known and discussed at dinner time in Ottumwa, Iowa. The latest fashions and the latest slang from Paris or Broadway or Hollywood no longer required months or years to seep into the hills of Kentucky but were communicated in hours or days by newspapers, radio and the movies.

In 1929, the Southern Pacific Railroad announced in an expensive series of advertisements in national magazines that it had completed plans for a de luxe boat train to run three thousand miles across country from New York to San Francisco (without a change and with assurance that "your companions will all be men and women of your own class") to make connection with the Matson Line luxury steamship *Malolo* for Hawaii, an eight-day trip in all. At Lakehurst Naval Air Station in New Jersey, the German dirigible *Graf Zeppelin* under command of white-haired old Dr. Hugo Eckner completed the first around-the-world flight of nineteen thousand miles in twenty-one days and seven hours carrying nine commercial passengers. An unidentified marksman shot a hole in the big silvery, cigar-shaped ship as she passed over Texas in the course of a wildly acclaimed voyage above a dozen big American cities.

Neither the zeppelin nor the New York–San Francisco boat train (which never ran) were going to mean much to civilization in the future, but the idea of more and quicker travel was here to stay. In London on a visit, William F. Kenny, a New

York contractor, was reported by the press to have put in an urgent telephone call for his barber in New York, told him to get the first ship to England and bring his scissors because Kenny needed a haircut. Louis Arico followed instructions, got a free trip to England and his regular fee for cutting his patron's hair. This report so angered London barbers that Kenny later explained it was just a gag. Actually, he had arranged some time earlier to give Arico a free trip to his birthplace in Italy, which he had not seen for many years. In New York, the management of a newsreel company suppressed a film of Colonel and Mrs. Charles A. Lindbergh—who were married in 1929—landing their small plane at a local airport after zipping around the country on a private trip. The reason for the suppression, according to *The New Yorker* magazine, was that the newsreel microphone had picked up a conversation in which the famous flier was reproving his bride for not wearing a petticoat.

Things were happening all over. In Chicago, a German named Charles Loeb had a friend pack him in a coffin-like box labeled "Statue—handle with care" and addressed to the Pathé motion picture studios at Culver City, California. The box arrived at the studios four days later and Loeb was discovered suffering from severe exhaustion and thirst. He told police that he merely wanted to get inside the studio gates, from which he had been turned away, so that he could ask the casting director for a job. From Pittsburgh, the United Press reported that a group of twenty prisoners "including some of the most prominent western Pennsylvanians ever sentenced to the federal penitentiary" had departed for Atlanta, Georgia, in a special railway coach. They include five politicians and ward workers, a former state senator and banker, a former receiver in bankruptcy, a former postmaster, a former prohibition agent and a bank robber. In New York, a man named Frank Latkowski did a jackknife dive from Brooklyn Bridge—the still higher George Washington Bridge over the Hudson River had not yet been completed—into the East River, 138 feet below. He sprained his thumb and revived discussion of whether famed Steve Brodie had actually jumped off the same bridge in 1886, as claimed. Opinion was divided.

In Chicago, it was announced that Dean Robert Maynard Hutchins of the Yale Law School had been appointed president of the University of Chicago, taking charge of an institution with an enrollment of fifteen thousand students and a faculty that included some of the nation's best-known academic names. Hutchins was thirty years and five months old at the time of his appointment. He later aroused the anger of many "old grads" of the University by abolishing football. In Ohio, the deans and doctors of philosophy at Defiance College celebrated a campus get-together by taking part in a kiddie car race with students. The deans and doctors won. In Pennsylvania, Bucknell University opened a course in sanitation and hygiene for barbers, who announced that in the future they hoped to be called chirotonsors instead of barbers.

From Paris after a long self-imposed exile came Raymond Duncan, who believed the world to be flat and who was an apostle of ancient Greek culture, clad in a homespun toga and sandals and with his shoulder-length hair bound by a narrow band. The brother of famed danseuse Isadora Duncan was ready to teach Americans—as he had taught Parisians—the Ancient Periclean dance steps and to organize groups for painting, weaving and singing in the manner of the early Greeks. In Cincinnati, Ohio, Mrs. Eva Sells Jaeger presented local clubwomen with a chart showing how Mrs. Jaeger traced her ancestry back through William the Conqueror, Solomon, Nathan and Seth to Adam in an unbroken line.

At a New York night club, the Lido, the management presented guests with air-inflated rubber bathing girl dolls that were clad only in grass skirts and could "shimmy violently when tickled." In Greenwich Village, Don Dickerman insisted that guests at his popular club, the Daffydil, observe the new 3 A.M. curfew on night life ordered by Police Commissioner Grover Whalen. At 3 A.M. everybody in the club was asked to

step out into the street. The doors were closed and then immediately reopened so that all guests could return to their tables
for breakfast.

An ancient Filipino toy, the yo-yo or "come-back" top on a
string, was introduced to American youngsters and received
with great enthusiasm by almost everybody except school-
teachers. One boy in Texas claimed to have set a world record
by spinning a yo-yo 121,111 consecutive times before it wob-
bled off the string. In Connecticut, a teen-age boy was hailed
as a champion of windy endurance after playing the harmonica
continuously for three hours and thirty minutes.

American department stores, upon receipt of the latest
fashion notes from London, blossomed out with perambulators
and expensive yellow dresses styled after those of a three-year-
old British child called Lilybet, who would grow up to be
Queen. At Elmira, Michigan, Doris Buell was chosen as "the
most intelligent farm girl" in America and promptly issued a
statement to the press. Said Doris: "I developed my mind by
driving a pair of mules."

3

Not all Americans, of course, were interested in yo-yos or
night clubs or even the idea of getting someplace in a hurry; a
great many were concerned about spiritual values, although
they frequently seemed to be all but submerged in the frantic
swirl of 1929. For a while in the mid-Twenties it had seemed
that the country's jangled nerves might be soothed by a little
French psychotherapist, Emil Coué, who attracted tremendous
crowds and had practically everyone saying: "Day by day in
every way I am getting better and better." But interest in the
latest stock market tip or in the new automobile models soon
overcame interest in Couéism. By 1929 the new humanist
school was in vogue among intellectuals, with Professor Irving
Babbitt, an American scholar from Ohio by way of Harvard and
Paris, as its leading spokesman. Babbitt looked to the classical

traditions and classical literature for guidance and preached a doctrine of moderation and restraint, an idea that seemed to make only a negligible impression on the nation in 1929.

Dr. Alfred J. Lotka, supervisor of mathematical research for the Metropolitan Life Insurance Company, took a long look at the American way and decided that while everybody was busy watching the curve of human knowledge shoot upward they had neglected to inquire whether people were getting any smarter at the same time. The fact was, he said, that the growth of human wisdom had lagged far behind.

"We are," Dr. Lotka told the American Association for Advancement of Science, "stuck in a morass of authority worship. We flatter ourselves that we live in an era of progress unparalleled in history. The generations that come may wonder at our skill in turning the powers of nature to our own ends. But will they not marvel even more at the incredible contrast between our skill in doing and our ineptitude in choosing what to do?"

The country, he added, was at a crossroads. One fork would lead to a world peopled by robots, stunted in mental growth, doing rough work for an aristocracy of "the best minds." The other fork could lead humans to take advantage of the leisure gained from mass production in order to work for the betterment of mankind. He was pessimistic, however, about Americans seeing the wisdom of taking the second fork.

Professor Harry Elmer Barnes of Smith College was disturbed about the spiritual development of the nation. He told the same meeting of scientists that our concept of God would have to be redefined in the light of discoveries in astrophysical science. This venture into metaphysics so shocked the distinguished gathering that Dr. Henry Fairfield Osborn, president of the association, promptly and publicly rebuked the Smith College sociologist for the "unwarranted intrusion" of a philosophical subject into sessions devoted to pure science.

Although Osborn made it clear that Barnes's opinions were his own, there were many signs of the times that disturbed religious leaders in America. Church attendance was at a low ebb.

Ministers spoke bitterly of men and women who chased golf balls on Sunday morning. There was increasing skepticism about religious dogma. The Rev. John Haynes Holmes, a notable rebel against orthodoxy, told his congregation at the Community Church in New York that there was "not the slightest shred of evidence that Jesus ever rose from the dead." Furthermore, he added, there is more of the religion of Jesus taught in the synagogues than in all of the Christian churches combined; Jesus taught the Jewish religion and his religion remains Jewish.

The intellectuals of the day delighted in deriding the red-hot salesman, the overworked businessman who relaxed with too much bootleg liquor on Saturday night at the Country Club, the apostles of standardization and mass production. The intellectuals, said Frederick Lewis Allen in *Only Yesterday,*

believed in freedom—but freedom for what? Uncomfortable as it was to be harassed by prohibition agents and dictated to by chambers of commerce, it was hardly less comfortable in the long run to have their freedom and not know what to do with it. . . . They also believed, these intellectuals, in scientific truth and the scientific method —and science not only took their God away from them entirely, or reduced Him to a principle of order in the universe or a figment of the mind conjured up to meet a psychological need, but also reduced man, as Krutch pointed out in *The Modern Temper,* to a creature for whose ideas of right and wrong there was no transcendental authority.

And later in *The Big Change,* Mr. Allen elaborated:

Along with [the] relaxation of the social code went a wave of religious skepticism—wasn't science making mincemeat of the old-time religion?—and of hedonism. Among young men and women who prided themselves on their modern-mindedness there was a disposition to regard church work or social service work or anything else to which the word "uplift" could be applied as "poisonous" . . . and besides, one had a right to enjoy oneself and taking a ride in the sedan of a Sunday morning was much more fun than going to church.

It should not be imagined, however, that faith had been

abandoned in the America of 1929. There were, in various parts of the country, remarkable displays of religious enthusiasm—as demonstrated by Evangelist Aimee Semple McPherson—and not a few direct-action attempts to combat the materialistic and worldly trend of the times, especially in regard to women's dress and the consumption of intoxicating liquors. Anna F. Doring wrote a song, published at Huntington, Indiana, for girls who desired to join in a crusade for more modest fashions

> Though standing or sitting, if you please
> With skirts we have well-covered knees.
> Our lines and our curves we don't reveal
> To strangers' stare; but modestly conceal—
> We belong to the Crusaders.

Another broad but equally unsuccessful reform campaign was launched in Chicago by one George Huntley Aron, Ph.D., A.M., who advertised in the newspapers for members to bolster the roster of the Fasting Club, which promoted the theory that "the key to world wide regeneration" was to be found in the psychological condition achieved while fasting. All who desired to assist in regenerating the world were invited to join the club in the Rocky Mountains for a hunger fast lasting from forty to ninety days. In Georgia, Governor L. G. Hardman, addressing the convention of the National Education Association, advocated the fingerprinting of school pupils because "fingerprint reading will be an aid in determining the mentality" of children. All cells of the brain, he said, are represented in some of the physical organs of the body. At Malden, Massachusetts, an estimated 150,000 pilgrims overran Holy Cross Cemetery to visit the tomb of a young priest where a number of miraculous cures of the sick had been persistently reported. Police and cemetery officials announced they were temporarily removing the stone from the priest's grave as the only method of clearing the crowds out of the graveyard.

In the last years of the Twenties some members of the clergy were making a valiant effort to bring their churches "up to date" and to attract larger congregations by employment of modern publicity methods. In Herrin, Illinois, a "railway sermon" was delivered at the First Methodist Episcopal Church by the Rev. Frank W. Pimlott, whose father had been an engineer. The ushers carried lanterns. A male quartet sang "Life's Railway to Heaven." The pastor called "All aboard!" and the orchestra imitated a railroad train—the exhaust was heard, the bell rang and the whistle blew. As the train speeded up the congregation sang "I'm Bound for the Promised Land." Far to the west, in San Francisco, a church notice listed as subjects for discussion the following: "Why They're Hot after Hoover," "I Want a Girl," "The He-Man," "Christ, the Wine Manufacturer," and "Weak Women and Strong Drink." Not to be outdone, a men's Bible class in Hollywood heard a series of lectures by W. W. Bustard, an "experienced athlete," on the following subjects:

> Samson—The World's Strong Man
> Jacob—The Great Wrestler
> Enoch—The Long Distance Walker
> David—The Pinch Hitter
> Saul—The Man Who Fumbled the Ball
> Jesus—The World Champion

Even with an up-to-date public relations approach, the churches of America had a hard time in 1929 competing with the country clubs and the stock market. "Wall Street, to multitudes, as well as to the custodians of the shrine, was a Holy of Holies," wrote Halford E. Luccock in *American Mirror*. And William Allen White added: "What a sordid decade is passing! . . . The spirit of our democracy has turned away from the things of the spirit, got its share of its patrimony ruthlessly, and has gone out and lived riotously and ended up by feeding it to the swine. . . . We sit in our offices and do unimportant things and go home at night and think humdrum thoughts. . . ."

"Of all ages," said an editorial in the *Saturday Review of Literature*, "ours is perhaps the most tolerant . . . largely because the spirit of science has descended upon us." Faith, it added, has been replaced by science and society is now a laboratory where it is fashionable to be open-minded, although the masses "are still in the shadow of Victorian morality."

The descent of science upon the United States, however, had failed to solve a good many social problems. Murder, for example. In 1929 Dr. Frederick L. Hoffman of the Prudential Insurance Company, figured up some statistics on crime and decided that Memphis, Tennessee, led all other cities in homicides per capita. Memphis recorded 115 murders in a year for a rating of 60.5 per 100,000 population. The most murders, however, occurred in Chicago which reported 498 for a rating of 16.5, with New York second—401 murders for a rating of 6.7. In Detroit there were 228 murders, in Cleveland 134, in Philadelphia 182, in New Orleans 111, in Atlanta 115 and in Birmingham 122. Although virtually all of these cities increased in population in the next quarter-century and some of them increased greatly, the prevalence of murder took a nose dive. In 1953, the murder rate dropped to 32 in Memphis, to 291 in Chicago, to 321 in New York, to 120 in Dertoit, to 71 in Cleveland, to 125 in Philadelphia, to 74 in Atlanta and 62 in Birmingham.

The gangster wars of the prohibition era accounted for a considerable percentage of the 1929 killings, but there were not a few commentators of the day who believed that the country was going to the dogs anyway. The editor of the *St. Mary's Beacon* in Leonardtown, Louisiana, for example, put down some sour notes on affairs in general and the honesty of the people in particular. "The man who was prompt in paying for his horse shoeing and buggy repairing," he wrote in a discussion of the changing times,

will not pay his garage bill if he can get out of it. He will even buy his gas on credit, and steal his spark plugs and tires, just to keep her going. Politics has eliminated justice; those who have the pull go free, and those who haven't go to jail. . . . Our country is overrun with lawbreakers and roughnecks. A man can't drive to the movies or a dance without having his automobile stripped, tires, motometers, spark plugs or pump stolen. . . . Our county officers seem to be asleep at the switch. They are paid good money to wear their pants out sitting in their swivel chairs or letting barnacles grow on the bottoms of their patrol boats.

4

People with money were not much concerned with whether the country was going to the dogs in 1929 or at least there were few evidences of concern in those spots where the free spenders were most in evidence. In California, for example, the Hollywood motion picture stars were just beginning to take to the desert at Palm Springs, where a new million-dollar hotel, El Mirador, had been constructed with a huge swimming pool that had a plate glass window to permit the taking of underwater photographs. It was only a beginning, but the Palm Springs publicity staff would be able to keep in the newspapers by introducing rickshas pulled by college students (an unsuccessful enterprise), shorts worn by women (so successful that by 1955 they would cause only a raised eyebrow on New York's Fifth Avenue), bicycling (unsuccessful) and movie stars in evening dress diving into swimming pools (successful). Eventually Palm Springs became known not only as an expensively fashionable vacation spot but as the place where "the sun shines on the stars."

In New York, a Vienna-born architect, Josef Urban, redecorated the Central Park Casino at a cost of a quarter of a million dollars as the most expensive restaurant in the city. Soda water sold for three dollars a bottle. Patrons had to bring their own liquor, but were kept cool in the summer months by a fountain that played on the roof. The orchestra—twenty-eight thousand dollars a month—included a young piano player named Eddie Duchin, who soon became leader and collected as much as twenty thousand for one evening's music at private parties. The Casino was patronized by free-spenders who on some occasions tipped the orchestra with a thousand-dollar bill. Mayor Walker retrieved his hat from the hat check girl one evening and tipped her two hundred dollars.

Not all New York restaurants, however, were so obviously money-minded. Some pinned their hopes on snob appeal. The Maillard, putting emphasis on the better things of life, ran a full-page advertisement in *The New Yorker* magazine showing a discreetly lighted and handsomely decorated dining room with the caption: *"Il y a une grande nombre de restaurants où on peut manger, mais combien y a-t-il où l'on peut dîner?"* The city's night clubs also set a high standard for customers. Three of them refused to admit patrons not in evening dress. Five others discouraged patrons from appearing in business suits.

Among the free-spenders were the racketeers turned respectable, or at least putting up a respectable front.[1] In New Jersey, a liquor racketeer who had cleaned up in the early days became a leading resident of a suburban community, a member of the country club set and a prominent owner of race horses. Nothing of his past was known to his neighbors until an unfortunate day when several of his former pals bumped him off on a country road for reasons that were never entirely clear to the police.

There was another racketeer with offices on Columbus Circle in New York, who had become so well known that *The New Yorker* magazine's Morris Markey did an article about him—no

---

[1] It would be a mistake for future historians to assume that all racketeers and gangsters were dumb brutes just because they could be hired to "bump off" a bothersome stranger—or a bothersome friend, for that matter. Many of them, outside of business hours, were sentimentalists who wept copiously at the first note of a blues singer's carol about that dear old mother of mine or even about the beauties of boyhood life in Dixie. Many of them, according to the Broadway columnists of the day, were true blue to their friends and often defenders of decency—outside of business hours, of course. On one occasion, according to Jim Bishop's biography of Columnist Mark Hellinger, Singer Al Jolson was on the verge of a nervous breakdown because Gangster Legs Diamond had demanded he hand over fifty thousand dollars or else. Hellinger found out about it and called up a much tougher gangster, Owney Madden, whose sense of decency was promptly outraged. Madden, who didn't care for Diamond anyway, telephoned the would-be extortionist and told him to lay off Jolson or get a hole in the head. The next day Diamond called up Jolson and said he had just been kidding and no hard feelings, eh, pal? In this way, friendship, loyalty and decency prevailed and nobody had to bother the police or an undertaker.

names mentioned—under the title "Fear, Inc." "Instead of having a private detective for his bodyguard," the article said,

he carries with him two dapper fellows who . . . are without peers at close-range pistol work. . . . He drives an automobile which is, within itself, impregnable. A certain romantic history hangs about this car. The King of the Belgians, it seems, has a hobby of building magnificent armored automobiles with his own hands—as Peter the Great built clocks. He turns out of his elegant shop about one car every two years. The first went to the King of Spain, the second to the Prince of Wales, and the third, through the devious channels of an American millionaire and a brokerage house, to our celebrated gentleman of Broadway. Its one-inch steel plate looks no more forbidding that the enameled sheet-metal that covers our Detroit models, but it turns back high-penetration bullets. Its cowling hides a sub-machine gun. Its speed and pick-up are almost uncalculable because the throttle has never been wide open.

Near La Salle Street in Chicago, still another and unreformed racketeer spent a good part of every day behind a desk in a handsomely decorated office suite that might well have been the headquarters of a law firm or an advertising agency. It had been years since he touched a gun or a blackjack. He had a great deal of business correspondence to attend to daily because he was the head of an organization of independent bakeries, each of which paid him a substantial fee to protect them from the possibility that racketeers would throw a bomb into their places of business. The authorities at one time had suggested that this was not a legitimate organization—that our racketeer himself had coerced the bakery men into joining his organization by having his henchmen throw bombs into the establishments of two or three bakery men who declined to join. But when the authorities tried to get members of the organization to testify that they had been coerced they were assured by every member they interviewed that their president had rendered him important services and that they would never appear as witnesses against him. None of them wanted bombs through their plate glass windows.

Mr. Racketeer, a moon-faced man wearing English-made shoes and a tailored silk shirt with a neat monogram on the pocket, wasn't worried. He was practically "legit" now; operating in the open. His wife and three children lived in an exclusive suburb. His girl friend had been making a modest reputation as a blues singer in a night club since he bought into the club ownership. His influence in one of the city's most powerful political clubs was increasing steadily and his occasional dinner guests included two municipal councilmen and a judge. He had acquired some valuable real estate holdings in the city and had recently bought a piece of a promising young heavyweight boxer. So far as he knew—and he knew most things—his potential underworld enemies had either left town or were at the bottom of Lake Michigan. There was just one thing that bothered him occasionally; his income tax returns were more than slightly misleading. He must have another talk with his lawyer about that problem. But it was nothing to worry about. Washington was a long way from Chicago.

5

The year 1929 was a kind of turning point for the famous resorts which had long been populated at various seasons each year by America's society families. Not that the wealthy families were going broke in many cases. On the contrary, tax records that year showed 513 Americans with incomes above a million dollars and a dozen with incomes of more than five million a year. George F. Baker, the stern guiding spirit of society at Tuxedo Park in the Ramapo Hills some forty-five miles from New York, was estimated to have added around fifty million dollars to his fortune in the last few years before he died at the age of ninety-one in 1931.

Yet a change was coming. The changing economy of the nation, the changing social patterns and especially the changing tax structure would soon begin to undermine the great mansions, villas and palaces—always called "cottages"—of Tuxedo, Newport, Bar Harbor, Fisher's Island and White Sulphur

Springs as well as other resorts where "society" had long circulated with the changing seasons. By 1954, there would be only 148 Americans with incomes of a million dollars annually. There would still be plenty of palatial homes at American resorts, more in fact than in the Twenties; but the vast hundred-room "cottages" of the past would be gone or going, divided into apartments, turned into museums or torn down. The rigid social barriers which "Western millionaires" were always trying to break through in the old days would be gone too, and a whole new pattern of resort living would be established by hordes of vacationers moving with the seasons all over the nation. The swimming pool on the lawn, once a reasonably sure sign of affluence, would become almost commonplace and no less than twenty-five thousand of them would be built in California alone in 1955.

But in the final fabulous year of the Twenties there were only vague signs of the impending change, and the very rich as well as the very social segments of society were going strong. High above the rugged California coast, William Randolph Hearst sometimes ran his newspaper empire from the seclusion of a lavish ranch establishment called San Simeon—a name that to different persons would come to mean a variety of things ranging from fear to distaste to high hopes. For Hearst editors all over the nation, San Simeon was the origin of messages from Mount Olympus, sometimes filled with blessings and sometimes with wrath. An editor might be summoned there from the Eastern seaboard on a moment's notice. Sometimes he went in high hopes and left looking for a job; sometimes he went as a favored guest. One editor dashed three thousand miles to San Simeon and never got past the gate, where he found waiting for him a message about some rather unimportant matter and a return ticket to his job. For writers who got inside the gates, San Simeon was a subject of endless adjectives—some laudatory, some bitter, some ironic—and for Aldous Huxley it was the setting for a novel called *After Many a Summer Dies the Swan*.

But for southern California it soon became a social pinnacle where, as one of a hundred week-end guests, you might never meet your host but you could swim in a vast pool fed by fountains copied from Michelangelo, sleep in Cardinal Richelieu's bed, walk in a huge hall made of panels from choir stalls of a Spanish cathedral, exercise in an underground gymnasium roofed in Venetian glass mosaic, attend a private theater decorated with Italian brocatel and eat excellent food at great antique tables where—because Hearst as a boy had camped on this spot—paper napkins were always substituted for table linen. San Simeon's buildings were dazzling white and included a twin-towered main house in Spanish mission style, three large guest houses and an ever-growing number of other buildings for play and work. The master had amassed a great, heterogeneous collection of famous paintings and art treasures from all over the world. There were dozens of servants, sports instructors, chauffeurs and cowboys in attendance. At a time when great display of wealth was almost going out of fashion, the publisher lived here like an ancient potentate and often entertained important guests in a style to which they were not accustomed. One such guest in 1929 was a British politician, Winston Churchill, who was going out of favor and on the downgrade as a statesman in his homeland but continued to be a popular contributor to American magazines and newspapers. Hearst, discussing the affairs of the world, talked his guest into "a most peaceful and profound slumber" which lasted until they went to luncheon with Movie Magnate Louis B. Mayer, where twenty-four chorus girls in peekaboo costumes appeared to bring Churchill back to a state of wakefulness.

Southern California was becoming a popular wintertime spot, especially for travelers from the Northern farming states and many thousands were buying retirement homes there. But for society-minded folk, the sands of Florida beaches were most attractive and the Palm Beach Bath and Tennis Club—in its infancy in 1929—was perhaps the most expensive and the most glamorous society resort spot in America. Founder memberships at ten thousand dollars a throw were so oversubscribed that a quarter of a million was returned to disappointed applicants. Palm Beach was booming and the Gulf Stream Club refused an offer of a million dollars for a small strip of its waterfront property because it would necessitate moving the eighteenth hole of its golf links. Mrs. Marjorie Post Hutton Davies imported the entire cast of a Broadway stage show to the resort to perform for a couple of hundred guests at her residence, Mar-a-lago, which boasted an inlaid marble dining room table and was modestly compared to Louis XIV's haven at Versailles.

"Important news from Palm Beach, where Prosperity gets its coat of Winter tan," Arthur Brisbane wrote in his front page column for the Hearst newspapers that year.

Ladies, "the very nicest," walk on the beach in silk pajamas, wearing sandals, no stockings. The sandals reveal their little toes and these toes are manicured, the nails nicely rounded, beautifully polished. Carlyle could have written about that. . . . There is good in everything and manicured toes will be good for the feet of generations to come. . . . The pleasures of our "upper classes" at Palm Beach will interest future historians. At one party, six clowns drove tiny pigs and another exhibited the smallest living mule, named Sparkplug. [Sparkplug was the name of a horse in a current comic strip called Barney Google.] That was intellectually most diverting. . . . Then there was a tacky party, all trying to look poor, wearing rags and tags . . . and how they did laugh when they saw each other. . . . Palm Beach's tacky party only rules Palm Beach.

In the summer season, the village of Southampton, on the South Shore of Long Island, was probably the most popular of the fashionable resort spots and certainly the most lively. But there were elaborate establishments and incredibly expensive parties—sometimes lasting for days—all over in the dying years of the Twenties. Marshall Field III had a $1,300,000 estate on Long Island and another of a thousand acres, with an airport and race track, in Virginia. J. P. Morgan had a mansion in New York, a huge estate on Long Island, an estate in Hertfordshire, England, a town house in London, a shooting lodge in Scotland and a winter house in Bermuda. In Boston, Frank H. Beebe had a mansion on Beacon Street in which he lived and another house on the same street which he had refurnished and redecorated every year but in which he never slept. In New York, John Markle, a coal operator, had a Fifth Avenue apartment with forty-two rooms and a dozen baths, a private switchboard with twenty-six extensions and a twenty-five-thousand-dollar black marble staircase. A Kentuckian named Preston P. Satterwhite owned a New York apartment that cost approximately a million dollars—the living room was sixty feet long—as well as a villa at Palm Beach and a half-million-dollar house on Long Island where he installed a hundred-thousand-dollar pipe organ.

In a survey of how the rich were able to spend so much money, Stanley Walker wrote that a utilities operator making a westward crossing on the *Berengaria* found a steward he liked, tipped him five thousand dollars and hired him as a butler. The steward retired five years later with sixty thousand dollars and his own country house. Publishers Condé Nast and Horace Liveright were famous party givers. Liveright frequently worked up parties on the spur of the moment at his offices, summoning the literary stars of the day by telephone. Nast entertained decorously and formally whether he had a hundred guests or a thousand. Sometimes he engaged two orchestras so that music would be continuous in his large ballroom and he served nothing but champagne.

The famous old resorts of Newport and Bar Harbor in 1929 were enjoying a mild revival of popularity that in retrospect would seem like the bright flare of a candle before it starts to die down. Later, the year would be called the end of an era in resort life. "Today," Cleveland Amory wrote much later in *The Last Resorts*,

the ragged remnants of the great resorts' Old Guards look back from their crumbling cottages to the era of the 1920's as financially the last of the Good Old Days. Those were the days, they say . . . the days of the private yachts and the private railroad cars, the private golf courses and the private polo fields, the private balls and the private art collections. Of all the personalities of those days, the two who are best remembered for cutting the largest swath in the era were unquestionably Philadelphia's famous pair of men-about-resorts, E. T. Stotesbury [a partner in the House of Morgan] and A. Atwater Kent [manufacturer of radios]; indeed, current resorters feel that the whole era of the 1920's was far better symbolized by this pair than by the late F. Scott Fitzgerald, a gentleman who, they feel, merely wanted to be in such rarefied Society.

There was one occasion, Mrs. Kent recalled later, when despite the fact that she had been doing her best her husband called her on the carpet about the expenses for entertaining and running the house.

"Mabel," he said sternly, "you aren't spending enough money."

So far as is known, nothing like that ever happened to Mrs. Stotesbury, whose husband gave her four million dollars as a wedding present. One day a visitor noted with something of a shock that all of the bathroom fixtures were of gold, a departure that he later mentioned in an awed tone to Mrs. Stotesbury.

"Yes," she replied, "they're very economical. You don't have to polish them, you know."

6

This is doubtless as good a place as any to point out that there were not a few qualified experts who believed there was something cockeyed in the national economy in 1929. The warm glow of prosperity that seemed to hover over the land tended to fade under the scrutiny of tough-minded statisticians, whose studies suggested that there were a great many contradictions in the American way of life.

For one thing, the mania for installment buying—make a small deposit now and try to scrape up the weekly payments over a couple of years—had grown so rapidly that radios were ordinary equipment even in homes where the table fare was sparing, indeed. Surveys showed that almost half of the nation's factory workers owned some kind of automobile—they almost had to have one to get to work—but ignored the fact that most of them were ready for the junk heaps which were becoming familiar eyesores on the outskirts of every city. Or ignored the fact that household furniture and equipment often was repossessed because of lagging payments. Installment buying of everything from washing machines to Wall Street stocks had become such an integral part of the economy that householders who failed to use their credit to the limit were likely to be regarded as unpatriotic shirkers.

Furthermore, although almost three million families owned two automobiles, America was not quite so richly endowed as a visitor from Mars might have imagined after reading the newspapers and taking a superficial look at life in the upper social strata. There were, for example, more than a million and a half unemployed persons in the country, according to Labor Department estimates which were regarded as very conservative. There were only around 115 billion kilowatt-hours of electric energy produced in the United States and less than 10 per cent of farms had rural electric lines, as compared to 328 billion kilowatt-hours that would be produced annually in the 1950's when electrification of farms mounted to about 95 per cent. A Brookings Institution survey indicated conservatively that approximately six of every ten families in the United States had incomes of less than two thousand dollars which "may be regarded as sufficient to supply only the basic necessities." Only eight families in every hundred had incomes above five thousand and only three in every hundred had incomes above ten thousand.[2]

---

[2] Such statistics are difficult to compare with similar figures compiled in the 1950's for various reasons such as differences in statistical method and reduced purchasing power of the dollar. However, the President's Council of Economic Advisers reported that at mid-century approximately four of every ten "spending units" (meaning families or individuals) had incomes of less than $2,300, another four of every ten had incomes ranging up to $5,000, and two families in every ten—more than twice as many as in 1929—had incomes of about $5,000 or more. About three families in every hundred, approximately the same as in 1929, were estimated to have incomes of more than $10,000. All such figures, however, can be deceptive because they do not distinguish

7

*Elizabeth Banks, her husband, Robert, and their two children
moved to a pleasant suburban town fifteen miles outside Philadelphia in 1929 because about everybody they knew was moving
to the suburbs to find better schools and playgrounds for growing
children. Robert Banks worked in the offices of a large corporation
which paid him seventy-five hundred dollars a year. This put the
Banks family well up in the Middle Class bracket. The Banks
home was a Tudor-style, seven-room house with a bathroom
upstairs and a powder room on the first floor, with a brick and
stucco exterior and a quaint gabled effect achieved by steep roofs
and imitation beams. It had cost sixteen thousand dollars. Robert
was paying twelve hundred a year on the mortgage, and if he
could hold on to it until 1947 it would easily sell for thirty
thousand.*

*Robert belonged to the country club, where he managed to get
in a round of golf almost every Sunday morning, unless the regular
Saturday night dance had led to consumption of too much poor
gin. He carried ten thousand dollars' life insurance at a cost of
$225 a year—life insurance of all kinds in force in the United
States in 1929 totaled one hundred billion dollars and would
more than double by the 1950's—and owned a two-year-old
thirteen-hundred-dollar Studebaker automobile that he had just
finished paying for. His total income tax payment for the past year
had amounted to $12.38. At thirty, Robert was doing well and felt
that he might boost his income above ten thousand dollars in the
next ten years.*

The weekday rising hour in the Banks household was seven A.M.
Elizabeth turned off the alarm clock on the table between the

---

between a young girl working in a store while living at home and a father with
six children to feed. Nor do they make allowance for businessmen who happened to have one bad year as compared to a marginal farmer who has never
had a really good year.

twin beds, pulled on a robe over her pajamas and woke the two
children on her way to the kitchen. Bob went directly to the basement, shook down the coal furnace and opened the dampers. He
reminded himself that next year he should be able to switch to one
of the new oil burners.

Elizabeth squeezed oranges to provide juice for breakfast—it
would be more than a decade before she would hear of frozen
orange juice—and put a bowl of bran cereal at each place on the
red-painted wooden table in the breakfast nook. All of the health
hints in the newspapers were recommending that everybody have a
daily dose of "roughage" and a cake of yeast for vitamin B.
Mothers were also being urged to stuff young children with
spinach, which Elizabeth tried without great success. She warmly
sympathized with the eager mother in a cartoon by Carl Rose that
had just appeared in The New Yorker—the mother saying per-
suasively to her small but stubborn daughter at the luncheon table:
"It's broccoli, dear." And the child replying: "I say it's spinach,
and I say the hell with it." The younger members of the Banks
family had about the same attitude toward "roughage," and Bob
agreed with them. Because of a slight tendency toward plumpness
Elizabeth had just started on one of the new eighteen-day diets
and was strictly limiting her calorie intake.

At five minutes of eight, Bob went down to the basement again
to close the furnace dampers and put more coal on the fire. He got
the Studebaker out of the garage and picked up the children and
Elizabeth, who had slipped on a dress and tied a scarf around
her head, at the front door and they drove two miles to the station
where Bob caught the 8:08 A.M. train for the city. The train and
a brisk walk would put him at his office in just fifty minutes.
Elizabeth drove home and got young Bob ready for school. One
reason they had chosen this suburb was that it had an up-to-date
public school modeled on Professor John Dewey's ideas of progressive education. Dewey preached against authoritarian

methods in education and emphasized that progress lay in experimentation and environmental control to facilitate the most effective integration of culture and vocation. Under this system, young Bob didn't seem to be making much progress in spelling or arithmetic but he was a good reader, his imagination was developing rapidly and he was the acknowledged leader of the second grade rhythms class.[3]

In connection with the children, Elizabeth also had become interested in Dr. J. B. Watson's book, Behaviorism, *which was popular at the time. Dr. Watson attributed practically all human behavior to environmental stimuli and argued that emotions other than fear, rage and love were conditioned by habit and could be learned or unlearned. Elizabeth's husband was left-handed and she had noticed that the baby, Betty, tended to use her left hand more than her right. According to the behaviorists, this was pure habit rather than heredity and could be changed by a little training which Elizabeth was now attempting. Betty had resisted rather resentfully, but she was awkwardly switching to her right hand.*

After young Bob had gone to school, Elizabeth and Betty got in the car again and drove four miles to pick up Mrs. Brown, the thrice-a-week cleaning woman and cook who was the only hired help at the Banks' house except on special occasions. The Browns lived in one half of a two-family house near a box factory where Mr. Brown earned thirty dollars a week for approximately nine months each year, being laid off during the other three months. Mrs. Brown charged forty cents an hour for cleaning, which Elizabeth considered high but she was a good worker. Most of the Banks' neighbors paid around twenty dollars a week for regular maids, who had Sundays and Thursday afternoons off.

[3] There were numerous jokes about progressive schools in 1929. For example:
VISITOR: How is your son getting along in the progressive school?
MOTHER: Well, his last report card said that he was only fair at spelling and that he was unco-operative in arithmetic but that he was "excellent" at recess.

Leaving Betty with Mrs. Brown, Elizabeth drove two miles to the village to shop at the Piggly Wiggly store, where things were usually a little cheaper because you served yourself. The prices were posted along the shelves: Leg of lamb, 39 cents a pound; pork roast, 35 cents; boneless rib roast, 51 cents; bacon, 50 cents; ham, 32 cents; porterhouse steak, 75 cents; coffee, 52 cents; butter, 58 cents; eggs, 61 cents; milk, 16 cents a quart; cream, 30 cents a half-pint; bread, 10 cents a loaf. She went next door and bought a pair of silk chiffon stockings for $1.95. She also took a pre-season look at bathing suits for herself and Robert. There was a green silk number with a V neckline and a short skirt that she liked but the most popular model was two-piece—a snug-fitting, woolen top of white and navy blue flannel shorts, also snug, with a white canvas belt. The men's suits were almost the same—white tops and navy blue trunks—or a plain-colored one-piece swim suit, but the arm-holes were often made so large that there were only a couple of narrow strips of suit above the waist. Elizabeth had heard that at some European resorts the men wore only bathing trunks and no tops, but she hadn't seen anything like that in America.

Back home again, she put a card in the kitchen window telling the ice man to leave an extra twenty pounds. She went to her bed-room, took off her dress and turned on the exercise machine. This was a small vibrator bolted to the wall. It had a six-inch-wide elastic belt which she fastened around her middle and which jiggled her stomach vigorously for fifteen minutes. Later, she had a cup of coffee on the enclosed sunporch, sitting on a pale green wicker settee with cretonne unholstery in a Navajo motif. The new issue of Harper's *had arrived in the mail and lay on top of the morning newspaper and an old issue of the* Saturday Evening Post, *featuring a fiction serial by Alice Duer Miller. On the table were two new books that she hadn't found time to read, Francis Hackett's* Henry VIII *and Ellen Glasgow's* They Stooped to Folly.

She picked up the newspaper, glanced at headlines about the

Paris Reparations Conference and an outbreak of violence in a textile mill strike somewhere in North Carolina, then skipped to the inside pages. There was an advertisement for one of the new aluminum waterless cookers made in three sections to fit over a single burner—"cook without water—the healthful way—hold in the steam—hold in the vitamins and minerals." One of the better stores in the city was having a sale on top-quality men's shoes, reduced from $10.00 to $8.99. Dorothy Dix was advising "Lonesome Miss" that petting in the back seat of an automobile was a bad idea regardless of what other high school girls did. The novel (and musical) Show Boat *by Edna Ferber, had been made into a movie with Laura La Plante as Magnolia. We must get into the city one night next week, Elizabeth thought, and go to the theater. Maybe we could even go over to New York on Saturday night— after all, Robert only works half a day on Saturday—and then dance for an hour afterward at the St. Regis where Vincent Lopez' orchestra is playing. There was a new play on Broadway called* Journey's End—*a war play—and the reviews were good. Eddie Cantor, whom she and Bob had seen in* Whoopee, *had announced he was through with show business and was retiring to a farm.*

Elizabeth dropped the newspaper and rushed to dress for the weekly bridge luncheon at the country club. She wore next to her skin a combination garment of light silk poplin with lace brassiere at the top and two circular lace trifles at the hips. There were elastic strips at the sides and garters at front and back. Her tailored dress was of bottle green silk crepe with a wide collar that draped loosely down the front. The waistline was nonexistent and the skirt came just to her knees. The over-all effect, while not quite as stick-like as drawings in the fashion magazines, was a straight and narrow silhouette. She wore a dark felt brimless hat that fitted tightly over her shingled hair, curving across her forehead and drooping down on both sides in a graceful arc that ended in large round felt discs below her ears.

At the club there was much excitement because one member whose husband managed a large department store was repeating a rumor that the Paris designers—Patou, Schiaparelli, Worth, Maggy, Rouff, Chanel, Molyneux—were going to come out late in the summer with radical changes in styles, including long skirts and definite waistlines. This frightening possibility, especially the threat of a waistline, was debated throughout luncheon with a majority of those present in opposition. The rumor, however, was correct. In August, the word would be flashed from Paris that short skirts were out and, on the basis of first reports, the old-fashioned corset was about to make a comeback. "Complaining loudly," one fashion expert cabled home, "lady buyers nevertheless are investing heavily in Patou trailing skirts and Chanel fitted waistlines. . . . We are all to have spindle shapes."

This Paris dictate met with initial cries of protest in America, but in no time at all skirts were down to four inches below the knee in daytime and to the ankle in front and the floor behind for evening dresses. The waistline, however, remained "happily nebulous" and the new Chanel models had a belt that could be worn "anywhere you wish." A typical model was a "robe de style" of black tulle with dipped bands of shirring, an immense bow at the back and a sudden flare from the hips before the skirt dropped toward the floor. There was even a faint suggestion of a brim in the new hats.

The change in skirt lengths was so drastic and so sudden that for a while all was confusion. Many national advertisers already had gone to press with expensive color plates in which the women were shown wearing short skirts. As a result, there was an embarrassing period in which magazines carried pictures of the sedate new woman in long skirts on one page while on the next page the manufacturer of automobiles presented a four-color picture of the latest model Lenhard straight eight with a custom body by Miffle being admired by hoydenish ladies whose skirts flapped freely above their knees. And The New Yorker *was able to get a big laugh with a cartoon of two young men turning their heads to look at a fashionably concealed young lady on the street, with the caption: "Gee, there's a swell ankle, Marvin!"*

But when Elizabeth Banks got home from three hours of bridge that afternoon she wasn't quite convinced that any woman was going to wear ankle-length skirts again, and Mrs. Brown heartily agreed. "Why, you couldn't drive a car with long skirts," she exclaimed, "and, anyway, long skirts collect germs. Don't you believe that rumor for a minute, dearie."

Elizabeth met the 6:14 P.M. train to collect her husband. After dinner, while she looked through Vanity Fair, *Robert fiddled with his new radio set for a couple of hours. She heard the voice of Milton Cross, who had just won the gold medal of the American Academy of Arts and Letters for excellence in radio diction, but Robert was more interested in trying to bring in some distant stations. He had at various times been able to get stations as far away as Cleveland and Minneapolis if atmospheric conditions were just right in the late evening, but one of the boys at the office claimed to have brought in Dallas. After twirling dials for half an hour, Robert did bring in Dallas but they were broadcasting hymns and he didn't listen long. He switched back to Station WLW at Cincinnati and got a voice that he had heard on that station before. It was a deep, young voice singing:*

> *S-a-int L-o-u-i-s wo-o-man*
> *Wi-th yo-our d-i-i-amond rings!*

He liked it and waited for the quarter-hour break in hope of finding out something about the singer. When the quarter-hour break came around, Robert didn't learn much. The announcer merely advised the unseen audience to tune in on the same station at the same time tomorrow night if they wanted to hear more popular songs sung by Jane Froman.

8

Americans in 1929 were intensely conscious of their native culture or lack of it, but there was a wide divergence of ideas as to just what cultural state the nation had achieved or just what it ought to try to achieve. During the early Twenties, this confusion of ideas had developed rapidly in various directions. Generally, the intellectuals were in revolt against the traditional American success story philosophy and the rigid conservatism exemplified by Big Business and the Coolidge administration. In *Babbitt*, Sinclair Lewis had bitterly downgraded the American business executive with his mania for mass production and standardization and his booster activities. Intellectuals were often scornful of the middle-class tendency to concentrate on "getting ahead" and Mencken's steady bombardment of the foibles of the "booboisie" created a picture of the Middle West as a Bible Belt in the grip of narrow-minded prohibition fanatics.[4]

But at the same time, the Babbitts, the mass producers, the go-getters, the White Ribbon League leaders of the Bible Belt —all these targets of intellectual scorn—were plugging right ahead, building great cities, demanding better roads and better automobiles, improving school facilities, supporting symphony orchestras and art galleries, inventing labor-saving devices, building bigger churches with bigger pipe organs, setting up magnificent hospitals, turning in better golf scores and boosting the American way. If they were short on culture, they were long on industry and they were making such radical changes in the American economy that by 1954 no less than 72.1 per cent of the population of the country would be described by the U.S. Information Service as "middle class."

[4] "Puritanism was the *bête noire* of Mencken," Edward Schindeler wrote in a letter to the *New York Times* in 1955 when Mencken was celebrating his seventy-fifth birthday. "But see what has happened. Mr. Mencken's boobs have all been gloriously freed from their puritanical inhibitions and repressions . . . followed, less gloriously, by the rapid deterioration in popular morals and ethics. . . . It has not cured the Menckenian boob of his boobism: unreliable, cynical, blasé—he is still a boob."

In 1929, America's Midwesterners were feeling all right about the kind of civilization they were helping to build as was illustrated by two developments in Omaha, Nebraska, then a bustling city of 225,000. The first event was the celebration of Nebraska's seventy-fifth anniversary as a territory, a tremendous civic affair in which practically the whole community participated for the benefit of many thousands of visitors from all parts of the nation and Canada. The celebration opened with a parade of the state's history that included floats representing Coronado discovering Nebraska, prairie schooners and oxcarts carrying early settlers, a Mormon handcart being pulled across the state toward Utah, a stage coach carrying eighty-three-year-old Deadwood Dick Clark, who wore a horse pistol with a notch for each man he had shot, elaborate floats of a dozen nationalities represented in the population of the state and a huge kettle—The Melting Pot—decked with flags and guarded by Miss Jean Redick, artfully draped in white robes as the Goddess of Liberty.

The climax of the celebration three days later was a pageant called "The Making of Nebraska," staged at the athletic field of Ak-Sar-Ben (that's Nebraska spelled backward and the name of a live-wire local civic organization) with a cast of thirteen hundred, including Omaha's civic and society leaders in colorful costumes. The pageant started at the geological beginning with men carrying torches to represent Volcanoes, girls in glittering costume as Stars, Seas, Land and Flowers and, in white garments, as Glaciers. Finally a group of young women in bulky dress appeared as Solid Land. Then there were Sioux Indians chasing a tribe of Pawnees across the landscape, the Spanish conquistadors, the French Jesuits, Lewis and Clark exploring the Missouri River and, at last, the frontiersmen and modern settlers. At the end, everybody stood, saluted the flag and sang the national anthem.

The second development in Nebraska that year also was cultural, but of a different nature. It was a simple evening at home with a few friends as recounted in a widely reprinted editorial in the Omaha *World-Herald,* one of the most respected news-papers of the region.

Table talk indicates what folks are thinking about, or whether they think at all. People say the art of conversation is dead, killed by the radio and the movies. They say that the trouble with America (someone always seems to be seeking to define the trouble with America) is that no one thinks of anything any more, except the making of money and various devices for spending it. Our rabble-rousers love to list the imbecilities of the Americano.

The other night there was a dinner party in Omaha where were to be found a newspaper man, a banker, a real-estate man and their wives. They were ordinary folk in the sense that none of them had a million dollars or anything near it. The men work hard and the women look after their homes and children. The dinner might have been expected to provide such a scene as perfectly suits the repor-torial venom of Sinclair Lewis when he views the American scene. There was, however, a complete absence of all that might be classed as Babbittry.

If this group were representative of Omaha citizenship, and of the country at large, then a report of its conversation should be reas-suring.

The writer then listed various topics of conversation that were taken up at the dinner table while soft music drifted in from a radio in an adjoining room. Among other things, the ladies discussed the books of Sinclair Lewis and decided, rather regretfully, that he had a "blind spot" in regard to the good qualities of the American businessman. They talked about music, expressing a friendly tolerance toward the "homespun glories" of programs over a near-by radio station directed mainly to farm families. Then, the writer noted with tongue-in-cheek, there was "some desultory speculation as to the proper place in a symphony orchestra of the musical saw that one of the dance bands utilizes so effectively." The talk shifted to a discussion of modern music, including the fact that a "modern-ist group . . . had been hissed at a symphony programme in New York."

The conversation turned to "the cult of hero-worship" surrounding such figures as Lindbergh, who was obviously admired by the ladies at table; and went on to the "satisfying fact that not a few dishonest state bankers had found lodgement in Nebraska's penitentiary" but this "was not stressed too much, out of deference to the banker guest." There was some "genuinely prideful talk" about Nebraska's new capitol at Lincoln— a skyscraper sticking up from the prairie—and a change of subject to novelist Elinor Glyn, whom one of the diners had recently met. "The women were interested in learning that Elinor Glyn was charmingly gowned, but the men were not surprised to learn that she is not beautiful, although her face has been lifted." When the subject of the "reds in Russia" was brought up nobody at the table "shuddered in fear of communism." But later the women seemed "vaguely to fear and resent the growth of chain stores in Omaha's shopping districts, but admitted that they liked to shop where the utmost in value seemed to be assured for the dollar spent."

Of such was the talk. It doubtless could be duplicated in scores of homes every night, where people gather. There was honesty of opinion, kindliness, a flash of wit and a lively interest in the things that made the day and its affairs pungent and interesting. It seemed to one who listened to it all that here, in this table talk, was every necessary guaranty that Americans are not dull and sordid money-grabbers, but rather people with a keen sense of the rich happiness that can be had in living life to the full, in giving rather than in getting, in cultivating the mind rather than the pocketbook, in cherishing virtue rather than pursuing vice.

Although the *World-Herald*'s editorial writer was fairly content about America's cultural development and willing to relegate the cultivation of the pocketbook to business hours, there were obviously discontented elements in the land. This had been made evident earlier by a number of debunking biographies and by the popularity of the *American Mercury*, especially among college students. The *Mercury* was highly skeptical about the state of American culture but it did a great deal to cultivate native American talent and in 1929 conducted a competition among college graduates for the best literary manuscripts based on their student days and their role in civilized society.

"What they reported," said the *Mercury* in an editorial that might have been reprinted twenty-five years later without drastic change,

was a society [on the campus] almost as completely dominated by mass production as the Great Society they must now enter. The campus swarms with youths whose talents, however gaudy, simply do not include a talent for ingesting the humanities. The hope they cherish is not that of increasing in culture, but that of increasing in efficiency. Their eyes are fixed on Rotary, and to its ideals they shape their grabbing of credits. Thus the dominant student is not a nascent Goethe but a nascent Hoover, and the whole academic scheme of things is thrown out of whack. . . . Going to college, especially in the more backward parts of the country, has come to be a sort of social necessity; it almost ranks with having a bathroom and keeping a car. Thus the hordes of the unteachable swarm in, and the poor pedagogues can only gasp in dismay. . . . There is more teaching in America than ever before, and it is less good. A learned degree, once a pearl of great price, has come to have no more value or significance than the ruby-studded insignia of the Elks. . . . The kind of education on tap in the colleges seems to be the kind that the country wants, and maybe it is also the kind that such a country needs.

At about the same time, a sad assessment of life in America was made by George Jean Nathan, who argued that intelligent men and women were becoming "expatriates at home." Nathan contended that America had been swept by a "tide of commonness, cheapness, vicious dishonesty and unAmericanism" and to support his argument he cited the manner of enforcement of the dry laws, the trial and execution in 1927 of Anarchists Sacco and Vanzetti for murder on what he regarded as questionable evidence; the imprisonment of Labor Agitator Tom Mooney—later pardoned—for a bomb outrage committed while he was elsewhere; the efforts of the Daughters of the American Revolution to "impose a censorship" on the public; and the "prosecution and conviction of an honorable and intelligent mother who tells her children how to order their lives."

The "honorable and intelligent mother" was, in fact, a grandmother—fifty-three-year-old Mrs. Mary Ware Dennett, who in 1929 was taken into federal court in Brooklyn at the instigation of a well-known sin chaser, John S. Sumner of the New York Society for Suppression of Vice, and of Canon William S. Chase of the Episcopal Church. Mrs. Dennett was charged with committing a criminal obscenity by sending through the mails a twenty-four-page booklet written by herself and called *The Sex Side of Life*. She was accompanied to court by her two sons and a daughter-in-law.

The booklet was based on an article Mrs. Dennett had written fifteen years earlier for the *Medical Review of Reviews*. It had been so highly regarded that many thousands of copies were reprinted and distributed by the Y.M.C.A., the Y.W.C.A., the Union Theological Seminary, churches and social organizations for the guidance of young men and women. The booklet was a frank discussion of sex with drawings by Dr. Robert L. Dickinson, a gynecologist and eugenist. "Don't let any one drag you into nasty talk or thought about sex," it said. "The physical side of love is the intensely intimate part of it, and the most critical for happiness." In summing up the case, the prosecutor said: "It may be true that to the pure all things are pure, and that we have to go down to the gutter for our information, but this woman is trying to drag us into the sewer." The jury of twelve men debated the case for forty-two minutes and returned a verdict of guilty. Mrs. Dennett was fined three hundred dollars.

Elsewhere in the nation there were a few faint but encouraging signs that bigotry was waning, although only a visionary could have foreseen the integration of Negroes and whites in the armed forces or the United States Supreme Court decision twenty-five years later that segregation in public schools is unconstitutional. One of the faint signs, however, occurred in Washington. Mrs. Oscar De Priest, wife of the first Negro to sit in Congress since 1900, was invited to the White House for the regular afternoon tea in honor of wives of senators and representatives. Slender and dignified in a Capri blue chiffon afternoon dress, a small gray hat, moonlight gray hose and snakeskin slippers, Mrs. De Priest was among the first to arrive, was greeted by Mrs. Hoover and "greatly enjoyed" herself.

The White House tea caused a furor in the Southern states. In Florida, the state legislature voted 71 to 13 to condemn "certain social policies of the Administration." Florida had gone for Hoover in 1928. So had Texas, but the Texas state senate voted 26 to 2 for a resolution saying that "we bow our heads in shame and regret and express in the strongest and most emphatic terms our condemnation . . . of said conduct . . . on the part of the mistress of the White House and her associates." One senator, in debating the resolution, used the expression "political nigger lovers."

A letter to the editor, printed in the Macon, Georgia, *Telegraph* said that

every Southern State should set aside one day to fast and pray for the preservation of our pure Anglo-Saxon race, for it is plain that if the South does not preserve it, that it will soon be a thing of the past. . . . I hope that no Southern Senator or Southern Congressman's wife will darken the doors of the White House as long as Mrs. Hoover is its mistress. When Mrs. Hoover has vacated the White House I hope our government will see the necessity to dynamite the White House . . . and build another one that its walls may not be contaminated with the odor of Mrs. De Priest. . . . I would rather that the Catholic had control of our government than the African race.

"The De Priest incident," said the Jackson, Mississippi, *Daily News,* "has placed President and Mrs. Hoover beyond the pale of social recognition by Southern people. Several weeks ago it was announced that [they] intend to visit several Southern States during the Autumn and early Winter. It is sincerely hoped they will not do so." [The trip was canceled, but for other reasons.] The Memphis, Tennessee, *Commercial-Appeal* said that the White House tea did not establish the social equality of the Negro race, but it did establish the social status of the President and Mrs. Hoover.

Most newspapers, in reporting the De Priest incident, recalled that in 1901 President Theodore Roosevelt had created a somewhat similar storm by having Booker T. Washington at the White House for luncheon. At that time, it was explained by White House spokesmen that the famous Negro educator just happened to arrive as the President was finishing his luncheon and had been invited into the dining room to avoid delaying his appointment. In connection with Mrs. De Priest's visit, however, a White House statement made it clear that she had been invited for tea; that the Hoovers had planned it that way.

...the blue of the night...

Nineteen Twenty-nine was a hell-raising year for Americans . . . for Harry Lillis Crosby, a relaxed young man with an unusual voice and a remarkable sense of rhythm, with an inclination to drink too much bootleg liquor and a disinclination toward taking life seriously.

As a boy in Spokane, Washington, he had played cowboy games with great enthusiasm and pursued imaginary Indians with a toy pistol, aiming and shouting: "Bing! bing! bing!" For this, or perhaps for some other reason, he was nicknamed Bing. The Crosbys had seven children but not much money. Bing was good at sports and not bad in an alley fight, but he also worked—driving a grocery truck, janitoring in a club, sorting mail at the post office, lumberjacking until he hacked his own leg with an ax. He wanted to be a lawyer and was studying law at Gonzaga University when a young friend named Al Rinker, leader of The Musicaladers dance orchestra, lured him away in the early 1920's to play the drums. Bing had to buy his drums on the installment plan, but it was worth it one night when they let him step up front and sing a chorus of "For Me and My Gal." He was nervous and his voice wavered, but he was on his way.

For the next half-dozen years, however, he wasn't sure which was his way. In 1925, Bing and Rinker formed a vaudeville team—Two Boys and a Piano—singing hot rhythms, Al at the piano and Bing beating a cymbal with a drumstick or sometimes using a kazoo which he moved in and out of a tin can to get a trombone effect. They went in for a kind of gibberish that became known as scat-singing, usually ending with a yowling boodle-dee-boo and yodle-dee-yo that was regarded as "hot stuff" at the time. Driving a decrepit, twenty-four-dollar jalopy, they got to Los Angeles and got a booking on the Franchon and Marco vaudeville circuit. Bing kept introducing new touches in his songs. Sometimes he hummed part of a chorus. Sometimes he put in "my boo-boo-boo" stuff. One night Paul Whiteman caught their act and offered them three hundred dollars a week to join his orchestra at the Tivoli Theater in Chicago. Whiteman was the country's best-known band leader. He had sponsored "symphonic jazz" at a concert in New York for which George Gershwin had written "Rhapsody in Blue." When he tapped a young singer with a signed contract, it usually meant success.

But Bing wasn't just another young singer. He was an expert golfer. He was good with his fists. He played top-notch pool. He liked crap games, fishing expeditions and a good time. He was quick-tempered one day and indifferent to everything the next. Sometimes he didn't show up for performances. He had many excellent qualifications for becoming a pleasant but confirmed bum.

In Chicago, Bing and Rinker did well enough with Whiteman. In New York, they flopped and were withdrawn from the orchestra's appearance at the Paramount Theater after two days. Whiteman was patient. He had to go to Europe, but he arranged a vaudeville tour for them as the Rhythm Boys, with a hot piano player named Harry Barris. The Rhythm Boys raised hell all around the circuit. They got on the wrong trains. They missed dates due to hangovers. They lost their shirts in crap games. Bing expected to be fired when Whiteman returned, but instead the bandleader offered him a solo in his forthcoming movie, *The King of Jazz*.

They had hardly arrived in Hollywood when Bing went to a party, got involved in an automobile accident that wasn't his fault, was arrested and ordered to appear three days later in court on charges of reckless driving and suspicion of drinking. He played golf that day and walked into court wearing a bright orange sweater, green plus-four knickers and checkered stockings. Bing was color-blind, but the judge wasn't.

"Had you been drinking?"

"I'd had a couple," Bing replied in a cocksure manner.

"Don't you know about the prohibition law?"

"Nobody pays much attention to that."

"Sixty days in jail. Next case."

Bing went to jail and another singer got the solo part in *The King of Jazz*, although friendly jailers later let him go under escort to the studio and the Rhythm Boys did a small bit in the movie. Bing made another tour with Whiteman's band. He was a fairly constant headache and they soon parted company in reasonably friendly fashion. It looked as if Bing had decided that his way was down—but he hadn't, because in a night club one evening in 1929 he saw a blonde named Wilma Wyatt of Harriman, Tennessee. She was introduced as Dixie Lee, a promising young actress. They fell in love promptly. Everybody from the studio boss to the night club doorman warned Miss Lee against Bing, saying that she would ruin her bright future, that she would have to support him and that the marriage could never, never last. Bing was also against the marriage because he felt he would become known as "Mister Lee," overshadowed by a famous wife. So they were married, and Bing could see that he'd been right. The newspapers in reporting the wedding misspelled his name.

Maybe it made him mad. Maybe he was just in love. In any event, he went to work in earnest. Radio was just opening up and Columbia Broadcasting Co. was looking for a distinctive popular singer. Bing was hired and his voice—"Old Gravel Throat," Dixie called him—was soon familiar everywhere. Hollywood beckoned. Bing permitted makeup men to glue back his big ears. He wore built-up shoes so he would be taller than his leading lady. He struggled through love scenes that never quite came off. He wore a toupee, or a hat, in all public appearances as his hair thinned rapidly. He recorded religious songs that were a great success. He was nonchalant with a wisecrack. He was a crooner, a groaner; everybody knew his theme song

> Where the blue of the night
> Meets the gold of the day . . .

His style changed with the times and with his age but he always had as many men as women among his admirers. In what seemed to be a lazy, almost indifferent fashion, he made close to a million dollars a year in the decade after 1929. His record sales topped five million annually. His radio program brought in $16,000 a week. His movie salary was around $150,-000 a picture and he might make several a year. "Call me lucky," he said. "I just did what I liked to do."

He still played hard between jobs, but he played on the golf course, on hunting trips, at the race track. One evening in 1939, he was with a friend at the New York World's Fair watching the Aquacade stars dive from the fifty-foot platform. His friend delivered a little lecture on how difficult it was to acquire the special skill and physique required for such hazardous dives.

"I bet I could do it," Bing exclaimed.

"I bet a hundred you wouldn't dare try," the friend replied.

"Okay. Sit right here," Bing said and departed.

Ten minutes later there was an announcement over the loudspeaker that "the next dive from the fifty-foot board will be by Singer Bing Crosby." In a light blue borrowed bathing suit, Bing came swooping off the high board and slipped into the water with scarcely a ripple. He never did tell his friend that as a boy he had been an expert swimmer and diver.

World War II came along. Television came along. Bing endured and, if some of the old zip was missing, few of his fans noticed it. But by that time, Dixie was gone after a long illness.

The hopeless marriage of the young star and the potential bum had turned out to be one of the longest-lasting in Hollywood. "I don't ever want anything more in life," Bing said later, "than the memory of all she did for me."

I Can Do Without Broadway
(But Can Broadway Do Without Me?).

—JIMMY (SCHNOZZOLA) DURANTE,
in the musical *Show Girl*

The Pulitzer Prize in recognition of literary excellence
that contributes to uplifting the American Scene has been
awarded to Scarlet Sister Mary, *the story of a harlot.*

—News Item

Boop-boop-a-doop!

—Singer HELEN KANE

M A Y , 1 9 2 9

show business

Everybody said in 1929 that Broadway wasn't what it used to be, and they were probably right. The famous old restaurants, richly furnished and fashionable, and the famous old saloons, richly furnished and discreetly run, had become casualties of the Prohibition Era. The fashionable folk who had once frequented the famous street were gone, too, and in their place were the tourists, the gangsters, the petty chiselers, the ballyhoo artists, the racketeers and their molls. Mrs. Astor's little dinners for sixty-five guests were replaced by friends of Harry the Horse eating cheesecake at Lindy's restaurant with Damon Runyon and playing the matchstick game to see who paid. Johnny Broderick, a two-fisted little detective whose beat was Broadway for many years, kept himself amused and the gunmen more or less in line by punching offensive characters on the nose and telling them to do their shooting elsewhere. Once, with Mayor Walker watching from across the street, he dragged Gangster Legs Diamond out of a theater, lifted him across the sidewalk and dumped him head first into a trash can with an emphatic suggestion that he get out of town. Broderick never bothered to carry a gun; he knew how cheap the Broadway crowd had become.

But Broadway means show business, too; and show business in 1929 was at the climax of a wild whirl such as would not be seen again. This didn't mean that a great new breed of playwrights was being developed or that everybody was making money, but it did mean that activity in the theatrical world was at a high-water mark.[1] In the course of the year no less than 224 plays of one kind or another, including revivals and holdovers, showed in New York's seventy-five theaters. There will probably never be another year so lush with theatrical fruit, good or bad. The great "go-for-broke" producers—the Shuberts, Arthur Hammerstein (whose *Sweet Adeline* lost money in 1929), Arthur Hopkins, Jed Harris (a newcomer who was estimated to have made two million dollars in three years), John Golden (who was said to have ten million dollars at the height of his career), and even aged David Belasco—represented a theatrical tradition that would give way in the future to "angels" or stockholders in a corporation formed to finance stage productions. By 1954 there would be only thirty-one playhouses in New York and they would present only seventy-three shows, including fifteen musicals, throughout the season; and about the nearest approach to a "go-for-broke" producer left in the entertainment field would be Hollywood's Samuel Goldwyn.

The normal run of even a successful show in 1929 was short in comparison to the runs of two or three years in later years, but the theatrical menu was varied. Walter Hampden was appearing in *Cyrano de Bergerac*; Helen Morgan was still in

---

[1] The hit shows made big profits but many others, including Florenz Ziegfeld's costly *Show Girl*, didn't. From a financial viewpoint, *Variety* reported 1929 the worst legitimate season in nine years.

Show Boat; and Beatrice Lillie and Noel Coward in *This Year of Grace*. Eugene O'Neill's *Strange Interlude*, so long that it required an afternoon and evening performance with a break for dinner, had opened in 1928 but was still running, as was the rowdy Chicago newspaper play, *The Front Page*, by Ben Hecht and Charles MacArthur. ("An extraordinarily vulgar play . . . entirely thug," commented the noted British critic, St. John Ervine, who was a temporary member of the staff of the New York *World* that season. "Displayed on the stage are finger signs labeled 'IT' pointing to a urinal.") Fred Allen, once a Boston librarian and later a poor vaudeville juggler, was wise-cracking his way through a musical called *Polly*; Katharine Cornell was in *The Age of Innocence*, and Mae West was swishing through the title role in her own story of a Bowery bordello, *Diamond Lil*, en route to a day when she would knock America dead with a single line: "Why doncha come up an' see me sometime?" Alfred Lunt and Lynn Fontanne were starring in *Caprice*.

Willie Howard and Frances Williams were in the tenth annual edition of George White's *Scandals*, which as usual was largely a display of scantily clad chorus girls. The dance routines were even more strenuous than the earlier Black Bottom and Charleston and the settings were reminiscent of European carnivals, with grotesque mechanical figures of shaggy animals and clowns looming in the background, swaying and rolling their huge eyes. One number featured a big swimming pool into which actors descended wearing rubber costumes. Another number featured a clown who, upon being ousted from the bed of a married woman, exclaimed: "Believe it or not, I'm a stowaway!"

W. C. Fields, a very good vaudeville juggler; Victor Moore, who would later immortalize Throttlebottom as Vice-President; Bert Lahr, who would eventually be a cowardly lion in *The Wizard of Oz*; and Eddie Cantor, who wanted to retire to a farm but didn't, were all stars of Broadway musicals that year, and the four Marx Brothers were still doing fine in a zany production called *Animal Crackers*. Minnie Maddern Fiske, at sixty-four, after three score years on the stage, was as expert as ever in a disappointing play called *Ladies of the Jury*, and Margaret Anglin was the whole show in *Lady Dedlock*.

There was a good deal of emphasis throughout the season on sex and psychology. O'Neill, for example, presented a second play, *Dynamo*, starring Claudette Colbert, a pert newcomer to the Theatre Guild, in which the hero (Glenn Anders) turns his back on both fundamentalism and atheism to search for a god that he will not have to fear. He ends up in rather confused and indecisive fashion worshiping electricity to which he sacrifices his earthly love. The critics of the day were charmed by O'Neill's poetry but otherwise somewhat confused and indecisive in their comment.

A more direct approach to both sex and psychology was made late in the year by George M. Cohan who wrote and starred in an involved murder mystery called *Gambling*. Cohan's characters were not exactly idealists. His hero was a gambler who spends most of his time making improper proposals in the apartment of a hard-boiled tart named Mazie, although eventually it turns out that he is not interested in debauchery after all but only in discovering the murderer of the daughter of his dead pal. Other characters included the debauched fiancé of the murdered girl, the debauched mistress of the debauched fiancé, the patrons of a gambling hell and the district attorney, whose idea of applied psychology is to accuse Mazie of murder. Mazie's wisecracks soon demonstrate the foolishness of *that* approach but the gambler's more subtle methods drive the real murderer to suicide before the final curtain. The critics thought the new Cohan show was exciting and persuasive "in the best Broadway manner."

To round out some of the headline attractions—and there were a lot of them—there were *The Kingdom of God* with Ethel Barrymore, *Street Scene* (a Pulitzer Prize winner) by Elmer Rice, *A Most Immoral Lady* with Alice Brady, *Paris*

with Irene Bordoni, *New Moon* with music by Sigmund Rom-
berg, *The Wild Duck* with Blanche Yurka, *Jealousy* with Fay
Bainter and John Halliday, *The Jealous Moon* with Jane Cowl,
Journey's End with an all-British cast, *Congai* with Helen
Menken, *Berkeley Square* with Leslie Howard, *Sherlock Holmes*
with William Gillette, *The Sea Gull* with Eva Le Gallienne,
Strictly Dishonorable with Muriel Kirkland and Tullio Carmi-
nati, *Fifty Million Frenchmen* with music by Cole Porter, *Sweet
Adeline* with music by Jerome Kern, *Major Barbara* by George
Bernard Shaw and some incomparable monologues by Ruth
Draper. Not all of these shows were running at the same time.
In fact, some of the stars appeared in one play early in 1929
and opened in another late in the year. And Miss Le Gallienne,
the moving spirit of the admirable Civic Repertory Theatre,
acted in or directed a whole series of classics during the year,
while Noel Coward not only appeared on the boards but wrote
a highly successful musical called *Bitter Sweet*, which opened
that summer with Evelyn Laye singing a new hit

> I'll see you again
> Whenever spring breaks
> Through again.

One of the most popular shows of the year was a highly
sophisticated satire on the life of song writers in Tin Pan Alley,
by Ring Lardner and George S. Kaufman. It was called *June
Moon*, dealt with young lovers, hard-boiled golddiggers, wise-
cracking Broadwayites and a little number entitled "Give Our
Child a Name" which posed a sentimental question:

> Should a father's carnal sins
> Blight the life of babykins?

But perhaps it was Libby Holman who scored the biggest
success of the season in a sophisticated revue, *The Little Show*
—also featuring Clifton Webb—in which she sang in husky,
torchy fashion:

> Moanin' low . . . my sweet man . . . I love him so!

All of this—and other—theatrical fare failed to prove much except that there were always tired businessmen and out-of-town visitors to pay fancy prices for first-row seats at the musical comedies. In 1929, about the only theatrical ventures that could be regarded as significant were Rice's *Street Scene*, a story of highly charged emotions in a New York tenement house, and O'Neill's five-hour-long psychopathic study, *Strange Interlude*, which, incidentally, was suppressed in Boston. In a lighter vein there was *Strictly Dishonorable*, a bright and sophisticated number by a new but promising author, Preston Sturges, destined for a long career on Broadway and in Hollywood. There was, too, an unusual development across the river from New York in Hoboken, where the Christopher Morley repertory company was drawing big and happy crowds to witness the revival of some old and hilarious dramas—such as *After Dark, or Neither Maid, Wife nor Widow*—costumed and acted in the spirit of the nineteenth century. The audiences drank beer and hissed the villain, but after a while the novelty wore off and everybody was bored.

There was among the drama critics of 1929 a high degree of discouragement over the state of the theater in general and over the ticket scalping racket in particular. Except for productions by the Theatre Guild, which had thirty thousand members who subscribed for seats in advance, and the Civic Repertory Theatre, which had a top price of $1.50 for its arty productions on Fourteenth Street, it was difficult to see a popular show without falling into the hands of speculators who were generally believed to be working in connivance with a number of producers and ticket brokers. The result was that a man in a hurry to get tickets for a Broadway musical hit would go to the box office, where top seats were listed at $6.60, only to discover that nothing was available for that evening. He would then proceed to a ticket broker's office, where the same seats cost $7.35. They, too, would be sold out and he would have to resort to a scalper whose price would range from $9 to $15, depending upon the demand. The customer not in a hurry might try to avoid this illegal racket by buying his tickets a week or two in advance, but he would not be likely to succeed because many of the big shows did not put tickets for a specific week on sale until the preceding Thursday—and at that time they could hang up the "sold out" sign at the box office and start the shakedown all over again.[2]

In addition to the high cost of tickets, the business of getting to the theater in New York was a difficult chore in 1929. Most of the city's seventy-five theaters were jammed into an area roughly bounded by Sixth and Eighth avenues and Fortieth and Fiftieth streets, which also was crowded by large and small motion picture theaters, vaudeville theaters, burlesque shows and the new Madison Square Garden. Until the winter of 1929 there were few traffic rules, automobiles parked at will along the narrow side streets off Broadway and a vast armada of low-fare taxicabs circulated through the district. Thus at eight o'clock each evening the world's greatest traffic tangle and the world's largest army of jaywalkers locked the area in a kind of "curtain time" paralysis that the police were helpless to handle. It might take a taxicab half an hour to cover four blocks and countless theatergoers would choose to get out and walk, which was considerably faster, rather than miss the first act.

But, in addition to all this, the critics and presumably the public as well were exceedingly unhappy over the lack of vigor in the theatrical fare of the day. There were many complaints among the critics that playwrights and producers seemed to be afraid of old-fashioned dramatics, that the new plays had gone overboard on psychological emphasis and sophisticated high-brow dialogue. Some of these complaints may have been due to the popularity of British drawing room plays that made a point of understatement and of lackadaisical third act climaxes instead of dramatic action. An article by Wesley Stout in the conservative *Saturday Evening Post*

---

[2] Twenty-five years and several official investigations later the situation hadn't changed much, except in regard to advance sales.

pointed out that "you will find no hint in the drama today that this is an extraordinary time and that America is an exciting place in which to live . . . that more history, as it affects the common man, is in the making than in all the centuries together between the fall of Rome and our Civil War."

The literary left wing was just as unhappy. "I think the drama is dying because of the blighting touch of intellectuality," wrote Heywood Broun in the *Evening Telegram*.

Managers have been fooled into heeding the cries of those who say they want to be able to think in the theater. In spite of certain evidence to the contrary, I have no objection to thinking. But why should anybody choose a playhouse as the place to do it? Within the last few years the man who went out for an evening's entertainment was as like as not to run into three acts of morbid psychology or some little thing concerning the nature of inherited disease. . . . The Drama League and kindred organizations . . . have introduced a new and fatal point of view about the stage. They ask their members to come forward and support good shows. . . . The simplest way to make any art dull is to uplift it. No one has to be implored to see *Animal Crackers* for the good of his soul.

Such complaints, such dire predictions had doubtless been heard before and certainly would be heard again, as late, for example, as 1955 when Critic Walter Kerr declared that the theater had "lost its hold on any sort of mass audience." Kerr wrote that when the average American is looking for a good time it does not even occur to him that "he might deliberately choose playgoing over poker, golf, movies, television or bourbon on the rocks. . . . The contemporary theater is extremely honest about trivia, and extremely indifferent to any activity more pronounced than the rustling of a leaf, a dress or a newspaper over coffee. Indeed it is hostile to the idea of activity. I am convinced that this is the main reason why the mass audience is hostile to the theater." Perhaps somebody is always predicting the death of the theater or perhaps, in view of the decline in the number of Broadway productions between 1929 and 1954, the critics were right both times.

2

Broadway, of course, was not the whole world of show business. Out in the country there were good repertory theaters, road shows, vaudeville, burlesque, traveling tent shows in the small towns and circuses. Some of them, especially vaudeville and burlesque, were on their last legs but the Greatest Show on Earth was really living up to its name under the guidance of John Ringling.

A big, nattily dressed man, Ringling was the youngest of seven brothers who dominated the circus world. They had started out in the 1870's with a concert troupe to which they quickly added acrobats and aerialists, a hyena, a lion and a kangaroo. At that time Ringling had never even seen an elephant but he had learned that freaks and a menagerie would keep the box office busy. He accumulated more and more and, in 1907, bought control of the famous Barnum and Bailey shows. Then the big money rolled in. He went into development of oil fields and railroads. He had a mansion in New York and an estate in New Jersey. He built a vast medieval Italian-style palace with elaborate boat landings on the bay at Sarasota, Florida. He built a huge museum of marble from ancient Greek temples and filled it with works of art from the Old World—Corots, Tintorettos, Romneys, Gainsboroughs and Rembrandt's "Descent from the Cross" which he acquired in 1929 for forty thousand dollars. And he kept on acquiring circuses.

In 1929, Ringling Brothers–Barnum and Bailey Combined Circus bought out the American Circus Corporation, which was practically the only rival left in the field, and thus acquired Sells-Floto, John Robinson, Hagenbeck-Wallace, Sparks and Al G. Barnes circuses. The Greatest Show on Earth was getting "better and better," as Ringling's remarkable press agent, Dexter Fellows, kept telling newspaper reporters all over the country. Not only was the beautiful Lillian Leitzel still "breaking the world record" almost every night by doing a hundred breath-taking turns on a rope caught in the glare of a spotlight high up against the top of the darkened tent. But a new and sensational act had been added as a result of Ringling's tireless search for new talent in the far corners of the world. In Egypt, he had found the "human cannon ball"—one Ugo Zacchini, an Italian war veteran, who had first discovered his talent by permitting himself to be "shot" by compressed air out of a cannon and into a haystack. By the time Ringling put him on display in America, Zacchini was fired, with a loud bang and a big puff of smoke, from the barrel of a realistic-looking cannon into a net some two hundred feet away.

Also under canvas every summer were touring repertoire tent shows, especially in the Midwestern farming areas. There had been about three hundred such tent shows employing possibly five thousand actors shortly after the war, but the number had been dwindling steadily and 1929 was the last full year for almost all of them. One of the few that survived the Twenties was the Neil E. Schaffner Players, which was still going strong twenty-five years later on an annual circuit through Iowa, Illinois and Missouri. Throughout that period Schaffner, a husky, deep-voiced man, and his petite wife, Caroline, wrote, staged and played in scores of unsophisticated comedies and melodramas. But they were best known for keeping alive an old-time theatrical character—a red-headed, freckle-faced comedy figure named Toby—and his freckle-faced girl friend, Susie. Some of the gags that they used in 1929 could still be revised in 1954 to get a laugh out of audiences that were familiar with all of the latest Broadway wisecracks via television but still admired Toby.

SUSIE: Oh, Toby! I bet you never even kissed a girl except in your dreams.
TOBY: I'd rather kiss 'em that way than any other.
SUSIE: You'd rather kiss a girl in your dreams? Why?
TOBY: You get a better class of girls that way!

Vaudeville and burlesque were failing as big-time circuits in 1929, although a few top stars—such as Bea Lillie at six thousand dollars a week—were still doing well in the big-city variety houses. In his history, *Vaudeville*, Joe Laurie, Jr., blamed the decline of vaudeville in part on the violation of an old rule laid down by Tony Pastor and B. F. Keith: "Keep it clean!" The actors, working hard to get laughs, worked more and more off-color gags into their numbers and patrons all over the circuits complained that vaudeville was no longer anything for the family to patronize. There were gags in 1929 about "a girl taking a tramp through the woods" and a scene in which a girl appears carrying a pair of oars and announces: "I just made the crew." One comic remarked that "children look more like their fathers since we have Frigidaires" and the climax of outrages was reached when a female bit player was "goosed" at the Palace Theater, the "cathedral of vaudeville." There were, of course, other reasons such as the motion pictures and radio to help account for the decline of vaudeville and it was becoming the practice to show a talking picture with a few specialty acts in many theaters. Burlesque was in bad odor generally (although it would enjoy a brief revival later) and in some instances it was in the hands of underworld characters. At the Gayety burlesque house in Washington, D.C., a special benefit performance was given in 1929 for four gamblers who had been sentenced to prison but had refused to "sing" about their gangster friends. An audience made up largely of rum runners, gamblers and racketeers paid five thousand dollars at the box office and bought many thirty-two-page program souvenirs while actors, musicians and stagehands "volunteered their services—after strong hints from certain circles that it might be healthy to do so," according to Abel Green and Joe Laurie, Jr., in *Show Biz*.

A number of good repertory companies were to be found in various parts of the country in the last year of the Twenties. On the Pacific Coast, the Henry Duffy Players were based at the Alcazar Theater in San Francisco but they made a regular tour of eight other playhouses. The Stuart Walker Players at the Murat Theater in Indianapolis made similar tours in such cities as Louisville, Dayton and Baltimore. One of the country's famous theaters was Elitch Gardens in Denver, located in the center of a park. The Little Theater and university theater movements were prospering, and included the Iowa University Theater, the Knox College Theater, the Pasadena Community Playhouse, the Peoria Players, who started out in an abandoned firehouse, and the University of Washington Theater. Students at Professor George Baker's famed Yale Drama School were busy in the summer of 1929 building scenery for the Berkshire Playhouse's production of *Outward Bound*.

3

One reason for worried brows in show business in 1929 was the great revolution that had struck sun-baked Hollywood, some three thousand miles across the continent in southern California. The motion pictures, since the days of Mack Sennett comedies and *The Birth of a Nation*, had grown into a billion-and-a-half-dollar industry by producing black and white films that ran in eerie silence in more than fifteen thousand theaters in the United States—silent except for whatever incidental music the management might provide by hiring an orchestra in the city theaters or a piano player in the small towns where patrons were pretty sure to hear snatches from the *William Tell* overture whenever cowboys chased Indians across the screen. The silent movies were a highly effective method of presenting the pantomime of Charlie Chaplin, the Wild West exploits of stern-faced William S. Hart or even the Biblical extravaganzas featuring thinly clad ladies in sinful Roman debauches under the direction of Cecil B. DeMille, an imaginative little man who wore leather puttees and carried a megaphone through which he shouted stage directions. Whenever words were necessary to keep the audience abreast of the simple plot, the picture disappeared from the screen and a "subtitle," explaining the action or quoting a few lines of conversation, was flashed on for a period long enough to permit a fourth-grader to read—frequently in a loud voice—all of the words. The writing of subtitles had become a work of art and movie critics liked to point out occasions when a skilled specialist like Herman Mankiewicz had saved a weak picture just by composing subtitles that made the audience laugh frequently.

The character of Hollywood had been changing throughout the Twenties as the silent movies blossomed into big business. The aroma of scandal that had been stirred up by the Fatty Arbuckle "wild party" incident, by the mysterious, never-solved murder of Director William Deane Taylor who was involved with two film stars—Mary Miles Minter and Mabel Normand— and by the narcotics death of the great Wallace Reid had more or less died out by 1929. Scandal-seeking newspapers could still get plenty of headlines from Hollywood, but the studios under leadership of "Czar" Will Hays, had made a determined effort to clean out undesirables and not a few of the more prominent stars were busy setting a more respectable, or at least a more lavish, tone for society in the film capital.

New and elegant homes were being built with little regard for cost. Pickfair, the huge home of Mary Pickford and Douglas Fairbanks, was the scene of many elaborate and extremely dignified affairs. A big park and formal gardens surrounded the house and the estate was enclosed by a high wall. An invitation to enter the gates was described by Lloyd Morris in *Not So Long Ago* as "the local equivalent of a command to Buckingham Palace. . . . Protocol established a high rank for representatives of literature and the arts, so native as well as foreign celebrities usually described *Pickfair* as their first intellectual oasis in Hollywood's glittering Sahara."

Harold Lloyd built a home that was said to have cost a million dollars. It had tennis courts, elaborate gardens with fountains and a big swimming pool. John Barrymore's home had three swimming pools as well as a bowling green, a skeet range and an English taproom. There were only two swimming pools at the home of Miss Marion Davies, but otherwise her residence was unquestionably the most spectacular in Hollywood and vicinity. Miss Davies had been elevated to stardom with the aid of William Randolph Hearst and his love of feudal pomp was reflected in her establishment on the shore of the Pacific Ocean. One of the swimming pools was eighty feet long and had a marble bridge imported from Italy. The ceiling of her drawing room was done in gold leaf and had been transported from a castle in England owned by the Earl of Essex. Many art treasures from Europe decorated the ninety-room establishment and when Miss Davies entertained she sometimes had a full-sized merry-go-round set up on the tennis courts.

But the world-wide reputation of Hollywood's fabulous movie kingdom was not achieved without anguish and in 1929 there were loud cries of despair echoing across the California desert. The movie industry had been stricken by a technological revolution called "the talkies." The first major talking picture threat had actually made its appearance in Hollywood as early as 1924 when the Western Electric Company demonstrated a method of synchronizing a movie camera with a turntable on which was a wax recording disc. A photographic method of recording sound on a narrow strip along the edge of the film also was being worked out by Western Electric and by Radio Corporation of America, using slightly different approaches to the problem, and Inventor Lee De Forest was producing short talkie features in New York. The Hollywood moguls, however, didn't pay much attention to such modern gadgets until 1927 when a secondary outfit, the Warner Brothers, decided to put their money into the disc method of making talkies and another operator, William Fox, took up the film method of recording sound for newsreels. Within a few years both concerns had turned small investments into millions and were the top dogs in Hollywood.

Warner Brothers made *The Jazz Singer* in 1927 with Al Jolson the first singing voice to be heard in a big Hollywood movie. Sam Warner, who had been the chief backer of the idea, died the day before the picture opened in New York, where it was an immediate success. Hollywood's first "all talkie" with conversation and sound effects recorded was *The Lights of New York* in 1928. Yet the talkies came in slowly and even a year later there were some who doubted that silent pictures would be outmoded entirely. There were various reasons for this slowness. Some of the most famous studios—those which controlled chains of movie theaters—were caught short by the popularity of sound and couldn't catch up quickly. It cost at least half a million dollars to build a sound stage and it took time. It also cost theater owners up to twenty thousand dollars to install sound apparatus and by the late spring of 1929 there were only about two thousand such theaters in operation. Since sound recording was by no means perfected there were also complaints from the customers and *Variety* said that it was fifty-fifty whether the public would take to talking pictures after the first novelty wore off. There was a certain feeling of opposition among theatrical producers who were concerned that talkies might cut into their business.

But the most tragic cries of anguish came from the ranks of the famous stars of silent movies when it dawned on them that a Brooklyn-born blonde could no longer play the role of a Grand Duchess in her native accent. Many of the silent stars had never appeared on a stage or learned a line, and their voices were not only untrained but often unsuited for sound. John Gilbert, for example, was an outstanding silent star but his high-pitched voice was too near a screech on the sound track. Pola Negri, a famous "vamp" from Europe, spoke little English. She retired. Many veteran stars secretly rushed to the voice culture studios for elocution lessons, often with poor results, and not a few movies magnates rushed to Broadway looking for trained voices. Fox, a native of Hungary who once was a seventeen-dollar-a-week cloak-and-suit pattern cutter in New York, announced that he had hired some two hundred "legitimate" actors, stage directors, dialogue writers, dramatists, singers and dancers and that in the future he would make only talking pictures. He had, remarked *Time* magazine, apparently become the top film producer, succeeding Adolph Zukor, head of Paramount–Famous Players–Lasky Corporation, in that post as a result of his "right guess" on the talkies.

As the talking pictures continued to pack in the crowds in 1929, the big but backward movie companies which owned theaters but couldn't yet produce sound films, had to buy from their rivals in order to keep up with the public's demands. Some of them tried to make up for their own delay in switching to sound by making records of music and sound effects that were synchronized with already completed silent films. This could be done, not very satisfactorily, by writing a musical score and then running the silent movie over and over while the orchestra and sound effects crew rehearsed their timing. For about eighteen thousand dollars it could be recorded on discs that were distributed to the theaters with the silent films. One of the first such productions in 1929 was *Lilac Time*, with Colleen Moore. Apparently in an effort to make people forget the talking films, Miss Moore's studio shot the works at the première of the picture in various big cities by blowing lilac perfume through the theater during certain sad scenes. The experiment was popular with patrons but all the critics would say about *Lilac Time* was that it smelled better than most of the recent stuff from Hollywood.

"Criticism terrible," reported a Dallas theater manager in regard to *Lilac Time*. "Business tremendous." The same was generally true of almost any talking or sound effects picture and some of them grossed more than a million dollars despite the fact that only a small percentage of theaters were wired for sound. The stock of one leading sound movie company jumped one hundred points in a year as a result of profits approximating twelve million dollars. The standard of living of not a few aging Shakespearean actors, who had been definitely on the downgrade, rose spectacularly as the Hollywood casting directors searched desperately for voices that could put a speech across. And the final seal of approval was put on the talkie fad by the *Saturday Evening Post*, which ran a cartoon showing a young lady accompanying an aged relative to the art gallery.

YOUNG LADY: Uncle, why did you bring your ear trumpet?

OLD MAN: Wal, one never knows when a picture will start talking these days.

Various companies turned out both silent and talkie versions of films in 1929, but the great percentage of all Hollywood production was frothy entertainment to which patrons were lured by advertisements that depended essentially on two words: supercolossal and sex. In contrast to the "vamps" starred in earlier movies, sex was epitomized in 1929 by a bright and smiling girl named Clara Bow, whom Elinor Glyn had endowed with "It." (Novelist Glyn, a product of the Victorian days and the famous author of some of the world's worst novels, had written a great deal about sex and naturally gravitated at the age of fifty-six to Hollywood where she was immediately recognized as an authority.) Miss Bow's new picture was *The Wild Party*—"Now she speaks from the screen; you know what 'It' is to see her." Another silent screen favorite, Lon Chaney, who achieved national fame by clambering over the roofs of Notre Dame Cathedral in the grotesque makeup of a hunchback, was appearing in something called *West of Zanzibar,* while Corinne Griffith was disclosing a slightly nasal but not unattractive voice in a dull version of Maxwell Anderson's *Saturday's Children.* Mary Pickford, the former Gladys Smith of Toronto, who had been perhaps the highest-paid American at about a million dollars a year, was struggling with her husband, Douglas Fairbanks, through a film version of *The Taming of the Shrew,* a picture that did practically nothing for the career of either America's sweetheart or her athletic husband.

Walt Disney's first animated cartoon, *Plane Crazy,* which had been made in 1928, was setting a new style in comedy attractions, and Ronald Colman was appearing in a good movie called *Bulldog Drummond.* Jimmy Durante, the big-nosed night club entertainer, deserted Broadway for a whirl at Hollywood, and Jack Benny, who had stuck with dying vaudeville until the last gasp, was now on the screen in *The Hollywood Revue.* Gary Cooper made *The Virginian*; Joan Crawford was a newcomer in *Dream of Love* and *Our Modern Maidens*; John Barrymore was in *Song of Songs* and brother Lionel in *Madame X*, an impressive picture with Ruth Chatterton as the star. George Arliss was widely ballyhooed by Hollywood press agents as a sensation in *Disraeli*, which turned out to be one of the best pictures of the year. Greta Garbo did not speak in *Wild Orchids*, nor did anybody else. Harold Lloyd, who ran a guileless smile and a fake pair of horn-rimmed spectacles into a fortune as a comedian in the silent movies, was doing his usual spine-chilling stunts (they were fake, too, but they were nonetheless chilling) on flagpoles and skyscraper window ledges in *Welcome Danger*.

There were other names that would be familiar a quarter-century later—Walter Huston, Adolphe Menjou, William Powell, Loretta Young, Dolores Costello, Gloria Swanson, Tyrone Power, Boris Karloff, Charles Boyer, Sidney Franklin, Norma Shearer, Constance and Norma Talmadge, Janet Gaynor, Joan Bennett, Marion Davies—either because they were still in the movies or had achieved a degree of fame elsewhere or had made a lasting impression on the industry. But perhaps the most talked-about movie character of the year was not an American but a former doll factory worker from France. Preceded by a masterful publicity and advertising campaign by Paramount's experts, Maurice Chevalier quickly caught the spirit and the fancy of America in 1929. A handsome, saucily droll character with jutting lower lip and a stiff straw hat, Chevalier had made a name for himself as a Paris café singer and as a dancing partner for the incomparable Mistinguette at the Folies-Bergère before appearing briefly in Florenz Ziegfeld's *Midnight Frolic* in New York. Paramount unveiled him in a sentimental story, *Innocents of Paris*, and later in 1929 in *The Love Parade*. As an entertainer he was good. About the only things that could have made him a bigger attraction were colored movies, which were still in the experimental stage, and the three-dimensional screen which wouldn't be along for practically another quarter-century.

3

In 1929 the radio industry was growing up. In 1924, Secretary of Commerce Herbert Hoover had said that radio had "passed from the field of adventure to that of a public utility" with 530 stations on the air and an estimated twenty million listeners. The National Broadcasting Company was formed in 1926 as "a great force for the cultural improvement of the American people" under the guidance of David Sarnoff, general manager of Radio Corporation of America, which was interested in selling radio receivers to the public. Merlin H. Aylesworth, a public utility lawyer from Utah, was made president and it was announced that NBC would be a public service concern. "If we make profits," a spokesman said, "they will go back into the broadcasting of better programs." By the end of 1929, NBC's profits were up around the two million dollar mark.

In January of 1929, William S. Paley, the sales manager and son of the owner of the Congress Cigar Company, organized the Columbia Broadcasting System. Paley, who was twenty-seven, had been impressed by the fact that a dramatic production on the Columbia Phonograph Broadcasting Company's radio stations had boosted sales of La Palina cigars from four hundred thousand to a million a day. When he merged the Columbia outfit with United Broadcasters the network had only forty-seven stations and Congress was just giving a Federal Radio Commission the authority to license stations. In the next dozen years, CBS acquired ownership of 8 stations and was affiliated with 121, while NBC boosted its station outlets to 221 including 10 that it owned. Mutual Broadcast System was not formed until 1934.

With more than ten million homes equipped to receive broadcasts in 1929, radio had become of great political importance. Huey Long used it lavishly in his climb to power in Louisiana. President Hoover used it frequently to get his ideas across to the nation, making ninety-five radio talks between 1929 and 1932 or only nine less than President Roosevelt would make—

with considerably greater effect—between 1932 and 1936. The greater impression left by the Roosevelt broadcasts, however, was not entirely due to a difference in the personality of the two men. Beginning in 1929, a vast change was taking place in the radio industry to give President Roosevelt a much larger audience.

Just for example, the ten million homes with radio receiving sets in 1929 had more than doubled by 1935. But in addition there were another two million sets in use in automobiles and still another five million in bars, offices and elsewhere; in all some thirty million sets. By 1954 the over-all number of sets in use in the United States would be close to 130 million, with three out of every four homes having two sets. In 1929, the total sales of radio equipment amounted to $842 million—a peak figure that would drop off sharply in the next few years but soar again in 1946 to nine hundred million, and climb to four billion dollars by mid-century, when manufacturers would turn out some twenty million radio and television sets in a single year. Over the same period, there would be an equally drastic change in the cost of broadcasting. The total advertising expenditures on radio in 1929 amounted to forty million dollars, but the net time sales for the entire broadcasting industry in 1938 had more than doubled and by 1954 the annual gross revenue of 3,481 radio and television stations, including talent costs, had mounted to more than a billion dollars.

What you heard on radio—as well as what it cost—was undergoing a radical transformation in 1929. The best-known voice on the air may have been that of Milton Cross, who first appeared at New York's WJZ—the station was really in the Westinghouse plant near Newark then—looking for a job as a singer. He got it and his tenor voice went on the air until one day when the station needed an extra announcer. Cross took the job and made a career of it. He had excellent diction and a thorough knowledge of music and he would still be going strong—an expert at handling Metropolitan Opera broadcasts— when the mid-century mark rolled around. Norman Brokenshire was another famous radio voice in 1929 as was Edward B. Husing, better known as Ted, who joined the Columbia Broadcasting System in that year and became an expert at the kind of blow-by-blow sports announcing that Major Andrew White had originated at the Dempsey-Carpentier world's championship fight in 1921. Still better known as a sports announcer at the time, however, was Graham MacNamee, an excitable talker who projected to listeners a feeling of great enthusiasm and high adventure as well as, on some occasions, a rather scrambled version of what was going on in the boxing ring or on the sports fields. One more voice that was familiar to radio fans was that of Floyd Gibbons, a rapid-fire (217 words a minute) and informal news commentator who always began with a cozy "Hello everybody!" Lowell Thomas, who had written a best-selling biography of Lawrence of Arabia, substituted for Gibbons one night in 1930. He was quickly hired for regular broadcasts and became, in the next twenty-five years, one of the best-known news commentators.

Much of the hour-by-hour music heard over the air in America during 1929 was produced by phonograph records, but some notable musical and entertainment programs were on "live" through the favorable evening hours. Walter Damrosch conducted a symphony orchestra over WEAF in New York every Saturday at 9 P.M., and the program was picked up on a coast-to-coast network of NBC stations. Paul Whiteman's dance orchestra was heard regularly over the CBS network, and Maxwell House Coffee put on a performance adapted from the musical *Show Boat,* with Charles Winninger as Captain Henry and Lanny Ross, a romantic tenor, as the singing star. The real originator of the radio variety show, however, may have been a young orchestra leader who had made a success in Maine, at Yale, in London and New York after learning to play the saxophone by mail. His name was Rudy Vallee, changed from Hubert P. Vallee because, when he didn't have money enough for lessons, the famous saxophonist, Rudy Wiedoeft, had written him instructions and sent him records so that he could learn to be a musician. "Mr. Vallee," said Francis Chase, Jr., in *Sound and Fury,* "brought to radio such careful production, such fine showmanship and originality in both idea and presentation that he might well be considered radio's first important producer."

Vallee played the saxophone, directed the orchestra, crooned through a megaphone, interviewed unusual people—Grand Duchess Marie of Russia, and Heavyweight Boxer Max Baer of California—and, for a while, almost turned the "Maine Stein Song" into the national anthem. Vallee and his Connecticut Yankees first made crooning (in this case, soulful singing with a nasal, New England accent) popular over WABC where he plugged two songs that he had written, "Deep Night" and "Vagabond Lover." He was then playing at the Heigh-Ho Club, but he later opened the Villa Vallee and in October of 1929 began a once-a-week hour-long broadcast called the Fleishmann Hour and paid for by Standard Brands. For the next decade the weekly hour remained under the same sponsorship and brought Vallee to the top in radio entertainment. His income from radio and other sources, however, never rose above two hundred thousand dollars a year in that period, which was small potatoes compared to the incomes of other radio stars during the same ten years.

And, speaking of making money, there was a chubby red-headed kid who showed up in radio in 1929 with the idea that he might pick up a few dollars on the side. He had been in vaudeville briefly and discovered that there wasn't any money there, or at least not for a guy who played the banjo and the ukulele. He had been in the Navy for a while, had sold cemetery lots door-to-door for a spell and was currently in the Coast Guard when he wandered into Station WFBR in Baltimore in 1929 to take part in an amateur hour program. The folks liked him and even before he got out of the Coast Guard service he went back to WFBR with a sponsor—the Triangle Pet Shop—who paid him five bucks for every show. He called himself Red Godfrey, the Warbling Banjoist, but a quarter-century later he was better known as Arthur Godfrey, who had a twelve-year contract with Columbia Broadcasting System that was expected to bring in more than two hundred million dollars in sponsors' fees.

Nineteen twenty-nine was the year in which Kate Smith began her long career as a radio songstress and it was the year in which the "Amos and Andy" show was created and broadcast on a coast-to-coast hookup by Pepsodent. Charlie Correll and Freeman Gosden, who did the whole cast of blackface comedy characters by themselves, had previously been on the Chicago *Tribune's* WGN was "Sam 'n' Henry." Their first shows as "Amos and Andy" were greeted with a marked lack of enthusiasm, presumably because the public was not accustomed to serials on the air, but within a short time they were tremendously popular and continued so for many years. The soap operas hit the air that same year with "The Goldbergs," originated by Gertrude Berg, one of the most successful. The radio quiz programs also were beginning with "Ask Me Another," an adaptation of a parlor game, originated over WTIC in Hartford, Connecticut, by W. M. Hickey.

But in some ways the most remarkable character on the air in 1929 was a doctor out in Kansas, John Romulus Brinkley, who was busy demonstrating (1) that radio had more pulling power than even the experts had imagined and (2) that the newly created Federal Communications Commission was badly needed to keep radio under control. Dr. Brinkley had long been known as "the goat gland man" because of his rejuvenation operations in which goat glands were transplanted into human bodies. He was a graduate of the Eclectic Medical University of Kansas City and had gained a reputation of sorts in Los Angeles before returning to Milford, Kansas, where he had earlier established a small hospital and performed his rejuvenation operations. He drove a sixteen-cylinder automobile and wore diamonds as large as marbles and, after he had set up a radio station—KFKB—in Milford, it became evident that he was a spellbinder. He gave medical advice over the air and urged listeners to write to him, which they did by the tens of thousands. In 1929 he started a program called "Dr. Brinkley's Medical Question Box" on which he answered questions sent to him in letters and advised the writers to take Dr. Brinkley's Prescription No. 24 or No. 67 or No. 78. At the same time, he organized the Brinkley Pharmaceutical Association which was joined by some fifteen hundred pharmacists across the country, any one of whom could supply Dr. Brinkley's prescriptions by number. The pharmacists then paid in so much per prescription to the association to help operate KFKB—payments that amounted to $27,856 in one three-months period.

"Don't get the impression that women are icebergs," Brinkley would say in his broadcasts, "and content with impotent husbands. I know of more families where the devil is to pay in fusses and temperamental sprees all due to the husband not being able to function properly. Now this operation, which I call 'Compound Operation,' consists of adding a new artery and nerve to the patient's own sex glands . . . which act as a charger. . . . My batting average is high. That is what counts. Well, what is my average? Oh, about 90 to 95 per cent! How's that?"

The success of KFKB, which broadcast a great deal of popular music by cowboy bands, and of Dr. Brinkley—at least in a financial way—was spectacular. He bought a yacht and a private airplane. He had a huge staff. He built a new hospital. He ran for governor of Kansas as a write-in candidate and lost by only thirty-three thousand votes to Harry Woodring, who later became Secretary of War. But he had long been under heavy fire from the American Medical Association, from the Kansas City *Star* and from the Kansas State Medical Board, which in 1930 revoked his license to practice. The Federal Radio Commission, by a vote of 2 to 3, refused to renew the license of KFKB. Brinkley promptly went to Mexico where he signed a twenty-year contract with the government to build the most powerful transmitter in the world—a hundred thousand watts— at Villa Acuna, just across the border from Del Rio, Texas.

From there he offered medical advice to a bigger audience than ever in the United States but had to keep reminding his listeners to enclose two dollars in each letter to cover "the cost of postage, stenographic hire, office rent and so forth."

In 1932, Dr. Brinkley went back to Kansas and again ran for governor. The state and the A.M.A. had thrown the book at him and the federal government had kicked him off the air. But his radio audience still loved him. He carried more counties than either of his two opponents but—protesting that he had been robbed—he lost by thirty thousand votes to Alf M. Landon, who would be the Republican nominee for President in 1936.

4

The jury of selection for the National Academy of Design spent many hours in 1929 picking the pictures that would be hung in the Academy's annual exhibition. One of those selected was "The Fossil Hunters" by Edwin W. Dickinson of Provincetown, Massachusetts, an unusual painting in which the casual observer could see a grindstone, a young woman who seemed to be sailing through the air, a man holding a twig and a mass of twisted draperies. The Academy's five-man jury of awards was impressed by Dickinson's painting and gave it second prize in the show. Only after the award had been announced to the press, did they discover that "The Fossil Hunters" had been hung sideways throughout the exhibition. The artist, upon being questioned by reporters, said that he had known the painting was hung sideways but didn't want to mention it to the jury. Furthermore, he added, the painting had also been hung sideways at the Carnegie Institute International Exhibition in Pittsburgh, where it didn't win any prizes.

Neither American artists nor modernistic paintings did very well at the Carnegie Exhibition, where European painters took the honors except for a second prize won by William J. Glackens with a lively composition called "Bathers, Ile Adam." First prize went to an "old-fashioned" nude by Felice Carena of Italy—a painting that attracted the attention of most critics only because it was the largest entered in the exhibition.

The most important event in the world of art in 1929 was the opening of New York's Museum of Modern Art in a temporary gallery pending erection of its striking new modernistic home on Fifty-second Street. A lumberman from Buffalo, Anson C. Goodyear, headed a committee of seven modern art enthusiasts who raised money to start the new museum after giving up hope that the staid Metropolitan Museum of Art would ever do anything to encourage contemporary painters. Exceedingly active in the new museum were Mrs. John D. Rockefeller, Jr., who was treasurer of the committee, and the courtly, modern-minded editor of *Vanity Fair*, Frank Crowninshield, who was secretary.

Under supervision of Director Alfred H. Barr, Jr., ninety-eight canvases by Gauguin, Van Gogh, Cézanne and Seurat were hung for the formal opening of the gallery in November. Among the first day viewers, by special invitation, were scores of society folk, art patrons, collectors and artists, including William Gropper, brilliant cartoonist for the *New Masses* who had just published a book of drawings made in Soviet Russia; Norman Bel Geddes, verstaile young designer who had just been selected to help plan the 1933 Chicago World's Fair; Chester Dale, owner of one of the best collections of modern art; and Sir Joseph Duveen, distinguished English art dealer who was busy spending fabulous sums for American millionaires who wanted to own a few old masterpieces. Sir Joseph was known to take a rather dim view of modern art but he strolled happily through the crowd, carefully inspected a yellow and green painting of Christ and politely murmured: "Wonderful! Marvelous!"

...I never pose except in public....

Nineteen twenty-nine was a year of ballyhoo for Americans . . . for Alexander Humphreys Woollcott, an obese and peevish man, whose tongue uttered clipped and bitter insults, whose pen often gushed sentimental treacle, whose idea of sophisticated dress was a kimono-like coat and gold slippers, whose friends swore undying loyalty one moment and hated him the next. Alex Woollcott was one of the influential critics and essayists in American literature as the Twenties came to an end, and an incomparable ballyhoo expert for himself or, occasionally, his friends. "I never pose," he once said, "except in public."

The most celebrated literary group of the 1920's was a luncheon club at the Round Table in the Algonquin Hotel, long a favorite spot for theatrical and literary folk. Membership in the informal club varied but included Woollcott, Franklin P. Adams, Robert Benchley, Marc Connelly, Deems Taylor, George S. Kaufman, Dorothy Parker, Edna Ferber, Brock and Murdock Pemberton, Heywood Broun, Harold Ross, and Robert E. Sherwood. Some of them were among the brightest of the postwar field of writers; all of them were known for a kind of hardboiled waggishness and all of them contributed to the legends of what became known as the Vicious Circle. But none was as vicious or as irrepressible as Woollcott.

A graduate of Hamilton College, he became a fifteen-dollar-a-week bank clerk until he could get a fifteen-dollar-a-week reportorial job on the *New York Times* where his writing quickly attracted attention. He began to get around town, once interrupted and took charge of a conversation being carried on by J. P. Morgan at a party and was so ingratiating that he got away with it. He became dramatic critic of the *Times* and wisecracked that he had taken the job only because he thought Jane Cowl went with it. Thereafter he was off to the races, attracting attention by the shock method of saying the unexpected, sometimes slipping sly off-color sentences into his copy, gradually developing a style that swung unaccountably from sentimentality to waspish bitterness. Later, as a writer for the New York *World* and for many magazines his bitter witticisms—often hoarded to be uttered for an audience at the Algonquin—were an integral part of the literary history of the Twenties.

To a friend who wanted to free himself from an agreement with Woollcott, he wrote: "I think your slogan 'Liberty or Death' is splendid and which ever one you finally decide upon will be all right with me." After three days' work appearing in a motion picture for which he was paid four thousand dollars, he said: "In the early days of the last war, I had to take care of the bedpans in an Army hospital. But never, no never, have I been so humiliated as on my few appearances in the movies." When an editor telegraphed him a request to change an article in conformity with office rules and thus to save the editorial face, he replied: "Sorry I cannot save your face only if for some museum. A. Woollcott." When he handed over a ten-dollar bill to some old but now broke acquaintance, he liked to say: "When you get through with it, pass it on to some other low character." Asked by the leader of an enthusiastic group of women, who had just presented him with a citation for his achievements, to take a bow and "just say one word" to the donors, Woollcott bowed, gave the crowd an angry stare and said: "Coo." Impotent since his youth, but in love with Artist Neysa McMein, he told her that he intended to write the story of their lives together and already had decided on the title— "Under Separate Cover."

He gambled—bridge, anagrams, poker at the Thanatopsis and Inside Straight Club—with great excitement and refused to lend taxicab fare home to a loser. He played croquet at a thousand dollars a game with "the guile of a cobra and the inhumanity of a boa constrictor." And in 1929 he went on the air as the Town Crier over the Columbia Broadcasting System network— a gabby man with a warm voice, with a host of famous theatrical friends (who appeared on his program without pay) and with endless, well-told stories (which he had written and rewritten for many different magazines in the past). His reading of Dickens' *A Christmas Carol* became an annual Christmas Eve event on radio, looked forward to by millions of listeners and rendered with greater sentimentality every year.

"Woollcott . . . read Charles Dickens with a sort of proprietary interest," the critic, Burton Rascoe, wrote later, "which was curious in that he . . . was sycophantically worshipful toward commercial success. . . . The chief occupation of the [Algonquin] group seemed to be the manufacture of wisecracks, and their concerns seemed to be mah-jongg, poker, the exploitation of themselves and their friends, and the touting of whatever contributed to their own sense of self-satisfaction." Rascoe admittedly was prejudiced and at war with Woollcott and his group but his opinion was not without support in other quarters. Woollcott had "the tongue of a viper, but the temperament of a schoolgirl," Historian Lloyd Morris wrote later. "He wisecracked cruelly, or he gushed. . . . He exemplified one phase of the times; for in any night club you could watch killers weeping whenever a torch singer broke out with a number about 'Mammy.'"

But, gushing or aspish, Woollcott was a remarkable figure in New York literary life for almost three decades and when he suffered a heart attack during a radio broadcast in 1943 and died, Edmund Wilson pointed out that "in the days of totalitarian states and commercial standardization, he did not hesitate to assert himself as a single, unique human being; he was not afraid to be Alexander Woollcott, and even when Alexander Woollcott was horrid, this somehow commanded respect . . . and made him a kind of folk hero."

Some of his articles for magazines were published in book form, but in a lifetime spent among literary folk he never wrote a book himself.

*Today Croesus is King. . . . Not thinkers but rich men
rule the world.*

— Elmer Davis

By "guts" I mean grace under pressure.

— Ernest Hemingway in a talk with Dorothy Parker

Literature has gone slumming among the sociologists.

— *Saturday Review of Literature*

JUNE, 1929

the printed word

One evening in 1929 Franklin P. Adams, a columnist on
the New York *World,* and Playwright Marc Connelly went to
dinner at a popular restaurant frequented by artists and literary
folk. Once every week Adams devoted his column to "The
Diary of Our Own Samuel Pepys" which was largely a day-by-
day record of what famous personages in the world of the arts
were doing and saying in their informal moments. Looking
around the restaurant with interest, he noticed three famous
artists seated at a near-by table and engaged in animated conversation. He made a mental note of their presence and then,
seeing how excitedly they were talking, decided that they must
have some news of great import to the art world.

I went to greet them, [he wrote later] thinking to hear some news
or comment of artistick matters, and they were deep in discussion of
the action of the Federal Reserve Bank [which had been attempting
feebly to cool off the stock market boom], and were so engrossed in
the subject that one of them did leave to telephone, in order to ascer-
tain what had happened at the long session this afternoon, and he

came back, and said the [rediscount] rate had remained the same, and they all seemed to be delighted, and so they fell to talking of this and that stock.

Like everybody else, the leading lights of American literature in 1929 were profoundly affected by what was happening in Wall Street and not a few seemed to be more interested in the daily fluctuations in the price of U.S. Steel than in the state of American letters. During the early Twenties, there had been a great deal of experimentation in structure and language by John Dos Passos, Ernest Hemingway, William Faulkner and others, who had exercised a marked influence on American writers. There had also been a broad strain of cynicism and disillusionment as a kind of hangover from the war. But by 1929 some of the bitterness was beginning to fade out. That angry, red-headed journalist from Sauk Centre, Minnesota—Sinclair Lewis —was still going strong, having married newspaperwoman Dorothy Thompson after a hectic courtship across most of Europe and having publicly slapped Theodore Dreiser on the mistaken assumption that Dreiser had plagiarized Miss Thompson's writings about Russia. But Lewis' new book, *Dodsworth*, a broad-stroke commentary on Americans traveling on the Continent, was written with a great deal less venom than *Main Street*, *Babbitt, Arrowsmith* or *Elmer Gantry*. It was the last of his major works. He had said about everything that he had to say on small towns, businessmen, the medical profession and the ministry, and he would not repeat his earlier triumphs in the next two decades before he died in tragic loneliness at a luxurious villa in the Italian hills outside Florence.

F. Scott Fitzgerald, the "laureate of the Jazz Age," was living largely in a blaze of liquor on the French Riviera, where he was vainly trying to work on a new novel and just as vainly trying to pick a quarrel with his old friend, Hemingway. Fitzgerald was drinking so heavily that he fancied Hemingway had snubbed him, possibly an outgrowth of Fitzgerald's increasing difficulties in writing at a time when Hemingway was moving steadily upward in the field of literature. Hemingway did his best to patch things up, but the author of *The Great Gatsby* remained suspicious and resentful.

Hemingway, who was regarded as the "he-man" of postwar novelists, was in a softer mood, too. A brilliant stylist, he had been acclaimed for his short stories and a novel, *The Sun Also Rises*, a hard-boiled story of cynical and restless society in Europe. In 1929, however, he published a deeply romantic novel of a young couple in Italy during the war, *A Farewell to Arms*. Hemingway's great skill was evident in a stark description of the savagery of warfare during the Italian retreat at Caporetto. Much of the new book, however, was devoted to what one reviewer called a glowing modern love story so profound and true that it was like reading the record of an overwhelming personal experience. The eloquent descriptive passages opening the novel and the poetic use of modern idiom in the final tragic dialogue between the lovers, which Hemingway said he rewrote seventy times, were often described as the finest in modern American literature. Two other novels that could be more accurately described as war novels were published in America that year, the first top literary works to come out of the conflict that had ended eleven years earlier. They were both antiwar books by Europeans—Erich Maria Remarque's *All Quiet on the Western Front* and Stefan Zweig's *The Case of Sergeant Grischa*—and both were best-sellers in America.

Late in the year two other important American novels were published, *The Sound and the Fury*, a story of the disintegration of an aristocratic Southern family by William Faulkner, and *Look Homeward, Angel* by a new writer, Thomas Wolfe. Wolfe's exhaustive, uncompromising study of a Carolina boy and his home town, his psychological probing into his hero's thoughts and his vivid delineation of character brought him speedy recognition, which would grow steadily until his death in 1938 at the age of thirty-eight.

A couple of literary debates aroused interest among intellectuals during the year. Professor John Dewey published a collection of writings in which he urged the extension of scientific experimentalism to human beings and social affairs. Education, he argued, should adapt the child to the world in which he lived, but that world should be constantly remolded to promote the social good. The other side of the coin was presented by a Baltic aristocrat, Count Hermann Keyserling, three of whose books were published in America in 1929. One of them, *America Set Free*, was critical of capitalism and materialism and gadgetry. Keyserling felt that America's labor-saving devices, which had replaced menial human help, would mean less leisure instead of more leisure for those capable of literary achievement. Actually, gadgetry meant that competent men would waste time on dishwashers and other household appliances, he argued, and would be worse off than under a system that utilized incompetents to do such work. Exactly the opposite viewpoint was taken by Stuart Chase later in the year when he published *Men and Machines* to prove that "engines have been enslaved by man." Chase argued that this was a fine thing but that there were certain dangers, particularly the possibility that the modern, scientific world might some day get itself involved in a war which would last only a couple of hours but practically destroy civilization.

The argument was carried on by Walter Lippmann in *A Preface to Morals*, which put forward the bold idea that traditional religions based in part on legends, superstitions and supernatural miracles were not in accord with modern science and had lost their moral authority. He suggested that a new "high religion" would emerge from capitalistic free enterprise, which was now well beyond the days of the "robber barons" when a few men controlled vast economic empires and had become a mass enterprise in which power was greatly dispersed and decisions were made by conferences of many executives rather than by a single man.

George Santayana promptly accused Lippmann of confusing religion with morals, and expressed doubt that the blind *laissez faire* of pushing individuals and uncontrolled forces would produce a new high faith. He argued that specialization did not

ritz von Opel pictured in the rocket plane which he flew and cracked
p in 1929. He predicted that rocket planes would soon travel at five
housand miles an hour. (Wide World)

tri-motored Ford passenger plane such as was used to travel from New York to Los
ngeles in forty-eight hours, flying by day and riding the train at night. (NBC photo)

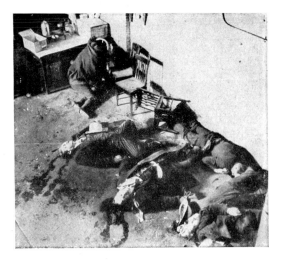

The Prohibition Era was marked by violence and murder as rival gangs battled for control of the bootlegging market. The Saint Valentine's Day massacre in Chicago in 1929 was one of the most brutal incidents in the underworld warfare. Seven members of the Moran mob were forced to line up against the wall in their beer depot and then machine-gunned to death by rival gangsters, who escaped with the aid of confederates disguised as policemen. (Wide World)

Loudest and best known of the speakeasy era hostesses was Texas Guinan, who was as important a figure in New York's café society as Mrs. Astor had been in New York's social Four Hundred. Otherwise they had little in common. This pose is from a movie, *Queen of the Night Clubs*, which Miss Guinan made in 1929. (Culver)

Bishop James Cannon, Jr., an ardent dry crusader, inspects the replica of a famous bar in Washington, D.C., shortly before the repeal of the 18th Amendment to the Constitution. (Wide World)

Illicit stills and speakeasies by the dozen were raided virtually every day by federal dry agents, but the number in operation increased steadily. Here Cleveland, Ohio, police bring in a number of stills confiscated during one day's raiding in 1929. (Wide World)

New York's opposition to the Volstead Act was symbolized by Mayor James J. Walker, one of the most popular figures along Broadway. Here he is performing the marriage of Fanny Brice, musical-comedy star, and song writer Billy Rose in 1929. (Wide World)

A redheaded woman was a problem for Vice-President Charles Curtis (left) and Secretary of State Henry L. Stimson in 1929. The redhead was Dolly Gann, sister of the widowed Vice-President, and the problem revolved around where she would sit at state dinners. Stimson passed the buck to the ambassadors. (Wide World)

The smiling lady shaking hands with Chief Justice Charles Evans Hughes is Mrs. Gann, photographed after the rumpus over her social status had died down and she was attending the George Washington Bicentennial Ball. (Wide World)

British Prime Minister J. Ramsay MacDonald was accompanied by his daughter, Ishbel, when he came to the United States in 1929 to confer with President Hoover. Ishbel observed that American and British girls wore their clothes "at different angles." (Wide World)

The long self-imprisonment of the Pope within the Vatican ended in 1929 when Pius XI was borne around St. Peter's Square following the signing of the Lateran Treaty. (Wide World)

Walter Winchell's newspaper column, filled with Broadway gossip, was switched from the New York *Graphic* to the *Mirror* in 1929 and syndicated for use in other newspapers. He is shown here at a somewhat later date. (Wide World)

One of the best-dressed and most widely read columnists in the late 1920's was O. O. McIntyre, an Ohio boy who made good by writing about the sins of New York. Here he is pictured (right) with Editor Ray Long, who "scooped" the magazine world in 1929 by publishing the memoirs of Calvin Coolidge in *Cosmopolitan*. (Brown Bros.)

The "Conning Tower" was a hi respected column in the New *World* under the signature F.P.A. (Franklin P. Adams), is pictured here in the 1 Adams became well known to audiences as a member of "Information, Please" quiz gram. (Wide World)

ree of the most popular maga-
es of the day were *Vanity Fair,*
Woman's Home Companion,*
l the *Literary Digest.* Of these,
y the *Woman's Home Com-
ion* survives today in much the
e form.

A typical cover in the days when a boy could win a bicycle by selling *The Saturday Evening Post*. When the cover design was later modernized, there were screams of anguish from many faithful subscribers.

Life, long a popular comic weekly, was on the skids in 1929. Playwright Robert E. Sherwood who won four Pulitzer Prizes, had just resigned from the editorship, and the magazine later would be bought by Henry R. Luce, who used the name for his new picture publication.

The New Yorker's cartoonists were different, usually more subtle than most. Compare the way in which this cover by Helen E. Hokinson shows the fashions of 1929 with the way the styles of the same year are presented by Russell Patterson on the cover of *Life*, on this page.

The 1929 front page of Bernarr Macfadden's New York *Evening Graphic*, one of the most blatant the tabloid newspapers of the day. In the picture on the left, Irene Ahlberg of the Bronx is being welcomed to City Hall by Mayor Walker after having been crowned Miss United States in a bathing beauty contest in Galveston, Texas. At the right is a picture of a three-year-old hit-and-run victim.

Thomas A. Edison (pictured in 1928) was the guest of honor at a celebration staged in 1929 by Henry Ford, but the famous inventor seemed to get the most fun out of recalling the days when he was a poor boy selling candy and fruit on a passenger train. (NBC photo)

Bernard Baruch took a great many gambles in his career as a speculator, but he preferred government bonds as the Wall Street boom soared to new highs in 1929. (Wide World)

Wall Street's J. P. Morgan at the Harvard commencement exercises in 1929. (Wide World)

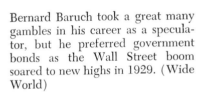

scene near the New York Stock Exchange during the market collapse in October of 1929. (Wide World)

Albert Fall, charged with accepting a bribe in the Teapot Dome oil scandal, was put on trial at his own insistence while ill and confined to a wheel chair. The spectators were sympathetic but not the jury. (Wide World)

Richard Whitney and Mrs. Whitney, photographed in costum of the 1890's at an equestrian meeting at Far Hills, N.J., son time before the former president of the New York Stock E change was arrested on charges of grand larceny. Whitney w one of the "heroes" of the 1929 market crisis. (Wide World)

En route to jail, Oilman Harry F. Sinclair alights from his limousine in Washington, D.C., following trial on charges arising from the Teapot Dome scandal. He was sentenced to ninety days. (Wide World)

William B. Shearer, who lobbied for a big navy, was the center of a major political hassle in 1929 after he sued several shipbuilding companies. He claimed they hadn't paid him for his efforts at the Geneva Naval Disarmament Conference, which he allegedly helped "wreck." Shearer (standing, right) and his lawyer, Daniel J. Cohalan, are shown with a Senate investigating committee composed of Henry J. Allen of Kansas, Samuel M. Shortridge of California, and Joseph T. Robinson of Arkansas. (Wide World)

Dr. Albert Einstein became a famous figure to the American public in 1929 when he disclosed that he had found a "key" to the formulation of a unified field theory. Nobody much understood what this meant but everybody knew it was important, and here Dr. Einstein is being interviewed by New York reporters when he arrived in America the following year. (Wide World)

An American scientist who added to his fame in 1929 was Admiral Richard E. Byrd, noted trans-Atlantic and polar flier, who led an expedition to the Antarctic. This photograph was taken before his departure. (Wide World)

Dr. Hugo Eckener (left), master of the dirigible *Graf Zeppelin*, which made a commercial passenger trip around the world, shown with New York Police Commissioner Grover Whalen during Eckener's official welcome to New York. (Wide World)

Lillian Andrus of Columbus, Ohio, won the title of Miss America at the National Bathing Beauty contest at Baltimore, but was later ruled ineligible. (Wide World)

...ris Duke, often called the richest ... in the world, won a society ...s' swimming race at Bailey's ...ch, fashionable bathing spot at ...vport in 1929. Here James B. ...kes presents the trophy to Miss ...ke. (Wide World)

Wearing sandals and Grecian robe Raymond Duncan returned hom from Paris in 1929 and provided lot of feature articles for the new papers. Here, the next year, he preparing to dip water from Ne York harbor to manufacture salt an act of sympathy with Mahatn Gandhi, who had been imprisone in India for illegally making salt defiance of British authoriti (Wide World)

Such zany fads as sitting for days on top of a flagpole or dancing day and night with only slight pauses for weeks and months were popular during the last years of the Twenties. Here, in 1928, a couple participating in a Harlem dance derby trip their way through the door of the marriage license bureau to apply for a license—doubtless an idea that originated with a press agent, who furnished a truck and a band to convey them to the bureau so they would not be disqualified in the derby. (Wide World)

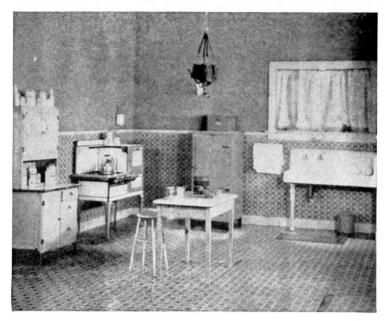

The average housewife in 1929 was just beginning to realize that electrical gadgets could make life in the kitchen a lot easier. But this "modern" kitchen of the day, with gas stove and gas refrigerator, would appear very inadequate a quarter-century later. (Courtesy Con Edison)

The yacht *Nourmahal*, owned by Vincent Astor, en route to the New York Yacht Club races off Newport, R.I., in 1929. (Wide World)

Several corporations in 1929 we building or planning to build "t tallest building in the world." He John J. Raskob (left) and Alfred Smith discuss how they will erec dirigible mast atop the Emp State Building, which easily w the skyscraper title but never m aged to snare a dirigible. (W World)

This is how Rockefeller Center looked in 1929 before John D. Rockefeller, Jr., began spending $125,000,000 to replace a group of run-down houses with a magnificent office building development that became one of the nation's leading tourist attractions. (Garber, courtesy Rockefeller Center, Inc.)

necessarily make for better morals because a great physicist could be lecherous or even moronic about other matters. Lippmann, he added, posed a perfect social equilibrium but there is no such thing and "here an individual, there a band, will be found ready to perish rather than continue subject to social equilibrium."

Many intellectuals in 1929 were gravely concerned with overemphasis on material wealth and scientific achievement and the neglect of spiritual values by Americans in general. "This mass culture, this semi-barbarism is a beast as powerful as the German hordes that swept over the Roman Empire," wrote Henry Seidel Canby in *American Estimates*, "as deadly for civilization as the swarms of the semi-civilized that welled up through the cracks of the classic world and drowned a society as well-organized as our own. . . . This is the danger. This is the beast of the Apocalypse. This is Mammon. This is the Twilight of the Gods."

Elmer Davis, writing in the *Saturday Review of Literature,* said that Croesus had achieved supremacy and "the successors of Solon, no longer law-givers, count themselves happy if they are not his hirelings. . . . In the reversal of the two roles lies the central problem of Twentieth century civilization." In *Harper's Monthly,* James Truslow Adams said that the enemy is "not Croesus but Mammon. Not the wicked conspiracies of certain rich men, but the materialistic standards of an age in which, for the first time, material comfort is within the reach of all."

A searching inquiry into American life was published in 1929 under the title of *Middletown,* a sociological study of a typical industrial community (Muncie, Indiana) by Robert S. and Helen Merrell Lynd. The Lynds' book, which had been started in 1924, presented to one reviewer the "disturbing wrinkles and crow's feet in our present day industrial and social face." They found a rapid trend toward labor-saving devices in the home, and the beginning of the idea that everybody should take an annual vaction of a week or perhaps even two weeks. They found that not a few working families would rather cut down on food and clothes than do without an automobile, and that in one run-down section of town twenty-one of twenty-six car-owning families did not have bathtubs in their homes. They found that children were more sophisticated at an earlier age than their parents had been, stayed out later on dates and, in nine cases out of ten, engaged in "petting parties."

2

A good many of America's prominent writers were spending much of the time in 1929 turning out articles, short stories and serials for the big-circulation magazines and newspapers. There were then about 125 magazines of all kinds listed in the *Reader's Guide to Periodical Literature,* although some of them were going broke and a substantial percentage would disappear in the next decade. Among the high-brow magazines the most widely respected included the *Atlantic Monthly,* under the command of Editor Ellery Sedgwick, *Harper's Monthly* and *Scribner's;* the *Saturday Review of Literature,* edited by Henry Seidel Canby; and, in a slightly different field, the *Nation,* edited by Oswald Garrison Villard. The *Literary Digest* was making a determined effort to stand off the youthful weekly news magazine, *Time,* but would go under within a few years after conducting one of its famous pre-election polls—this one showing that Alf Landon would be elected President in 1936.

The so-called popular or mass circulation magazines of the day—neither *Life* nor *Look* had yet been born—were booming, with the *Saturday Evening Post* regularly running around 200 pages each issue and sometimes going above 250 pages. In December of 1929 one issue of the magazine broke all records for size with 272 pages of reading matter, pictures and advertisements at the bargain price of five cents. A single copy weighed a pound and fourteen ounces and contained 295 square feet of paper. It carried the advertisements of 214 concerns which paid an average of $9,000 a page. A total of 2,977,000 copies was printed and advertising revenue amounted to about $1,512,000 for the single issue. At the same time, *Collier's Weekly,* which had almost folded in the early Twenties, was back on its feet, conducting a spirited campaign against the Volstead Act and the manner of its enforcement. Big name writers were much in demand for magazines and under the editorship of George Horace Lorimer the *Saturday Evening Post* was publishing such authors as Thomas Beer, Booth Tarkington, F. Scott Fitzgerald, John P. Marquand, Joseph Hergesheimer, Struthers Burt, Bernard DeVoto, and Kenneth L. Roberts in every issue in addition to serials by such popular writers as Clarence Budington Kelland and Mary Roberts Rinehart. In a single issue, the *Delineator* published stories by John Galsworthy, Edith Wharton and Kathleen Norris—all writers who demanded fancy prices. *Liberty* magazine's big splurge for the year in an effort to compete with the *Saturday Evening Post* and *Collier's* was a lurid serial of "the next war"—a Communist invasion of America—by a high-priced journalist, Floyd Gibbons, who had lost one eye during World War I and wore a black patch that was almost as familiar to the public as was that of the man in the Hathaway shirt advertisements at a much later date.

The magazine competition for big name writers, however, was won by Editor Ray Long, a short, breezy man who would eventually renounce modern civilization and flee to the South Seas but who, in 1929, was very much in the midst of things as the guiding spirit of *Cosmopolitan* magazine. One Sunday in the winter of 1929, Long called a secret conference of a few members of his staff and revealed to them that he was throwing out the lead article in the April issue in order to make room for a "scoop" that he had been working on for months. The scoop article was divided into a number of sections before being sent to the printer so that no linotype operator could make much sense out of what he had a chance to read. Private detectives were hired to guard the plant where the article was assembled and plates were made and 1,850,000 copies of the April issue were run off. Then the magazines were distributed by express rather than by freight—an extra cost of twelve thousand dollars —and wholesalers were sworn not to reveal the contents. But by this time the cloak-and-dagger scenario had run out and rumors of the great scoop seeped out into publishing circles. Three days before publication date Long announced that *Cosmopolitan* was publishing an article, "On Entering and Leaving the Presidency," by Calvin Coolidge. Mr. Coolidge also had contracted, at a dollar a word, to write a daily, hundred-word syndicated newspaper commentary on the state of the world, and his income from writing that year amounted to more than two hundred thousand dollars or almost three times his annual salary as President. Not to be outdone, Mrs. Coolidge wrote an article, "Opening the Gates of Silence," which appeared in the April issue of *Pictorial Review*. Long's scoop proved to be a good prestige builder for *Cosmopolitan*. But Mr. Coolidge, whose fellow authors in the April issue included Irvin S. Cobb, Beverly Nichols, E. Phillips Oppenheim and Theodore Dreiser, proved to be even less exciting in print than he had been in the White House. The style as well as the content of his newspaper commentary can best be illustrated by one excerpt: "When more and more people are thrown out of work, unemployment results."

Perhaps the most unusual and interesting venture in the magazine field was *The New Yorker*, which had been started in 1925 as "a reflection in word and picture of metropolitan life" and which by 1929 was beginning to work up a reputation for wit, sophistication and good writing all over the nation. Compared to the circulation figures of the popular "slick" magazines, *The New Yorker* was a small operation centered in Manhattan. But it attracted some of the most remarkable writers and cartoonists of the day and some of the most remarkable publishing legends of any day centered around its editor, Harold Ross, and his staff, which included such writers as Robert Benchley, James Thurber, E. B. White, Dorothy Parker, Alexander Woollcott, Wolcott Gibbs, and, for a brief time, Ellin Mackay, the wife of Irving Berlin.

The spirit of *The New Yorker* was portrayed from the beginning by a sophisticated drawing by Rea Irvin showing a gentleman of the Regency period in top hat and ruffles, gazing through a monocle at a butterfly. This character, who still appears on every anniversary issue, was later christened Eustace Tilley by Corey Ford. Behind Eustace Tilley, however, was quite a different character. Editor Ross was a Colorado boy who quit school at some indefinite but early age, became a newspaper reporter before he was fifteen and acquired a vocabulary of profanity that was considered remarkable even during his service in the Army. He disapproved of swearing in the presence of women, however, and worried constantly over the possibility that something off color or in bad taste might accidentally get into the magazine.

To Woollcott, Ross was a homely man who "looks like a dishonest Abe Lincoln." To Allen Churchill, his "leathery features combine the cowboy look of Will Rogers with the moon-mad expression of Harpo Marx." Ross was profoundly ignorant on many subjects but he was a tireless worker, a painstaking editor and, to most of his staff, some kind of a genius. *New Yorker* articles were checked and rechecked and rewritten and then torn apart and written again before Ross's search for perfection could be satisfied. Captions under cartoons, usually limited to one line, were worked over by half a dozen staff members. One such caption under a cartoon by Peter Arno was around the office for three years before Ross was satisfied and published it.

The practical jokers on the staff and among his friends added to Ross's anguish—or so he contended—and there were countless stories about the goings-on around *The New Yorker* offices. One day Ross was complaining to a vistor that staff members were always needlessly bothering him about minor things. At that moment an office boy rushed in and said: "I hate to bother you, Mr. Ross, but I don't know what to do. A man is trying to commit suicide in the men's room." Ross gave his visitor a triumphant look. "See what I mean?" he asked. The editor of *The*

New Yorker also had a mania for rearranging the offices of the magazine. At one period, he was having walls knocked out and new walls or new doors put in almost every other week. His staff complained that the noise was driving them crazy and Thurber finally posted a sign outside his door: "ALTERATIONS GOING ON AS USUAL DURING BUSINESS." Ross kept right on making changes.

Nobody ever quite explained why Ross was so successful as editor of the magazine, although a great many people tried to analyze his methods. Perhaps as good an explanation as any was his own: "An editor prints what pleases him and if enough people like what he likes, then he is a success."

In an entirely different way, the same thing might have been said for another successful publisher, DeWitt Wallace, who started *Reader's Digest* in a Greenwich Village basement with nothing more than an idea that people were in such a hurry they would appreciate a magazine that gave them all of the significant articles of the day in abbreviated form. Wallace came from a family of preachers and the *Reader's Digest* tended to reprint, in abbreviated form, many "inspirational" articles, to emphasize the necessity for self-reliance and thrift and hard work, to point out that spiritual happiness was more important than material success. It would be difficult to imagine a more successful formula in the publishing business. From a circulation of fifteen hundred in 1922, *Reader's Digest* rose in less than twenty-five years to more than twelve million circulation printed in many languages and supervised from a handsome plant in a New York village called Chappaqua.

A comparative newcomer to the publishing field was Henry R. Luce, who with Briton Hadden had founded a weekly news magazine called *Time*, and was getting ready to publish a plush business magazine called *Fortune*. The pithy, and abbreviated style developed by *Time* and its inventive manner of combining several words into one to save space caused considerable distress among some old-time journalists, but the magazine caught the public fancy during the late Twenties and by 1929 was a flourishing foundation for Luce's magazine empire, which later included *Life* and *Sports Illustrated.*

3

The last year of the Twenties was not only a lush period for the magazines—they would not enjoy such a year again in the next decade or longer because of depression, wartime paper rationing and new competition for advertising revenue—but for the nation's newspapers as well. For some years the number of newspapers in the United States had been decreasing slowly but the over-all circulation had been rising steadily. During the war, for example, there had been some twenty-five hundred daily newspapers with a total circulation of twenty-eight million copies. In 1929 there were less than two thousand newspapers but total circulation was up to thirty-nine million. (By 1954 there would be less than eighteen hundred newspapers with fifty-four-million circulation.)

Expenditures for newspaper advertising space in 1929 also were at a new peak of about eight hundred million dollars a year for almost two billion agate lines, and the Sunday editions of such papers as the Chicago *Tribune* and the *New York Times* were so swollen that subscribers groaned as they lifted them from the front doorstep. The *New York Times* averaged two hundred columns or twenty-five pages of news matter—to say nothing of space devoted to advertising—in its daily edition and 891 columns or 111 pages of news alone on Sunday. The Chicago *Tribune* was about the same size—so close, in fact, that the two famous newspapers engaged in a rather bitter dispute in the pages of the trade journal, *Editor and Publisher,* regarding which had carried the most advertising during the year. Both claimed to be first in advertising linage.

Smaller in size but potent in their field were such newspapers as Pulitzer's St. Louis *Post Dispatch,* under famed Managing Editor O. K. Bovard; the fat and complacent Los Angeles *Times;* the flamboyant Denver *Post,* owned by an ex-Mississippi River gambler, Frederick Bonfils; the Cleveland *Press,* edited by "Boy Wonder" Louis B. Seltzer; the sedate, world-minded *Christian Science Monitor*; the Atlanta *Constitution*; the Louisville *Courier-Journal*; the New York *Herald Tribune*, which had a reputation for outstanding editing and writing with such staff members as Beverly Smith, Stanley Walker, Grantland Rice, W. O. McGeehan, Mark Sullivan, Leland Stowe, Rodney Gilbert and Percy Hammond.

A subject that came in for a great deal of debate among newspaper publishers was the rapid growth of newspaper chains such as the twenty-five Scripps-Howard papers under command of Roy W. Howard and the Hearst group of twenty-eight papers. There were around fifty chains or groups of newspapers in all, and they controlled a total of more than three hundred newspapers. Critics of the chain system complained that individual newspapers were being robbed of their independence, that there was a trend toward monopoly and that independent papers were faced with unfair competition. Colonel Frank B. Knox, who was then general manager of the Hearst papers, made a wordy reply to these complaints at the annual convention of the American Society of Newspaper Publishers, contending that the complaints were groundless and that the more efficient operation of chain papers enabled them to give readers more for their money. Nothing much came of the discussion except that the weaker chain papers were weeded out in the next few years, while Colonel Knox shifted from Hearst to the Chicago *Daily News* and, in 1936, was the Republican nominee for Vice-President.

Actually, almost all newspapers were giving their readers more of everything due to the rapid growth of syndication and a steady improvement in the big news services, but there were so many newspapers that not all of them could operate profitably except in boom times. In New York City, for example, there were eighteen daily newspapers of some stature—not counting specialized newspapers or foreign language journals— in 1929. But in the next quarter-century ten of them would fold or be merged, including the *American*, the *World* and *Evening*

World, the *Evening Graphic,* the Brooklyn *Eagle* and the *Evening Sun.*

Syndicated newspaper columns were not new, but the syndicates were just entering a period of tremendous growth. Among the most familiar columns were two that appeared in the Hearst newspapers. One was written by a bald and busy editor, Arthur Brisbane, who also liked to turn out editorials about the wonders of nature. In 1929, the *American* was sued by Stanislaus Zbyszko, an egg-shaped wrestler of international fame and also a classical scholar, because it printed a Brisbane editorial accompanied by a picture of the wrestler and a picture of a gorilla. "Zbyszko," the editorial remarked, "is not fundamentally different from a gorilla in physique."

In his column "Today," Brisbane usually managed to avoid such controversies. A typical excerpt from the column concerned the 1929 Galveston, Texas, International Beauty Contest, won by Lisl Goldarbeiter of Austria. "Queen of the Universe seems rather a large title," Brisbane wrote. "Miss Goldarbeiter would probably be amazed if she could see the young ladies on some planet one million light years away from this corner of space and those far off interstellar young women, perhaps 1,000 times as big as Miss Goldarbeiter, and each with 1,000 eyes, perhaps, would be surprised to see her." Or on a subject a little nearer home: "We read that in Russia young people expel from their associations a boy or girl guilty of indecent jazz dancing in public. . . . This up-to-date nation [the United States] laughs. It need not laugh. If Russia takes life and decency seriously and we do not, Russia will win and we shall lose."

The other well-known Hearst columnist was a suave, graying and slightly pompous man, O. O. McIntyre, who liked to wear double-breasted waistcoats and to stroll sedately along Fifth Avenue, swinging his lacquered stick and thinking how much happier he had been as a boy in Gallipolis, Ohio. Or at least that was the impression his column gave to readers of some four hundred newspapers. He wrote about shadowy, unidentified figures (obviously dope peddlers) slinking through China-town rather than about the latest divorce scandal and was more likely to tell of glimpsing J. P. Morgan on his way to church than to relate who had been seen with whom in what night club. Some of McIntyre's critics claimed that he had a very simple formula for writing his column, which was called "New York Day by Day." They said he sat in his suite at the Ritz Hotel, read the newspapers and wrote about the wickedness of big cities and the phoniness of big city slickers—thus enabling his readers in small towns to participate vicariously in what seemed to them a glamorous life but at the same time to realize that they were better off at home. In return, McIntyre realized an income of about seventy-five thousand dollars a year.

The columnist business, however, was changing rapidly in 1929. The New York *World* had built up a famous stable of columnists on its "opposite-editorial-page" which was one of the best-read pages in the city. The *World's* columnists at one time or another included F.P.A. (Franklin P. Adams), William Bolitho, who also wrote *Twelve Against the Gods* in 1929, Frank Sullivan, Alexander Woollcott and Heywood Broun, who was fired after he bitterly criticized the *World* in an article he wrote for the *Nation* implying that there were no real liberal journals left in the United States. Broun was soon hired by Roy Howard, who had purchased the New York *Telegram* and within a short time would purchase the failing *World*, too.

But in 1929 a new breed of columnists was coming to the fore. Of these, the foremost was a hurrying little man who was not a newspaperman at all but a former vaudeville trouper who gathered a column of Broadway gossip and theatrical news for the raucous New York *Graphic*, a tabloid owned by Health Fad-dist Bernarr Macfadden. The *Graphic's* Broadway expert was Walter Winchell, who first sang in a Harlem theater at the age of thirteen, soon quit school and went on a tour as a hoofer and singer. He ended up broke, joined the Navy during the war and later got a job on *Vaudeville News*. Macfadden hired him in 1924 to write a column called "Your Broadway and Mine" and

he covered the city's night spots so thoroughly, reporting ro-
mances, quarrels, divorces, births and marriages among the theatrical and gay society folk, that his column soon became
famous along "the main stem" and his vocabulary notorious.
Winchell's reputation was built on his ability to be first in reporting which couple had "gone phfft" or which couple was
"middle aisling it" or which was "infanticipating"—and, upon
arrival of the offspring, its sex. On the rare occasions when he
happened to err that fact was blithely ignored if possible. He
invented many words that became popular: "sealed" for "married," "moom pitcher" for "moving picture," "hush parlor" for
"speakeasy." And in 1929 he was lured away from the *Graphic*,
which had originally paid him a hundred dollars a week, by the
New York *Daily Mirror*, which offered him five hundred a week
and half of the income from syndication by the Hearst organization. By syndication, and later on radio and television, Winchell
became known all over the country, rose to great affluence and
had many imitators.

Unquestionably, Winchell introduced a new note into journalism, or at least into the newspapers. But a definite change
in ways was taking place anyway. In the past, the only way to
get the news in a hurry was through the newspapers. But now
radio was carrying news everywhere instantaneously, and radio
was a keen competitor for advertising revenue. Publishers were
fearful of such competition and began searching for special
features that would hold the attention of readers. The syndication of columnists—Broun, for example, was published in most
of the Scripps-Howard papers—was one appeal to readers. More
and better pictures was another. Photographs of the inauguration of President Hoover were snapped in Washington in the
early afternoon, developed in a special "dark room" on an airplane en route to New York and published, after being transmitted by telephoto process, in many newspapers on the same
day. When Charles Lindbergh and his wife made a crash landing in Mexico City, the N.E.A. service sent pictures by airmail
to Laredo and thence by special plane to St. Louis where they

were transmitted by telephoto to New York, San Francisco, Chicago, Los Angeles, Boston, Cleveland and Atlanta for publication within thirty-six hours. The Akron, Ohio, *Times-Press* delivered football extras by "blimp" to Alliance when the Akron University played the Mt. Union football team. Unhappily, the blimp flew low over a cornfield and frightened the horses of Thornton Neiswonger, a farmer, who sued the *Times-Press* for ten thousand dollars for injuries sustained when he was thrown from his wagon. The McClure Newspaper Syndicate came to the aid of publishers with an imposing array of writers: Glenn Frank with editorial comment, Fannie Hurst with a regular fiction story, Dr. Logan Clendening to advise readers on health problems, Bruce Barton with a regular "inspirational" message and William Lyon Phelps with essays every Monday, Wednesday and Friday. Reporters—including David Lawrence—of "inside stuff" from Washington were very much in demand.

In addition to all of these features were the "comic strips," which had become a big-time industry. "Winnie Winkle, the Breadwinner"; "Mutt and Jeff"; "Bringing Up Father" with Jiggs and Maggie; "Polly and Her Pals"; "Our Boarding House"; "Skippy"; "Moon Mullins"; "Orphan Annie"; "Krazy Kat"; "Wash Tubbs"; "Freckles and His Friends"; and "Gasoline Alley" were among the popular strips. But perhaps the most avidly read comic was Andy Gump, a bald-headed, windy man who was endowed by Sidney Smith with all of the frailties of the average man. In 1929, Andy was involved in a melodrama that centered around the invention of a perpetual motion machine. The inventor, Tom Carr, was a clean-cut American boy who had been falsely accused of stealing ten thousand dollars from Andy. Tom's sweetheart, Mary Gold, was faithful to him but she was being relentlessly pursued by a wicked banker, Harry Ausstin, who may or may not have stolen the money. When Tom was sentenced to prison, national indignation reached a fever pitch. The Arkansas Senate formally adopted a resolution demanding his release. A petition for a pardon was signed by the Mayor and other prominent citizens of Clarksdale, Mississippi. It came out all right in the end, with the wicked banker brought to justice, Andy Gump still looking like a sap and the Chicago Tribune Syndicate making money by the basketful.

A staunch believer in the pulling power of comics was Captain Joseph Medill Patterson, who had launched the tabloid New York *Daily News* in 1919. Patterson was a wealthy man from birth, the grandson of the founder of the Chicago *Tribune*, and was educated at Groton and Yale. He was far from being an intellectual but in his youth he was an advocate of socialism, was elected to the Illinois legislature and wrote a novel exposing the vulgarity and corruption of high society, *A Little Brother of the Rich*. By 1929 he had reverted to mild liberalism (he would later become very conservative) and his newspaper was setting the pace for a new era in journalism. The *Daily News* grew fat on pictures and sensationalism. In 1928 it had published a photograph—it filled the entire front page—of Ruth Snyder, the instigator of the murder of her husband by her lover, dying in the electric chair at Sing Sing prison. The photograph was taken by a photographer who strapped a small camera to his ankle and managed to get a front-row seat in the execution chamber, where he could pull up his pants leg and snap the shutter with a wire that extended to his pocket.

The *Daily News* was often denounced, but Patterson had an unfailing instinct for popular success. By 1929 the newspaper had a Sunday circulation of 1,600,000 and was building a new ten-million-dollar plant on Forty-second Street, and it was being read avidly not only in the kitchen and the butler's pantry but in the drawing rooms along Fifth Avenue. Its headlines dealt with divorce proceedings, alienation suits, love nests and murder:

TORCH FIEND KILLED BRIDE
TO MASK ILLICIT LOVE LIFE

Earl Peacox Strangled Dot,
Burned Body in Woods

TRACE PYRE FIEND'S ALIBI GIRL
TO NIGHT VIGIL AT WIFE'S BODY

Torch Killer's Head
A Vacillating Type

The *Evening Graphic* went a step farther in its efforts to keep up with the *Daily News*. It produced what it called "composographs"—photographs that were pasted together and touched up by an artist or were posed by models to illustrate a news story. Thus the *Graphic* could present a vivid if faked picture of the sinking of the S.S. *Vestris* late in 1928, with the ship going down in the background and wild-eyed men and women struggling with sharks in the foreground; or an intimate bedroom scene in which unidentified persons posed as the principals in a current news story. Such extreme irresponsibility did not continue long, but the trend that had been set would continue and would expand—a trend that some people approved as a sign of franker and more thorough reporting, that others regarded as an invasion of privacy and still others denounced as just plain bad taste.

...we were given final proof that war is death....

Nineteen twenty-nine was a year of opportunity for Americans . . . for Henry L. Stimson, a thoughtful, gentle, graying man who believed that mankind progressed toward the good life through sacrifice and sufferings, who had labored arduously for peace, who eventually would lay before the President of the United States a piece of paper on which were written the names of two cities—Hiroshima and Nagasaki. "The face of war," he later said, "is the face of death."

Stimson was born only three years after the end of the Civil War, in which his father had almost lost his life, and his playground was the cobbled streets of New York until he went to Phillips Academy at Andover, Massachusetts, where he developed an undying enthusiasm for outdoor life. After one year at Yale, he journeyed with George Bird Grinnell to the Far West, explored and mapped the area of Glacier National Park, had a mountain named after him, hunted with Blackfoot Indians, rode, shot buffaloes, cooked, canoed happily through a lonely wilderness. But he came back to finish his studies at Yale and, after two years at Harvard Law School, he became a clerk in the sedate New York law firm of Root and Clarke; was made a member of the firm in 1893.

Elihu Root was a towering figure in Republican party affairs. Stimson, who had voted for Democrat Grover Cleveland in 1892, became Root's assistant in many cases and his lifelong admirer. He met Theodore Roosevelt as a member of the Boone and Crockett Club and they talked about bear hunting. In 1905, he was making more than twenty thousand dollars a year when President Roosevelt asked him to take a ten-thousand-dollar job as U.S. Attorney in New York. He took it, waged successful war against the big corporations that were violating the law by illegal rebates, prosecuted James Gordon Bennett for indecency in his newspaper's personal columns (Bennett was fined twenty-five thousand dollars), indicted Publisher Joseph Pulitzer's New York *World* for criminal libel and, after resigning in 1909, waged a vain battle for the governorship of New York as the hand-picked candidate of T.R.

In 1911, President Taft was fearful of a major split in the Republican party because of the increasing rebelliousness of former President Roosevelt and as a gesture toward peace he offered Stimson the post of Secretary of War. With T.R.'s approval, Stimson accepted but when he spoke for Taft in the 1912 presidential contest among Taft, Roosevelt and Wilson, the Bull Moose leader was incensed and refused to be reconciled for three years. With Wilson's election, Stimson returned to private practice but kept up his fight for progressive leadership in the Republican party. During World War I he was opposed to what he regarded as Germany's illegal submarine warfare and, in 1917, he entered the Army as artillery major at the age of forty-nine, served in France with the Seventy-seventh Division and, in a sector near Baccarat, gave the order that to the best of his knowledge caused the first shell to be fired against the Germans by the National Army of the United States.

After the war he was, except for some official missions, a private citizen until President Coolidge made him Governor General of the Philippines in 1928. In 1929 President Hoover sounded him out about a cabinet job, but Stimson wasn't interested in anything except the State Department and, after saying so frankly, he got the job. He was sixty-two years old when he took office and the world was not only at peace but had succeeded in erecting since the end of the war a structure of treaties and agreements which, with the League of Nations, offered for the first time a hope that war might be abolished. Stimson jumped at the opportunity of strengthening that structure.

The path was long and tortuous, and his luck was bad. The war debts that Britain and France owed the United States, which had made great economic progress during the war, were a constant irritant to international harmony. Stimson thought cancellation would be economically wise and politically advantageous; Mr. Hoover didn't. The 1930 London Naval Disarmament Conference was at best only a partial success. The United States high tariff policy caused bad feeling abroad and the world-wide economic depression added vastly to Stimson's difficulties. Then, in September of 1931, the Japanese Army began taking over Manchuria.

Japanese aggression against China—slowly, cautiously begun but stubbornly pursued—was a direct challenge to the world's peace structure, in Stimson's opinion, and he felt that it was "almost impossible" that it would not lead to an armed clash in later years with the United States. But to deal with this threat was quite another matter. No American wanted to fight a war in the distant Orient for some vague principle; nor did Stimson. But he felt that the moral force of the great powers might influence Japan; perhaps even economic sanctions might be invoked against the aggressor. Mr. Hoover disagreed with any proposal for sanctions. The British Foreign Office at first refused to join Washington even in a formal note reminding Japan of her treaty obligations not to resort to war and declaring a policy of "nonrecognition" of conquests made by armed force. The League of Nations in the beginning could agree on nothing but to dispatch an investigating commission. As he acknowledged later, Stimson moved cautiously and perhaps timidly, although at the time he felt he was almost too bold, particularly in co-operating with the League of Nations. But he was armed only with "spears of straw and swords of ice." "What happened . . . was that we lacked the courage to enforce the authoritative decision of the international world," he said later. "We condemned . . . war . . . but it was a moral condemnation only. . . . Our offense was thus that of a man who passed by on the other side." There were many complex factors that influenced the attitude of the great powers toward the Manchurian crisis, but in the end there was a sense of dismal failure and inadequacy and, in Stimson's heart, a belief that "somebody has got to show some guts" if the world was to avoid a grim tragedy.

With the Democratic victory in 1932, Stimson went back to a busy private practice, but throughout the 1930's he exerted his influence against the spread of Fascist aggression in China, in Ethiopia, in Spain and Middle Europe. And when World War II had come and the President asked him in 1940 to become Secretary of War again, he returned to active duty on the eve of his seventy-third birthday. He was there throughout the conflict, throughout the Japanese conquest of the Philippines and Southeast Asia, throughout the long struggle in Africa and Europe and back across the Pacific Ocean to Okinawa. Under his direction, the atomic bomb was developed "with full understanding of the responsibility involved" and in his mind there was never any doubt that, once perfected, the bomb should be used if necessary after giving the Japanese an opportunity to surrender. "In the light of the alternatives . . . open to us I believe that no man . . . holding in his hands a weapon of such possibilities for accomplishing this purpose and saving [the] lives [of American soldiers] could have failed to use it and afterwards looked his countrymen in the face."

At the Big Three Potsdam Conference on July 26, 1945, the warning to Japan was issued. On July 28, it was rejected by the Japanese Premier as "unworthy of notice." When the President returned to Washington, he and Stimson studied a list of targets and agreed to strike off the city of Kyoto, a shrine of Japanese art and culture. "I approved four other targets," Stimson said later, "including the cities of Hiroshima and Nagasaki." With the bombs, dropping in swift silence, "we were given final proof that war is death . . . [they] made it wholly clear that we must never have another war. . . . There is no other choice."

I am blazing a trail for peace.

—PRESIDENT HOOVER to Prime Minister
J. Ramsay MacDonald, 1929

*To me, America is a dreamland. I would like to work
in an American automobile factory.*

—ALFONSO XIII of Spain, 1929

*The thought that the Japanese will never land on the West
Coast and burn Los Angeles fills me with inexpressible regret.*

—HENRY L. MENCKEN, 1929

J U L Y , 1 9 2 9

farewell to arms

More Americans went abroad in 1929 than ever before in history, and most of them visited Europe. They were in a gay mood and had money in their pockets. They swarmed through historic cities on hurried sight-seeing tours; paid outrageous prices for trinkets and treasures from Picadilly to the Ponte Vecchio; and infested the night spots of Paris and the Riviera. The British spoke bitingly of their "star-spangled manner," the French overcharged them and the Italians happily assured them that Benito Mussolini was a great statesman who made the trains run on time. It was a boom year for travel and it would be almost a quarter of a century before so many Americans—an estimated seven hundred thousand—again visited Europe as tourists.

One of the American visitors was a thirty-nine-year-old Army officer Major Dwight D. Eisenhower, who spent almost all of his time tramping over the battlefields of World War I with a notebook in his pocket. He was assembling a guidebook for American tourists as part of his duties as a member of the United States Battle Monuments Commission, headed by General of the Armies John J. Pershing. But he was doing a great deal more than gathering tourist information. He was studying and committing to memory the entire terrain from Brest to the banks of the River Rhine, walking mile after mile over every battlefield that had grown out of the war, examining the small and large towns, studying the narrow country roads and the main highways, investigating the railroads and the huge marshaling yards. By the time he had completed his tour, he was probably as well informed as any living man on the part that American forces had played in the European conflict. It didn't seem likely, however, that such information would ever be of much use to Eisenhower except in an academic way.

There was nothing that Americans wanted less in 1929 than to get mixed up in the political intrigue of world affairs. Among the nation's hundred and twenty million population were fourteen million men and women who had been born in other countries and more than two hundred thousand who had just arrived as immigrants, but few of them wanted to go back and fewer still wanted to violate George Washington's warning against involvement in entangling alliances abroad. Popular sentiment throughout much of the Middle West was more or less in line with the fiercely isolationist attitude of the Chicago *Tribune.* A newly elected and highly popular United States Senator from Michigan, Arthur H. Vandenberg, who kept in close touch with public feeling at home, was an outspoken foe of "meddling" in foreign affairs.[1] "American businessmen," Thurman Arnold wrote much later, "believed with a religious faith that the world was composed of independent civilized states, whose function was to keep order at home so that international finance and investment could be free. In 1929 this kind

[1] Vandenberg changed his mind after the start of World War II and announced his conversion to international co-operation in a famous Senate speech. He later was a leader in the founding of the United Nations.

of world no longer existed. But the symbols still remained and were mistaken for the reality."

While it was "good business" for American manufacturers and dealers in agricultural products to sell as much as possible abroad, Americans in general favored high tariffs to prevent the "dumping" of cheap foreign-made goods in this country. And most people were a little suspicious of anybody, especially Easterners, who talked about "our responsibilities" abroad; just as they were a little scornful of the American artists and writers who preferred Paris and the Riviera to Dallas and Des Moines, or of the American heiresses who married penniless but titled Europeans. After all, America had won the war—or at least turned the tide—and what did it get us? A lot of abuse from people who didn't want to pay their war debts and called us "Uncle Shylock" when we suggested that they put a little cash on the barrelhead. The thing to do was to tend to our own knitting and not get mixed up in a mess like that again.

Yet, in 1929, America was a great world power and steadily becoming a greater one. You could close your eyes to it, and a great many Americans did, but the facts remained. When the First World War began, the United States was a debtor nation and our investments in foreign lands amounted to no more than two and a half billion dollars, much of it in branch factories of a dozen American corporations. Eleven years after the war, American interests abroad had grown to fifteen billion dollars [2] and this stake was increased to around twenty-five billion when you counted the war debts of something like ten billion owed to the United States by our former allies. And in 1929 we were still lending money abroad at the rate of more than a billion dollars a year by the sale of foreign securities in the United States.

Some of these facts were pointed out to Americans in an article by Isaac F. Marcosson in the *Saturday Evening Post,* but

[2] A quarter-century later, in 1954, United States private investments abroad amounted to twenty-six billion dollars and government credits abroad totaled fifteen billion for a grand total of forty-one billion dollars.

without making any noticeable change in the public attitude of the time. "Since 1914," Marcosson wrote,

we have done for Europe financially what England, Holland, Switzerland and, to a lesser extent, France and Germany, did for our enterprises and some of our states between 1860 and the outbreak of the Great War. The new world of money has redressed the credit balance of the old. . . . With a mountain of gold and a huge reservoir of surplus capital, we hold the international financial bull by the tail. We cannot let go . . . financial isolation is unthinkable.

Another reason why financial isolation was "unthinkable" for America was that our foreign sales had increased to $5,440 million annually in 1929, when we exported goods worth $686 million more than the goods that we imported. In the next quarter-century, such figures would not seem large because during the Second World War we exported more than fifteen billion dollars worth of goods a year and, in 1954, the United States foreign aid program alone (mostly gifts to allies in the cold war against Communism) amounted to more than five billion dollars. But in 1929 the dollar went almost twice as far as it would in the 1950's and the nation's sales abroad represented a vital 5 per cent of the gross national product. Whether we liked it or not, the economic welfare of the United States was now inextricably linked to the affairs of other nations and Americans would have to accept that fact—even if it took a second world war to make us do it.

2

The economic and financial ties linking America to the rest of the world were not easily visible to the ordinary citizen, nor was he much interested in them. One of the most important international conferences of 1929—the meeting of a new Reparations Committee of Experts—was a flop as far as newspaper readers were concerned if you looked beyond a comparatively small group of financiers and specialists who perused the pages of the *Wall Street Journal* or the *New York Times*. The sessions started with plenty of fanfare at the Hotel George V in Paris, under chairmanship of Owen D. Young, a tall, relaxed American farm boy turned financier. In addition to Young, who was chairman of General Electric Company and of Radio Corporation of America, the conference brought together a remarkable collection of famous figures in world finance.

There was Wall Street's mighty J. P. Morgan, shyly hiding away in an old-fashioned Paris hotel, and his partner, Thomas W. Lamont. There was Sir Josiah Stamp from Britain's Threadneedle Street and Emile Francqui, the famed Belgian financial expert. Emile Moreau represented France, Alberto Pirelli sat in for Italy and Kengo Mori for Japan. And last, but no means least, was the sharp-tongued, bespectacled and often insufferable genius of German monetary affairs, Dr. Hjalmar Schacht, who would outtalk and outlast all the rest. After starting to work amid a great flurry of publicity, the committee's wrestling and wrangling with highly technical financial matters soon became a deadly bore to most Americans. But, as a matter of record, the sessions emphasized several significant developments that would later assume vital importance.

For one thing, the annual report of the Agent General of Reparations was issued prior to the meeting of the new committee. The agent was S. Parker Gilbert, an American closely associated with the House of Morgan. His report was so technical that it could be interpreted in various ways but the main point was that the Germans had made a remarkable economic recovery in the eleventh year after a war in which they had been defeated and saddled with reparations amounting to almost six hundred million dollars annually. Germany, Gilbert's report said, was capable of keeping up her reparations payments.

This statement was greeted with cheers in France and with cries of outrage in Germany, where Dr. Schacht said it was a plot to bleed the German economy to death for the benefit of the French and British. Gilbert later modified his report somewhat by another interpretation qualifying his comment on

Germany's economic recovery, but events demonstrated that he was right the first time. The Germans had gotten farther on the road to recovery than had their conquerors. They would soon resume their dominant position in the European economy and renew the rivalry with the British Empire that had led to World War I. In retrospect, the German situation in 1929 would present some rather startling parallels—as well as some great contrasts—with the position of Germany in 1956, just eleven years after she had again been defeated in a great war with the Allied Powers. Controlling about two-thirds of the nation's area and fifty million population, the West German Republic surprised the world by the speed of its economic recovery in the decade from 1945 to 1955. Aided by United States assistance totaling three and a half billion dollars, German industry was rebuilt and, by 1953, was sending machinery and other products all over the world. The nation's gold reserves increased by four hundred million dollars in that year to a billion dollars and by 1954 West Germany was the third largest trading country in the world, outranked only by the United States and Great Britain. There were marked differences in the political and military position of Germany eleven years after the Second World War as compared to eleven years after the First World War, but in scarcely more than a decade the nation had again made an amazing economic recovery that outdistanced most of her conquerors.

The possibility that a resurgent Germany might again upset the peace of the world was not a subject on the agenda of the Paris Reparations Conference in 1929. The committee of international bankers was concerned with getting these huge obligations—reparations and war debts—on a "business-like basis" and, if possible, getting them out of the way of world trade. The United States officially refused to discuss the war debts in the same breath with reparations, but they represented a single problem because Britain and France refused to pay any more on their debts than they could collect in reparations from Germany. In the end, the bankers agreed on a plan for "commercialization" of reparations by creation of a Bank for International Settlements. They established for the first time the total of reparations owed by Germany—nine billion dollars—which when paid over a period of fifty-eight years in annual installments of almost half a billion dollars would amount to around twenty-seven billion dollars. The Germans would be permitted to raise most of the money by the sale of bonds which would be financed and guaranteed by the Bank for International Settlements and would represent a kind of mortgage on German railroads and industry.

As it turned out, the long, wearisome wrangle over how much Germany would pay Britain, France and other European nations in reparations and how much those nations would pay the United States on their war debts was mostly a waste of breath and energy, except for the creation of the Bank for International Settlements. In 1931, President Hoover proposed a one-year moratorium on all intergovernmental debts in an effort to check the world economic recession. Later, some efforts were made to arrange for resumption of payments, but the whole subject seemed to be out of date by then. The final solution was simple: the Germans simply declined to pay any more reparations and the other nations simply declined to pay any more on their debts to the United States, with the exception of Finland and Hungary.

3

World War I had failed to "make the world safe for Democracy" but it had pretty well convinced people in 1929 that another big conflict—this time with airplanes to shower bombs and poison gas on the world capitals—would mean the end of our civilization. In books, in magazines and in the newspapers, expert writers on military affairs were wont to explain in gruesome detail how New York City, or London or Paris or Berlin, would quickly be reduced to a jumbled pile of stones by aerial bombardment. The rubble, some of them predicted, would be piled twenty feet deep from one end of Fifth Avenue to the other and the biggest city in the world would be abandoned forever if war came again. The British Isles obviously would be devastated and any survivors reduced to the status of cavemen.

The general public took such predictions calmly because in 1929 nobody seemed likely to be foolish enough to start another war. Oh, there were troublemakers around, and there were some uncivilized revolutionaries trying to shoot their way into power in places like Afghanistan where old-fashioned Moslem tribesmen had risen against the King because they didn't like the fashionable short skirts worn by Queen Thuraya. But there was nothing to be taken seriously. Look at what was going on in Germany, for example: an angry, frustrated little egotist named Hiedler or Hitler, an Austrian by birth, was getting some susceptible people excited about his National Socialist party, which was dedicated to restoration of full German sovereignty and destruction of the potent German Communist party. It was just a lot of talk. Hitler had proved to be a kind of comic opera figure when he led a *Putsch* in 1923. He had been tossed into jail for a couple of years and most people regarded his demagogic speeches as foolish and futile. Experienced political observers in Germany were agreed that he wasn't the kind of man who could ever gain real power.

The Russian Communists, of course, were making trouble where they could and embarrassing the United States whenever possible, despite the fact that they wanted to establish diplomatic relations with Washington. They launched the two largest freighters ever built in Russia with considerable ceremony at Leningrad and, as the ships slid into the water, spectators could read the names painted across their prows. One was the *Sacco* and the other was the *Vanzetti*—the names of two anarchists who had been executed in Massachusetts after a celebrated murder trial that aroused national controversy. The Russians also spitefully took out after old John D. Rockefeller, who was trying to get in a little golf on his private course in Florida. The antireligious newspaper *Besbozhnik* charged that Rockefeller money was behind the printing of sixty-five thousand Baptist

Bibles in Russia. An article written by Krupskaya, the widow of Nicolai Lenin, said that "the need is imperative that the State resume systematic antireligious work among children. . . . But skill and persuasion must be used. I do not approve of . . . teachers tearing off every crucifix which they espy on a child's neck. We must be more subtle."

There was a threat of trouble in the Far East during the year when Chinese President Chiang Kai-shek and his momentary ally, Manchurian War Lord Chang Hsueh-liang, seized the Russian-built Chinese Eastern Railway running across Manchuria to Harbin, and expelled 174 Soviet railroad officials and employees. Both sides mustered troops along the frontier and there were sporadic outbursts of fighting. But the United States, Britain and Japan made it clear that they regarded China's action as illegal and Chang Hsueh-liang, abandoning Chiang Kai-shek, soon agreed to return of the Russian railroad officials. This proved to be a severe blow to the prestige of Chiang's campaign for complete unification of China. Several of his Army divisions mutinied, a forerunner of greater chaos to come.

There was a rattle of gunfire much closer to the United States than the fighting in China. In Mexico, an ambitious group of Army generals organized a revolt against the regime of President Emilio Portes Gil, who had been criticized for his stern enforcement of laws directed against the Catholic Church. The rebels, hoping for popular support, seized the port of Vera Cruz on the East Coast as well as the state of Sonora and other territory on the United States border in northwest Mexico. Portes Gil summoned a military hero and former president, General Plutarco Elias Calles, to take over the Ministry of Defense and suppress the rebellion. The United States sent ten thousand rifles and supplies of ammunition to the government forces. Calles quickly regained control of Vera Cruz and then dispatched an army of eighteen thousand men to the north where fighting had spread so close to the frontier that stray bullets were dropping into El Paso's streets. The rebels retreated cleverly to the northwest but were finally overtaken at the town of Jiménez by federal forces under thirty-seven-year-old General Juan Almazan, who ended the revolt with a climactic blow that might have been thought up by a Hollywood movie director. As rebel forces attempted to escape on an overcrowded railroad train, Almazan launched an attack through the air with fighter planes and an attack on the ground with hard-riding federal cavalry. More than a thousand rebels were killed.

Outbreaks of military violence in Mexico and China, however, were comparatively minor affairs in the peaceful world of 1929 and they were overshadowed by a surprising gesture of peace performed in Italy by Europe's most skillful professional sword-rattler, Fascist Premier Benito Mussolini. One momentous day the Italian dicatator entered a side door of the gloomy old Lateran Palace, which contains the Mother Church of Christendom, and sat at a long redwood table with Pietro, Cardinal Gasparri, the witty and massive Papal Secretary of State. In deepest secrecy, both signed a concordat that ended the self-imposed "imprisonment" since 1871 of the Pope within the Vatican. The imprisonment had begun with Pope Pius IX after the newly unified Italian nation restricted the papal sovereignty to a few buildings plus an annual indemnity for loss of the Papal States. The Catholic Church refused to recognize such a settlement and never accepted the indemnity. Now the long quarrel was ended. In the 1929 agreement, Mussolini's government recognized the City of the Vatican as a sovereign state where there could be no other authority than the Holy See. The Holy See recognized the Italian government, with Catholicism as the absolute state religion, and accepted indemnity reported to be around one hundred million dollars.

The Lateran Accord brought joy to Catholics throughout the world. "God has been restored to Italy," the Pope said, "and Italy has been restored to God." In July, on the Feast Day of St. James, a great serpentine procession moved out from the portal of St. Peter's Cathedral before the eyes of two hundred thousand hot and weary spectators. There were Papal gen-darmes, the famed Swiss Guard in red and yellow uniforms carrying halberds, the Palatine Guards in plumed helmets and some five thousand seminarians from all over the world bearing lighted tapers. At last there was a cry of "*Viva Il Papa!*" and Pius XI was borne from the cathedral on a podium beneath a scarlet and gold canopy, flanked by two lines of cardinals in scarlet robes. After almost sixty years, the Pope had left his "prison"—thanks to the political ambitions of a pompous little Socialist newspaperman who had turned into a Fascist dictator and who, with his mistress, would one day be hung head down-ward in a public square at Milan and buried in an unmarked grave.

4

Comparatively few Americans in 1929 were familiar with the name of Salmon Oliver Levinson, a lawyer living in Chicago. Yet on one occasion when President Hoover, Secretary of State Stimson, members of the diplomatic corps and a bevy of gen-erals and admirals gathered in formal array at the White House, Levinson was the only private citizen invited to be present. The invitation was issued because Levinson was the chairman of the American Committee for the Outlawry of War. His committee represented the hopes of American citizens that war could be banished from the earth and, to that end, it had proposed and worked for an agreement among nations never again to resort to armed force. Levinson saw a dream come true that day in the White House when the President promulgated a General Treaty for the Renunciation of War.

The treaty, informally known as the Kellogg-Briand Pact or the Pact of Paris, was ultimately signed by sixty-two nations, which solemnly agreed to settle all conflicts by pacific means and to renounce war as an instrument of national policy. The authors of the pact were strangely different: French Foreign Minister Aristide Briand, a short, rumpled man with drooping mustaches, a chain smoker of cigarettes, a compelling orator, a

Socialist and—with Gustav Stresemann of Germany, who died in 1929—an earnest worker toward a solid European peace. Frank B. Kellogg, who had just retired as Secretary of State, was a little man, too, and a laborer for peace. But otherwise he seemed far removed from the sharp-tongued, bohemian Briand. Kellogg had first gained fame as a corporation lawyer and later, as a "trust buster" in the administration of Theodore Roosevelt, he guided the prosecution and break-up of the great Standard Oil monopoly. His smooth white hair was always carefully brushed. He dressed with meticulous care. In later life, his hands trembled and he was known to Washington newspapermen as "Nervous Nellie" Kellogg.

The collaboration of Briand and Kellogg on the treaty to outlaw war was an odd and ironic chapter in international relations. The treaty contained no machinery for enforcement. Most "practical" politicians were of the opinion that it was a meaningless gesture. Yet the people everywhere were in favor of its purpose and no great power could afford not to sign. The treaty was invoked late in 1929 when there was a threat of conflict between Russia and China and it might have been employed successfully at later dates but for the timidity of the big powers. It was perhaps significant that the aggressor nations of the early 1930's were sufficiently impressed by world opinion to resort to "undeclared" wars—Japan in Manchuria, Italy in Ethiopia and Germany in Austria—rather than brazenly break the treaty. But it was soon apparent that no penalty was attached to international immorality, and the Kellogg-Briand Treaty became meaningless. Still, twenty-five years and several wars later, statesmen had found no better formula for abolishing war.

President Hoover's immediate problem on the road to permanent peace was a deadlock between the United States and Great Britain in regard to limitation or reduction of naval arms. The 1927 Naval Disarmament Conference at Geneva had ended in failure because the British wanted to limit construction of heavy cruisers but not of light cruisers while the United States wanted exactly the opposite. As a result of this deadlock, the United States Congress had passed a "big navy" construction bill and appeared ready to start an armaments race instead of co-operating in a general reduction. Mr. Hoover, however, instructed U.S. Ambassador to Belgium, Hugh S. Gibson, to appear before the League of Nations Preparatory Disarmament Commission with a compromise plan under which the powers were urged to agree on a common formula for measuring the combative strength of naval vessels and then seek an all-around reduction.

The British welcomed the idea of any kind of compromise that would avoid a competitive naval building program and newspaper correspondents reported that the Hoover proposals were a "bombshell" surprise. Most surprised of all, perhaps, was chubby, bespectacled Maxim M. Litvinov, chief delegate of Soviet Russia. Two weeks earlier, with Gibson present, Litvinov had reiterated a series of Russian disarmament proposals which, as one correspondent noted, were "almost exactly similar" to the main points made by Mr. Hoover. As usual, the Soviet proposals were largely ignored by the other delegates. After the Hoover "bombshell" had been exploded, one newspaperman asked Litvinov for comment.

"I scarcely know," the Russian diplomat replied, "whether Mr. Gibson spoke in support of my plan or in spite of it!"

But before anything could come of the Hoover proposals there was a general election in Britain and, surprisingly, it resulted in a victory for the Labor party and J. Ramsay MacDonald, who became Prime Minister. MacDonald promptly stopped construction of several new British warships and announced that he would go to Washington to talk with Mr. Hoover about holding another naval disarmament conference. The President met this gesture by announcing postponement of construction of three new American cruisers.

The courtly, white-haired MacDonald, accompanied by his daughter, Ishbel, arrived in October, 1929, to be given an enthusiastic welcome in New York City, where a press agent named Hector Fuller, who was serving as Mayor Walker's master of ceremonies, announced him to the Mayor and the radio audience as "the Prime Minister of the United States."

"I second that," exclaimed Socialist Party Leader Norman Thomas, who was a member of the welcoming party.

"I was only expressing a hope, sir," Fuller explained to Mac-Donald.

For a while, it seemed likely that Ishbel would steal the newspaper headlines from the statesmen. The reporters went slightly mad with joy when she said that she never took a drink, didn't even powder her nose, didn't know how to drive an automobile, didn't like to dance and didn't intend to pay any attention to letters from American boys who had proposed marriage. "American girls," she added, "seem much the same as British girls except that they wear their clothes at different angles."

But, having slept in Abraham Lincoln's bed at the White House and having talked over the state of the world with Mr. Hoover while sitting on a log at the President's Rapidan fishing camp, the Prime Minister eventually got back into the news. A statement issued by the two leaders said they were so close to agreement on naval disarmament that past obstacles seemed to have been substantially removed. Another conference on naval disarmament was called to meet in London early in 1930. There was, however, a degree of uncertainty behind the high hopes expressed by the President and the Prime Minister. The Japanese, for example, were suddenly demanding an increased ratio of naval arms compared to the United States and Britain. This was generally regarded as rather foolish but troublesome. Most experts were ready to testify that Japan was really a second-rate world power; that there was no actual danger to the United States from that quarter because the American naval base at Pearl Harbor in Hawaii was an impregnable bastion against any threat from the Orient.

More important, perhaps, in the long negotiations for disarmament were groups in America that opposed any move to reduce the strength of the United States Navy. Just how skillfully these forces could operate was demonstrated by a congressional investigating committee that looked into the activities of an angry and disappointed man named William B. Shearer.

5

Late in August of 1929 William B. Shearer filed suit in New York against the Bethlehem Shipbuilding Corporation, the Newport News Shipbuilding Company and the American Brown-Bovari Corporation. His suit stated that these companies had paid him $51,230 but that they still owed him $275,655 for professional services. It further stated that he had been employed to speak, to write, to talk to public officials and newspapermen in behalf of American shipbuilders—and he made clear that this meant in behalf of a big navy that would bring more profits for shipbuilding concerns.

The public had never heard of Shearer, a big and handsome man with a deep bass voice, but he was known to congressmen, to diplomats, to admirals and to reporters in Washington, Paris, London and Geneva. He had been a Navy recruit during the Spanish-American War, a real estate agent, a race-track betting operator, a Colorado mine superintendent, a prize fight promoter, a cabaret and theater manager, and an actor in *Ten Nights in a Bar Room*. He had at one time invented an amphibian tank and a one-man torpedo boat, and had been employed as a naval expert. Since 1924, he had been a kind of press agent for a big navy. He had lobbied in Washington for an "investigation" of the Navy, asserting that tests at the Naval War College at Newport demonstrated that the British fleet could destroy our Navy in an hour and a half. In 1927, he appeared at the Geneva Naval Disarmament Conference to entertain lavishly and to attack the British even more lavishly. In 1928, when Congress was debating a bill for fifteen new cruisers, he appeared in Washington with statements that the American Navy was inferior to the British.

"He has been everywhere," wrote the New York *Evening World* correspondent. "He seems to know nearly everyone worth while in the capitals of the world. Pin him down and you find he is not a cheap drawing-room boaster." To which the *New York Times* correspondent at Geneva added: "Some felt [at Geneva] that his game was to wreck the conference at any cost. . . . If he was employed to help wreck the conference, the opinion at Geneva would be that he earned his money."

President Hoover, in a statement to reporters, said he could not believe that "the responsible directors of these shipbuilding companies have been a party to these transactions as reported in the law suit" but he added that he had directed the Attorney General to consider what action could be taken. There wasn't time, however, for the Attorney General to consider. Senator Borah introduced a resolution for a Senate investigation and a three man subcommittee—Samuel M. Shortridge of California, Henry J. Allen of Kansas and Joseph T. Robinson of Arkansas—was directed to look into the whole affair.

The committee summoned Clinton L. Bardo, president of New York Shipbuilding Company, a subsidiary of American Brown-Bovari; Norman R. Parker, secretary of Brown-Bovari; and Charles M. Schwab and S. W. Wakeman of Bethlehem Shipbuilding Corporation. These distinguished businessmen assured the committee that nobody was more enthusiastic about naval disarmament than they and that they had been grievously misled or perhaps merely mistaken in regard to the activities of Shearer—if, indeed, they had even known of his existence. And, in any event, Shearer's reports were worthless, he was overpaid and they had fired him as soon as word of his activities began to trickle into the newspapers.

Bardo, who had paid a third of Shearer's expenses and salary at Geneva, complained that he had been "disarmed by the man's plausibility" but soon discovered that his reports were "bunk." "I regard Shearer as an undesirable man to have around," he added. "He wouldn't stay hitched. You might send him after the cows and he might take an idea to shoot the farmer's pigs instead. I wouldn't pay him twenty-five cents now to go anywhere."

Gentle, patriarchal Charles Schwab first said he'd never met Shearer and wished that every battleship afloat would be sunk. Later he modified his statement to acknowledge that there might have been a casual meeting but he stuck by his desire to sink all battleships. He then pointed out that he was practically retired and referred questions to "my boy"—Eugene G. Grace, president of Bethlehem. Grace explained that he didn't really know anything about Shearer, except that he had ordered him fired, and referred the senators to Vice-President Wakeman. Wakeman was somewhat better informed. He identified a letter from Shearer saying that he had "saved" the shipbuilding industry by lobbying for a big navy and that failure of the Geneva Conference had led to introduction of a $740-million naval construction program in Congress. Asked who had hired Shearer, Wakeman had a simple explanation. He admitted that he was to blame and that "it was a damn fool decision. I was just jazzed off my feet by Shearer." But Shearer's name was never shown on the payroll.

Having thus demonstrated that the shipbuilding industry was gravely disappointed by failure of the Geneva Disarmament Conference and that the hiring of Shearer was an unhappy aberration on the part of a subordinate official, the tycoons departed and the committee invited Shearer to the witness chair. Shearer fairly leaped to the stand, his voice booming. He identified himself as William Baldwin Shearer, "American, Christian, Protestant and Nationalist." He denied as "utterly false" a report that Scotland Yard had once suspected him of being a German spy. "I was a big bass drum and how could a bass drum by a spy?" He was incensed when the committee refused to permit him to read a prepared statement, roared "This is my party!" and complained that the cards were stacked in favor of the wealthy shipbuilders.

"Whether a man is in purple or in rags," Shortridge replied, "I propose to give him . . . a fair hearing."

"Well," snapped Shearer, "if I'm not given a break pretty soon you'll get your man in rags."

He said he had never received money from patriotic organizations but had received letters of approval from the American Legion, the Daughters of the American Revolution and the National Security League. He said he had helped Paul McNutt, Legion Commander, write a "big navy" speech. His contract with the shipbuilders was verbal but he had been assured that he would be amply rewarded if he "brought home the goods." At Geneva, he had worked hard getting out publicity, providing data for naval experts and reporters showing that the British were falsifying their figures on cruiser tonnage. He had turned over "secret" British documents to the American delegation. One such document was a pamphlet supposedly written by the head of the British Secret Service explaining how to convert prominent Americans to the British viewpoint by giving them medals and honors at a cost of fifty-eight cents per convert. This document, which a Naval Intelligence officer eagerly copied in Shearer's presence, was later described in London as a practical joke that had been perpetrated on Shearer by a British publicist in 1919.

"Did you have sumptuous quarters at Geneva?" asked Shortridge.

"It was not a villa but an apartment," Shearer said. "Some people here don't know the difference." It had a twenty-foot hall, an office, a salon, dining room, servants quarters and a number of sitting and bedrooms.

"I guess," said the Senator, "we won't need to go into that any further. . . . Why did you conceal your connections with the shipbuilders?"

Shearer said he had been ordered not to reveal his connections because of the American pacifist influence, especially that stirred up by a "bunch of lobbyists headed by Rockefeller, trying to get the country into the League of Nations." To inquisitive newspapermen at Geneva, he had said that he represented a Pittsburgh doorknob company which was interested in naval building "because ships have doors, don't they?"

"Do you mean to say," continued Shortridge, "that the Navy people, seeing you living in this impressive style, doing all that work, being glad to associate with you—that they didn't know who was paying you?"

"They didn't ask me. They're not inquisitive."

Shearer said he had met Schwab a number of times and it was Schwab who first suggested that the company might employ him. He added that the shipbuilders were now making him walk the plank because of pressure brought by former Secretary of State Kellogg. (Kellogg replied that it was "all rot.") He said that he was paid forty-five hundred dollars during the Hoover presidential campaign to "attack the British and get out the Irish vote" and that the material he wrote was mailed out from offices of Brown-Bovari. Later, he added, Senator Allen, who was directing publicity for the campaign, told him he should "go out and make Hoover campaign speeches." (Allen, a member of the committee, cried: "I wanted to get rid of you around publicity headquarters.") Senator Moses of New Hampshire, he added, "urged me to make a big navy speech in Boston to fool the simple Irish." (Moses made no comment.) Shearer said that Adolph S. Ochs, publisher of the *New York Times,* and Colonel Robert McCormick of the Chicago *Tribune* told their editors to use his material. (Both denied it.) He added that William Randolph Hearst paid him two thousand dollars a month to write articles against the League of Nations but fired him when he was called before the Senate committee. (Hearst said he had hired Shearer "among others.")

Shearer was scornful when Shipbuilder Bardo at one time said his conscience was bothering him because it was alleged that Scotland Yard had suspected Shearer as a German spy. "I hope," Shearer shouted when Bardo fired him, "that your conscience doesn't hurt you so much you won't build those cruisers!"

By the time the committee was through with Shearer—or vice versa—the American people had a somewhat better idea of how international negotiations were conducted, but the prospects for harmony and good will at the 1930 London Naval Disarmament Conference were not improved. Both Mr. Hoover and Mr. MacDonald, however, were persistent men. They went right ahead with their plans for discussing a reduction in the world's naval armaments, just as vigorously as Shearer went on demanding payment for services rendered. None of them got very far.

EIGHT

...is it power I'm after...
or what?...

Nineteen twenty-nine was a critical year for Americans ...
for John Llewellyn Lewis, a big, hard, bushy-browed man who
liked to recite Shakespeare, who once beat hell out of five
strikebreaking thugs hired to attack him, who clawed his way
to dictatorial power over unionized miners and who would not
hesitate to call the Vice-President of the United States a whisky-
drinking, poker-playing, evil old man. "What makes me tick?"
he once was quoted as asking a friend. "Is it power I'm after, or
am I a Saint Francis in disguise, or what?"

Lewis was born on Lincoln's birthday in the little Iowa mining town of Lucas. His father was from Wales, a miner descended from a long line of coal miners, and in America he
joined the Knights of Labor. The Iowa coal owners blacklisted
him as a union member and he moved his family to Illinois,
where his six sons also worked in the mines. John was the eldest
and the biggest. He was the leading actor in local theatricals,
he was shortstop on the baseball team, he was a wonderful
dancer and a gay companion. They said he ate three helpings
of raw beefsteak for breakfast, once knocked down a balky
mule with a stick of timber. For half a dozen years—"my years
of irresponsibility," he said later—he roamed through the tough

mining towns of the West, working for a while in Colorado, for a while in Utah, always moving on. In the early 1900's he returned to Illinois and settled down with his brothers in the town of Panama, where in 1908 he married Myrta Edith Bell, a serious and intelligent young schoolteacher.

Mrs. Lewis interested him in union activities, encouraged him to study the classics, helped him polish and rehearse his speeches, gave him the incentive to become self-educated and the opportunity to develop his natural bent for leadership. He represented the United Mine Workers in a legislative battle for a workers compensation act in 1910 at Springfield and caught the attention of Samuel Gompers, president of the American Federation of Labor. Gompers sent him all over the country as an A.F. of L. organizer and in 1916 he became chief statistician for the U.M.W. Two years later he was president and leading more than three hundred thousand miners in a nation-wide strike in defiance of the wartime no-strike legislation, which was still in effect. He declined to be intimidated by threats from Washington, journeyed to the national capital with a copy of *The Odyssey* under his arm, was put in jail and, in the end, won a compromise settlement of the strike. Overnight, he had become a national figure.

Lewis' troubles, however, were just beginning. He was determined to run the U.M.W. but he had many enemies within the organization. Not a few of the older officers regarded him as a bumptious interloper. A long, bitter and often bloody struggle began, with both sides determined to gain the upper hand even if they destroyed the union. Both sides used bombs and guns. Mines, offices, private homes, bridges were destroyed. Literally hundreds of men were killed. His enemies accused Lewis of betraying the miners. He roared back that they were "Reds" —the hirelings of Moscow. The United Progressive Miners union was launched in an effort to destroy him, and it almost did. Lewis fought back, brutally and effectively. Slowly, he won concessions from the coal owners. But many mines were closing down and "the Reds" were always after him.

In 1929, he was forty-nine years old and discouraged. He was still a big man, 230 pounds with hardly an ounce of fat on his powerful body. His massive, round head was crowned by a thick mane of dark hair that now showed threads of gray. His speech, even in casual conversation, was slow and formal and heavily sprinkled with polysyllabic words. He was still an actor —an amateur, a ham—but he was a highly effective orator, and he was always a fighter. By 1929, however, the unions had lost ground, and his own U.M.W. had shrunk from a membership of four hundred thousand to hardly two hundred thousand. The union treasury was almost empty. Lewis himself had failed in his bid to succeed Gompers as president of the A.F. of L. Even when, in 1929, he drove his bitter foe, John Brophy, out of the U.M.W., he could not view the future with any satisfaction. He said later that if he had had to face such a bitter struggle again he might not have gone on.

But the critical year of 1929 ended and in its wake came the New Deal, with labor a chief beneficiary. Lewis, who had voted for Herbert Hoover in 1928 and again in 1932, saw the door of opportunity open wide. He fought the A.F. of L. leadership because it insisted on organizing craft unions instead of lining up the great mass of workers in industrial unions. He knocked down Bill Hutcheson, the most influential champion of craft unionism, at the national convention in 1935 after Hutcheson had called him an offensive name. He created the Committee for Industrial Organization as a rival to the A.F. of L. and became the dominant labor figure of the 1930's.

He was never far removed from the center of controversy. Ruthless and opportunistic, a big man smoking a big cigar and riding in a big twelve-cylinder automobile, he dreamed of the White House but, when it came to a showdown, the working men voted as they pleased. Otherwise, they admired Lewis. "All right," he said to the Governor of Michigan, who had threatened to use the National Guard to end an illegal sit-down strike at General Motors, "you've got the Guard. . . . What kind of bayonets will they use? The flat sharp kind they can push in a long way . . . or the square kind they can twist around and make a big hole?" The Guard wasn't called, and the strikers got a contract that breached the open-shop fortress of America's greatest corporation.

He was denounced as a labor "Mussolini," he was derided by the newspapers for acting against the national interest, he quarreled with Presidents, he affiliated himself with and "disaffiliated" himself from the A.F. of L. as it suited his purpose. But he never quit fighting. "I want to see created social sluices or chutes through which the benefits of civilization will come down to every man, woman, and child in this country," he once remarked fuzzily in an attempt to explain his long-range views. "No one can guarantee the future, but I am certain that if labor does develop great power it cannot possibly make a worse mess of things than did big business."

Except in 1936, Lewis always voted the Republican ticket.

*The Lord made the land, and he put me here to raise
crops on it . . . and that's what's intended.*

—JEETER LESTER

*The lamp cleaning contest at the Farmers Fair was called
off this year because almost everybody is using electricity.*

—The Cooper County *Clarion*

*A six-day week is all right for machines
but a five-day week is enough for men.*

—HENRY FORD

*Oh, God, drive the devil out of the mills. . . .
The poor people have rights, too.*

—Prayer by REV. CICERO QUEENS at funeral
of workers killed in a Carolina strike riot

AUGUST, 1929

the troubled land of plenty

All that summer under a hot sun the harvesters moved
northward across the face of America, gathering the crops on
six million farms. More than eleven million men joined in the
work from the cotton fields of Georgia to the vineyards of
California, from the rice paddies of Louisiana to the wheat
fields of North Dakota. They plodded through brown fields
with sacks on their backs, they prodded mules and horses drawing wagons and mowers, they followed combines that cut vast
swaths through the prairie grainfields and they drove so many
tractors—827,000 of them—that old-timers were saying by
heck! it wouldn't be any time at all before farms would be as

mechanized as factories and a man could wear a white collar out to plow the cornfield.[1]

"At last," the *Country Gentleman* exclaimed editorially in 1929, "scientific agriculture has arrived." Twenty years before there had been only one farm tractor operating in the United States. But now, the magazine pointed out, the old-style farmer was done for, unable to compete with the scientific farmer who used new methods of conservation, of planting and of harvesting to reduce costs by half in many instances and to increase his yield per acre.

There seemed to be a lot of horse sense in the words of the *Country Gentleman*. Throughout the 1920's the farm population, which included three million hired workers, remained fairly steady and it would not drop below ten million until 1945. But in the same period production per man edged steadily upward due to mechanization and improved methods—it would increase by almost 40 per cent in the next two decades—and the area harvested in 1929 set a record of 355,295,000 acres. Even sixteen years later, in the war year of 1945, there would not be as much land under cultivation by almost ten million acres. The American farmland in 1929 was a land of plenty, with the harvest bringing in 2,515,000,000 bushels of corn and 824,000,-000 bushels of wheat, which was only a little less than would be produced a quarter-century later. The storage bins were full and overflowing.

Yet in the midst of plenty there were moans of anguish. For several years the agricultural situation had been deteriorating in the United States. Almost five thousand farms were legally placed in bankruptcy during 1929 and many others were losing money or on the verge of failure. The total debt of American farms on property valued at fifty-eight billion dollars was approximately ten billion dollars in 1929, and many farmers

---

[1] A quarter-century later there would be only 5,200,000 farms in the United States but there would be 4,500,000 tractors operating on them. By then, not even old-timers said "By heck!"

didn't know where the next interest payment was coming from because the bottom had dropped out of market prices. Wheat, which had reached a peak of $2.34 a bushel a decade earlier, was down to $0.98. Corn which had sold for $1.50 a bushel brought not more than $0.79. In 1919, the net income of farmers had been more than nine billion dollars but by 1929 it was down to six billion [2]—off more than one-third during a period in which income of other occupational groups had increased almost 50 per cent. And the net income per farm family was only $942 a year.

The trouble was that farmers had greatly expanded production during and immediately after the war when they could sell all they produced at high prices. In the 1920's they kept on producing at wartime levels. Meanwhile, European nations had resumed farm production and reduced the foreign market. At the same time, the United States had followed a high tariff policy designed to protect American industries from foreign competition. This not only kept prices of manufactured goods at a high level for the farmer and everybody else but it prompted other countries to boycott American farm exports of crude foodstuffs, which declined from almost a billion dollars in 1920 to less than one-third that amount in 1929. And the farmers were compelled to take whatever price they could get for surplus crops dumped on the world market. "This amounted to nothing less than a determination to appropriate what remained of agricultural wealth for the benefit of eastern business and finance," Representative Thomas R. Amlie of Wisconsin, wrote later in *Common Sense*. During the late Twenties, he said, the "average farmer has been able to stay in business solely because he has been able to consume part of his capital eac year while living in hopes of better times to come."

[2] A quarter-century later the income of farmers of the United States was something like sixteen billion dollars, but the purchasing power of the dollar then was perhaps half as much as in 1929. Farm income reached a peak of about twenty billion dollars in 1948, following World War II.

2

The night John Henry was born, the Mississippi River ran up-stream for a thousand miles because the South had produced a legendary hero to rival the superhuman feats of Paul Bunyan in the forests of the North. John Henry came into the world with a cotton hook for a right hand and a river song on his tongue. The first thing he did, according to Roark Bradford, was to sit up and yell for food.

"Don't make me mad!" he roared, and the thunder echoed across the sky. "Bring me four ham bones and a pot full of cabbage. Bring me a bait of turnip greens treetop tall and season hit down with a side er middling! Bring me two hog jowls and a kittleful of whipowill peas. Bring me a skilletful er red-hot biscuits and a big jugful er cane molasses."

Once John Henry consumed at a single sitting a river of honey and a whole tree of biscuits. Wherever he went, the land magically produced food and he was always eating. He was the symbol of the hungry Negro sharecropper reaching out for a share of the world's goods. He could roll and "coonjine" more cotton than any man alive. When he worked on the railroad, he could drive spikes with a sledgehammer in each hand. Casey Jones was the great engineer, but John Henry was his fireman. He could work and he could produce at a superhuman pace but by the time he had finished eating there wasn't much left.

3

The cotton crop in 1929 was three million bales under the eighteen million [3] record set in 1926. But there was still too much of it. Cotton that had sold for twenty-eight cents a pound in 1923 was down to seventeen cents and surplus stocks of several million bales were being piled up in storage. In Georgia,

---

[3] A quarter-century later approximately one-third less cotton would be produced in the United States.

the net income of the average farmer was not more than three hundred dollars a year, perhaps a third of it in cash and the rest in credit. More than 80 per cent of the Negroes in the state were tenants or sharecroppers and in the ten chief cotton states of the South the rate of tenancy had gone up to 61 per cent of all farmers.

The sharecropper's life usually was so meager that many of the younger people jumped at any chance to get away from it, rushing to the towns and cities to work in factories. The reason that the number of farmers remained about the same during the 1920's while the nation's population was increasing was that hundreds of thousands—some 546,000 in 1929—left agriculture and took up urban life. In 1929, the over-all farm population of twenty-seven million was the lowest in twenty years. Compared to the shanties in which they had grown up, some company villages erected near the mills in Southern towns seemed like luxury to many of the migrants and the pay represented more cash in a month or so than most of them had ever seen in a year. "You ought to see some of those folks from the hills," said one agent who was recruiting workers for newly established mills in the South. "They don't know nothing—just enough to follow the path to the mill and then take the path to their houses again when the whistle blows."

But the change in agriculture was a great deal more than just the migration of young people to the cities. The land was wearing out in many places—in the cotton states, for example—and cotton was moving westward. By 1929, 47 per cent of the nation's large-scale cotton farms (those grossing better than thirty thousand dollars a year) were in Arizona and California, where the yield would be pushed up to more than five hundred pounds per acre or double the national average. For the first time official concern over misuse of the nation's land became serious enough to prompt Congress to make appropriations for investigation of the effects of erosion and of methods for its control. But even then it was not easy to get farmers to change their wasteful ways, and it would take the great, destructive dust storms of the 1930's to convert some of them to the necessity for modern conservation methods.

Later studies of land conditions demonstrated how the old methods had damaged productivity. The government Resettlement Administration would find 650,000 families—more than 3,000,000 persons—living on 100,000,000 acres that were "virtually incapable of producing an adequate livelihood." All topsoil was gone from 51,465,000 acres, which is six times the arable land of England and Wales, and some 4,443,000 acres were ruined by wind erosion. In *The Wasted Land*, Gerald W. Johnson wrote that the South had "thrown away 3,500,000 people" who were forced to migrate because of failure of the soil and "had lost 97,000,000 acres of land."

"Why, the land down in this part of Tennessee has got so bad," an old planter said of the red clay gullies, "that the crows have to carry their own rations to fly over it."

As agriculture moved westward, the small "family-size" farm lost ground, unable in many instances to compete with large-scale, mechanized farming enterprises. More than 40 per cent of the farmers in Mississippi, for example, had given up their small farms to become hired hands on big agricultural operations, often owned by corporations. In Hardin County, Ohio, onion growing had become a big-scale corporation enterprise. In California, 40 per cent of the cultivated land was in farms of more than five hundred acres and there were a number of mass-production farms comparable to one in the San Joaquin Valley which employed as many as twenty-five hundred men and women on six thousand acres during the fruit-picking season, operated a refrigerator plant with a sixty-thousand-crate capacity and shipped out two dozen freight car loads of fruit a day at the peak of the season.

The advantages of the big farms were obvious. They could be operated more efficiently. They could afford a greater degree of mechanization. They could eliminate much of the waste of the small, family farm and increase the yield by modern methods of conservation, or by using airplanes to spray insecticides over the crops. By 1929, machines had taken over much of the work that previously had been done by men or by horses, but it was only the beginning of automation on the farm. Not even the most visionary farmer at the end of the 1920's could foresee the day twenty-five years later when a machine would do the work of fifteen men picking and husking corn or of fifty men picking cotton. Nor could he imagine that Western farms would operate fleets of tractors and trucks equipped with two-way radio communication to co-ordinate and speed up big-scale cotton production.

The trend to mechanization in 1929 already had begun to change the status of farm labor. Once huge gangs of workers, estimated at more than two hundred thousand men, had followed the wheat harvest northward every year, working from farm to farm. The increasing use of machinery made such gangs unnecessary in the grain country but fruit still had to be picked by hand and some two hundred thousand migrant pickers were required each season in the Far West. They were perhaps the poorest of the farm population; the foreign-born, the dispossessed. Citizens of the towns through which they moved scorned them. Ranch owners too often provided them with disreputable shacks as living quarters. Storekeepers were not always innocent of overcharging them. And the migrant family, working long hours in the orchards or the fields of sugar beets, lettuce, melons, asparagus, or Brussels sprouts, was not likely to make more than five hundred dollars in a season.

Labor organizers frequently went into the workers' camps in an attempt to interest them in a union that would demand improved conditions, but the migrants were usually uneducated, suspicious and, in many instances, illegally in the United States. And local law-enforcement officers or vigilante gangs were ready to break heads rather than see their community suffer heavy losses because of a strike called at a time when highly perishable crops had to be picked immediately. "You see the owners crying for cheap labor," said an article in the *New Republic*, "for . . . fruit tramps who make no fuss over dirt and disease, half-starvation and insecurity. . . . When they asked for more wages or objected to the stench and filth of their shanty-towns and ditch-side squatters' camps, [officers] drove them out of the fields at bayonet point, herded them in corrals and stock-ades, beat and jailed them and even murdered."

4

About the only time that the farmers felt the government at Washington was paying much attention to their troubles was during an election campaign or a disaster. In 1928 there had been an election campaign and in 1929 there was a disaster. The election campaign had resulted in a promise by President Hoover to call a special session of Congress to be devoted to farm legislation, and it met in April, 1929. In the same month, a United States Department of Agriculture expert bit into an orange in Orlando County, Florida, saw that it was full of maggots and turned in the disaster alarm. For the first time in history, *Halterophera capitata*, better known as the Mediter-ranean fruit fly, had invaded America. The invader was small, about a third the size of a house fly and colored brown, yellow, black and white, but deadly. It laid as many as eight hundred eggs which hatched in about four days. Not only Florida but large areas of the rest of the country were endangered by the insect that had in some mysterious, never-to-be-discovered manner slipped past the nation's border guards. War was declared at once.

Mr. Hoover transferred four million dollars to fight the men-ace in Florida, where crops in Seminole, Orange and Lake counties already had been badly damaged and six other coun-ties were affected. Congress later appropriated another twenty-three million for the fight to save as much as possible of the state's sixty-million-dollar citrus crop. The National Guard was called out to patrol every highway and byway and to inspect all vehicles. Cars and trucks were sprayed with poison. Farms where fruit was diseased were placed under guard. Five thou-sand volunteers were enlisted to dig long trenches into which thousands of tons of infected fruit were dumped, treated with lime and covered again. Almost six hundred thousand boxes of citrus fruit were destroyed, in addition to large amounts of vegetables and noncitrus fruit. By the time the danger was under control, at least eight million acres were involved at a huge loss to Florida growers who, however, were reimbursed by the government for the fruit that had been destroyed. The disaster, following severe hurricanes and collapse of the Florida land boom in the previous two years, was a serious blow to the state's economy but nothing that couldn't be corrected by sunshine and a good publicity man.

Meantime, Mr. Hoover's farm relief program had been enacted without pleasing anyone. The basic feature of the program was a Farm Board with a fund of half a billion dollars to make low-cost loans to farm co-operatives, thus enabling the farmers to market their own crops. At that time, there were farm co-operatives in the nation with a membership of two million and doing business of more than one hundred million dollars a year. When the administration sought to expand this movement, however, the grain elevator operators and grain dealers were incensed. The phrase "creeping socialism" hadn't been invented yet, but they accused Mr. Hoover, of all people, of "paternalism." The American Bankers' Association denounced the legislation, saying no such relief was needed and that farming would be healthy if it undertook "the proper application of business methods." A suggestion that price supports for basic crops be written into the bill was denounced by business experts who said it would lead the farmers "to peasantry." It is difficult to imagine what they would have said if anybody had suggested that twenty-five years later the federal government would be guaranteeing farmers 75 to 90 per cent parity prices and would have more than seven billion dollars of taxpayers' money invested in surplus crops.

The farmers were unhappy, too. They said the Farm Board was moving too slowly and that by the end of the year it had lent less than fifty million dollars. "If any substantial change for the better has taken place," said Frank O. Lowden, a farmer, a former governor of Illinois and once a strong contender for the Republican presidential nomination, "it has escaped my notice."

Perhaps the only persons not unhappy about the situation were politicians who might profit by embarrassment to the administration. When the Senate Agriculture Committee, at the instigation of a Democrat, proposed to call a group of business-men and financiers, including Henry Ford, Owen D. Young, J. P. Morgan and John D. Rockefeller, Jr., for advice on the farm problem, Senator Lynn Frazier of North Dakota, asked: "Having robbed the farmers all these years, do you think these gentlemen would know how to help them out now?"

"At least," replied paunchy Senator Tom Heflin of Alabama, "we might find out how they robbed the farmers."

5

The long-cherished theory that if business is booming and the rich are getting richer the benefits of general prosperity at the top will trickle down to the working man at the base of the pyr-amid seemed to be flourishing in 1929. The working man was doing well. Not everywhere, of course, but in most parts of the country and in most industries. Charles W. Nash, head of the Nash Automobile Company, personally handed out eight hun-dred thousand dollars in bonus checks to his twelve thousand employees. Alexander Legge, the hundred-thousand-dollar-a-year president of International Harvester Company, startled the industrial world by announcing that the concern's forty thousand employees in more than thirty plants would hence-forth get an annual two-weeks' vacation *with pay*. It would, he added, cost the company about a million dollars a year.

There was even more sensational news from Detroit. At the Ford Motor Company it was disclosed that employees would work only five days a week. There were, the announcement said, jobs for about thirty thousand more workers at the Ford plants at a minimum of five dollars a day. Crowds of job-seekers ranging up to twenty-five thousand a day gathered outside the employment offices, where about five hundred were being hired every day. The five-day week had been widely discussed but rarely practiced until 1929 when, in addition to Ford workers, the strongly unionized bricklayers and ironworkers in New York City and job shop compositors in Chicago forced employers to give them two days of leisure a week without a pay decrease. "The five-day week is inevitable," said Fred T. Ley, New York real estate and construction executive. "It may reach throughout the land."

In addition to getting more leisure—a trend that delighted automobile manufacturers, sports promoters, hot-dog salesmen and all others who catered to vacationists—the American worker was finding it easier to get a job and was paid higher wages when he got one. The national labor force had increased 14 per cent since 1919 to about forty-eight million and unemployment —around 1,600,000—was not severe. The average hourly wage rate in 1919 had been forty-seven cents for a forty-six-hour week in factories but by 1929 it had increased to fifty-seven cents an hour or twenty-five dollars for a forty-four-hour week.[4] This upward trend in wages and downward trend in hours was destined to continue for a number of reasons, including the discovery that better pay usually meant better production. In 1929, for example, Gerard Swope, president of General Electric, published a study of his company's pay and production statistics. He found that in 1919 when the average employee earned about twenty-five dollars a week and the company's business amounted to $237 million the ratio of production-to-pay was 2.23 per cent. By 1929, the average pay had gone up to about thirty-five dollars a week but sales had mounted to $348 million and the production-to-pay ratio had increased to 2.61 per cent. Thus, higher pay seemed to mean better production.

[4] By 1954, the nation's labor force had again increased by about one-third to sixty-four million and the normal working week had been cut to forty hours. The purchasing power of the dollar was perhaps only about half what it had been in 1929, but wages had more than doubled. The average factory worker's take-home pay in 1954, after deduction of income tax, social security, etc., was approximately seventy dollars.

Wages in 1929 varied considerably, of course, in different industries and in different parts of the country. United States Steel, which employed a quarter-million workers, paid sixty-eight cents an hour or around thirty dollars a week. In some Southern areas, according to a booklet issued by the New Orleans Association of Commerce in a bid to persuade Northern factories to move south, mill wages were twenty-five cents an hour for men and from fifteen to twenty-five cents an hour for women, with a ten-hour day customary except for workers under sixteen years old. Low wages and poor working conditions in many Southern mills were the subject of a great deal of controversy and a number of prominent Southerners attending the University of Virginia's Institute of Public Affairs were outspoken in criticizing the "repugnant, rotten and archaic" practices of some Southern industrialists.

Homer L. Ferguson, president of the Newport News Shipbuilding Company, former president of the U.S. Chamber of Commerce and a stockholder in several textile mills, had a ready answer to such criticism. "The condition of the Southern cotton mill worker is very much better than it was a generation ago when he had no work at all," Ferguson said. "When they talk about twelve-dollar-a-week wages, they do not tell you about the free homes, the good country food, water and light for nothing. . . . Perhaps children do work, but in juvenile vagrancy North Carolina is so much better off than Ohio that there is no comparison. . . . The hours may be long and the pay small, but the textile industry is highly competitive." Twenty-five years later it might be difficult to realize that Ferguson's words rather accurately reflected the business attitude, particularly in the South, at the time. Nevertheless, he had an even more forceful argument in defense of low wages. "If the Southern textile owners and operators tie up with the labor unions," he concluded, "then they will see the textile industry move elsewhere, as it has already moved once."

Another interesting comment on the status of labor came from Alabama, where the use of convict labor in coal mines had been ended after a long crusade led by a peppery club-woman, Mrs. Julia Harris. A coal operator congratulated Mrs. Harris on the success of her campaign, and added: "You are right. I had convicts on lease from the state. Now the bottom has dropped out of the coal market and I don't want to mine any more coal but under the old system I would have had to pay the state whether I mined or not. Now all I have to do is shut the mines and fire the other workers. You saved my life."

6

A rather amazing thing had happened to the labor movement in the 1920's. Immediately after the First World War there had been a period of serious agitation and strikes. Many persons were quick to blame the trouble on "alien agitators"—the Communists had come into power in Russia—and, in 1919, the U.S Attorney General authorized a series of raids and wholesale arrests for the purpose of shipping such aliens back to the lands from whence they came. These raids were directed by an able young lawyer in the Department of Justice named J. Edgar Hoover. Some agitators including Emma Goldman were deported but the courts directed the release of many of those arrested and the entire project was a rather dismal failure.

Then, in the next decade, the labor movement lost its fire and began fading away as the wave of business prosperity mounted. At the beginning of the 1920's the American Federation of Labor had a membership of about five million and some four million workers—almost half of those employed in factories —were involved in strikes. But by the beginning of 1929, the A.F. of L. membership had dropped to 3,442,600 [5] and there were no really big strikes that year. For example, there were half a million workers in the automobile industry in the last years of the 1920's, yet there were only a few thousand who belonged to unions—and the union leaders were quarreling over

[5] By 1954, trade union membership in the United States was around fifteen million, including virtually all automobile factory workers.

whether the automobile workers should be organized by craft or by industrial unions.

The decline of the unions in the middle Twenties was attributed to various factors, including the rising standard of living and a drastic change in the leadership of the labor movement. The aggressive, crusading Samuel Gompers, a onetime cigar-maker who had ruled over the A.F. of L. from its inception, was gone and in his place was William Green, a former preacher, who preferred compromise. By 1929, the organization seemed to be as much interested in avoiding anything that would disturb the business boom as it was in questions of hours and wages. At the annual A.F. of L. convention in Toronto, the biggest news was provided by William J. McSorley, head of the building trade unions, who joined Wall Street in attacking the Federal Reserve Board because it had boosted discount rates on loans in a timid effort to reduce stock market speculation. This, McSorley said, had done nothing except to reduce home building, which had decreased almost 25 per cent since 1925 when homes were constructed for close to half a million families.

The degree of prosperity enjoyed by the working man in 1929 was not easy to establish statistically because his family was buying everything from vacuum cleaners to automobiles on the installment plan and because cost-of-living figures can be deceptive. A government committee's study found that the cost of living had declined seven-tenths of one per cent between 1922 and 1929 and that, with wages increasing, the purchasing power of the working man's family had gone up about 14 per cent. Yet there were signs of discontent. The decrease in union membership, for example, was halted during 1929 and the A.F. of L. enlisted 37,482 new members before the end of the year. There was mounting unemployment in some New England towns where textile operators, complaining about union demands for higher wages and increasing local taxation, closed down their mills or moved to new locations in the South.

And in the South there was labor strife, and bloodshed and murder.

7

The South, generally speaking, was unfriendly toward labor unions and when textile mills first moved into Tennessee and the Carolinas their workers were unorganized men and women recruited from the hill country. One ten-million-dollar mill in Tennessee making artificial silk operated on a fifty-six-hour week for which wages ranged from $8.90 to $14.00 a week. At a group of mills in South Carolina the "stretch-out system" was introduced to increase the work of each employee without commensurate pay. One weaver, for example, had been working twenty-four looms and was paid $18.91 a week. Under the new system he tended 114 machines for $23.00 a week. "In the stretch-out system," said Representative Dowell E. Patterson, chairman of a state investigating committee, "it is the employee who does the stretching out."

By the spring of 1929 union organizers had moved south, too, and were trying to convince individualistic Southern workers that they should band together to demand higher pay. But this was slow and dangerous work. After one strike, the company fired three hundred union workers and brought in new recruits from the hills. Two prominent union officials were seized by a masked mob, carried across the state line and threatened with death if they returned to Tennessee. When strikes were called, the National Guard usually was ordered out to patrol the streets and protect strikebreakers. Groups of local vigilantes frequently made night raids on union offices or threatened outside organizers.

One of the New England textile mills that looked hopefully to the South was the Manville-Jenckes Company of Pawtucket, Rhode Island, which by 1929 was producing yarn for cord tires at the Loray mills in the North Carolina town of Gastonia. That spring, however, organizers for the National Textile Workers

Union—not connected with the A.F. of L.'s United Textile Workers Union—persuaded a thousand Loray workers to strike for a twenty-dollar minimum weekly wage, a forty-hour week, elimination of the stretch-out system, reduction of rates for utilities in the company-owned houses and recognition of the union. Mill owners replied that the National Textile Workers Union was "Communistic" and that one of its organizers was a representative of the Communist newspaper, *Daily Worker.* They closed the Loray mill and Governor Max Gardner called out two hundred state militiamen to keep order in the worried, restless town of Gastonia, where nine of every ten men were now jobless.

After a few days, the mill owners began hiring other workers and resumed operations on a limited scale under protection of the militia. Bitterness mounted in the town as the strikebreakers moved in and the strikers went hungry. One night a band of masked men broke into a ramshackle building that was serving as headquarters for the strikers. Ten men sleeping there were dragged to their feet. Holding revolvers and other weapons, the invaders ordered the strikers into the street and then systematically wrecked the building with sledgehammers and axes. Files and records were torn up and thrown into the street. A sign was erected on the ruins: "We have quit your damn union." Then the attackers vanished into the night as militiamen, most of them in their underwear, rushed to the scene—and arrested the strikers on charges of starting a riot.

The sign left by the raiders obviously was to suggest that discontented strikers had decided to drive the National Textile Workers Union out of town. Nobody believed it, but the heat was on. Strikers were evicted from company-owned houses. Their food supply was low. Their ranks dwindled and the remnants of the striking band gathered in a tent camp on the edge of town. The union modified its demands, but Loray manager, J. A. Baugh, would not talk to them, asserting that they were merely "discharged employees." Militiamen continued to patrol the streets, breaking up demonstrations and, on one occasion, attacking several score of strikers with clubs and bayonets. Two strikers, aged sixteen and fifteen, were arrested. Even the store-keepers of Gastonia were beginning to complain that they could not stop for a conversation with friends on the street without being prodded by a bayonet and told to move on. In Washington, proposals for a congressional investigation of the strike situation were blocked temporarily by North Carolina's senators —Lee S. Overman and F. M. Simmons—but later approved after a delegation of Gastonia strikers appeared at the Senate and fourteen-year-old Binnie Green, weighing sixty-nine pounds, told how she had been paid $4.95 for sixty hours' work a week in the mills. Senator Overman patted Binnie on the head and remarked that she "ought to be in school."

But the trouble was not over at Gastonia. One day Police Chief Orville F. Aderholt, who was said to have been informed that a fight had broken out in the strikers' tent camp, rushed there with a group of armed police. The "guard" at the camp opened fire on them, asserting later that in view of past tactics of police and militiamen he was convinced that the camp was being attacked. General firing ensued. Aderholt was fatally wounded and three policemen and one union organizer, Joseph Harrison, were wounded. The next day, Harrison and fifty-eight others were arrested on various charges, including murder.

By now the nation was taking a second look at the newspaper headlines reporting strife in North Carolina, fearing that a new Sacco-Vanzetti case might be in the making. Communists obviously had been active in the original flare-up at Gastonia. But that did not soften the story being published everywhere of life in the Southern mills, of instances of police irresponsibility, of vigilantes who flogged union organizers or of violence and death. In the town of Marion, at the foot of the Blue Ridge Mountains, the highly respectable A.F. of L. United Textile Workers of America called a strike and closed the Marion Manufacturing Company mill. The strike spread to the Clinchfield Company and National Guardsmen were summoned. When the companies attempted to evict strikers from company-owned shanties there was a riot in which many were injured and 148 persons arrested for "riot, insurrection and rebellion."

A few days later, Sheriff Oscar Adkins and a group of deputies were trying to maintain order outside the mills as strikebreakers arrived for the early shift. "Now, folks," Adkins shouted to the strikers, "everybody will have to stand aside and let all who want to work come to work."

"Over our dead bodies," somebody shouted, as strikers grabbed a man heading for the mill gate. Adkins pulled out a tear-gas pistol and fired it. Many in the crowd thought he was shooting a revolver. They began striking him with sticks and throwing rocks. The deputies began firing their guns. Two dozen persons were wounded—most of them in the back—and four died; one of them was a widower with eight children who had handcuffs on his wrists when he was carried to the operating table at the hospital. The union organizers lost no opportunity to capitalize on such tragic incidents. When the four victims were buried in a hillside scrub oak grove, John A. Peel, vice-president of the state Federation of Labor, was one of the orators. Four girls led a solemn crowd of mountain men and women in hymn-singing and a chant:

> We are building a strong union,
> We are building a strong union,
> We are building a strong union,
> Workers in the mill.

A little and aging man, Rev. Cicero Queens came down from the mountains to preach the funeral under a hot sun. "This is one of the most saddest times," he cried. "It is a cloudy day today in our hearts. Here lies four people dead. It's an awful pity. The devil's come into the world and confused people." He dropped to his knees. "Oh, God, we know we are not high society. But we know Jesus lives. Oh, what would Jesus do today if He passed through Marion?"

Meanwhile, sixteen persons including three young women were brought to trial at Charlotte on charges of murder in connection with the death of Police Chief Aderholt at Gastonia. Both sides made the most of the national spotlight that centered on the trial. A defense lawyer, Tom P. Jimson, told reporters the trial was a "frame-up" and that they should not be "fooled into believing that this is nothing but a murder trial because it is a Labor Case and will take its place in history with notable struggles against oppression and exploitation." When a prospective juryman said he believed all the defendants were guilty, another defense lawyer—Arthur Garfield Hays—leaped to his feet and pointed dramatically at a small, nineteen-year-old girl among the prisoners, crying: "Do you say this little girl is guilty of murder?"

The prosecution was not to be outdone. As it opened its case, court attendants wheeled into the courtroom a stretcher, covered with a white sheet. In deathly silence, the prosecutor stepped before the jury box and whipped off the sheet—revealing a plaster effigy of Aderholt in blood-covered police uniform, his face white and ghastly beneath a big black-brimmed hat. The jury shuddered at the grisly sight. That night one juror begged a deputy sheriff for a pistol so that he might kill himself. He confessed his sins and asked to be buried face down. Then he crawled under a bed and officers had to drag him out. A physician declared he was the victim of "acute emotional insanity" and the judge declared a mistrial.

It was a month before the trial could be resumed and, meantime, there were various outbreaks of violence—three union men were kidnaped and beaten after being threatened with hanging and a group of strikers in a truck was fired upon by men in several automobiles. A women was killed and several others wounded. But when the trial resumed, the state agreed to reduce the charges against seven defendants to second-degree murder and to release nine others. The star of the second trial was Prosecuting Attorney John G. Carpenter, a handsome man with a flower in his buttonhole. He described the labor organizers as "fiends incarnate, stripped of their hoofs and horns, bearing guns instead of pitchforks, creeping like the hellish serpent into the Garden of Eden" that had been Gastonia without a union. In dramatic fashion, he acted out the death of Aderholt, falling mortally wounded to the courtroom floor, moaning and writhing before the jury box. He tenderly held the hand of Aderholt's widow as he recited a poem on motherhood. He said that Gastonia was a town with "vine-clad doors where the kindly light of the autumn sun kisses the curly hair of happy children." He described the mill owners as "a holy gang, a God-serving gang."

The jury was out only an hour. It found the defendants guilty. Four organizers from Northern cities were sentenced to from seventeen to twenty years in prison. Three strikers who were natives of Gastonia were sentenced to shorter terms. "Justice," said the Gastonia *Gazette*, "has triumphed."

...12 hot dogs, 8 bottles of pop and 729 home runs...

Nineteen twenty-nine was a bumper year for American heroes . . . for George Herman Ruth, a big, ugly, vulgar man who was young in heart and still younger in mentality. Kids everywhere—and adults, too—adored him because they didn't know him with his uniform off. They called him the Babe.

He was some babe! In 1902, when he was seven years old, his parents left him at St. Mary's Industrial School in Baltimore, a semicorrectional institution for underprivileged children. Later, he never willingly spoke of either his father or mother and whatever memories he had of them, if any, must have been bitter ones. He was a rough, crude boy, growing up in back streets and dreary slums. Profanity poured from his wide lips with almost every breath. He was warmhearted, kindly and engaging in many ways but his environment was such that he seemed a good bet to end up as a mobster, a hoodlum. Everything was against him—except that he could throw a baseball.

Baltimore was a famous baseball town. Even on the dusty vacant lots where kids knocked a ball around, a boy with big hands and a strong arm was likely to be noticed by scouts for the Big League teams. They couldn't miss the Babe. At an age when most boys were in high school, he was playing semiprofessional ball and at the age of nineteen he joined the Baltimore Orioles, then in the International League, as a left-handed pitcher for six hundred dollars a year. Before the end of the season, he had been sold to the Boston Red Sox and was a Big Leaguer earning thirteen hundred dollars a year.

The Babe was a big guy now, and rougher than ever. He stood about six feet, with a big head, broad shoulders and a torso like a fat beer keg above slender, tapering legs that seemed too slight to carry his bulk. His face was broad and round under a mop of dark hair, his eyes so small as to be piggish, his nose flat and wide. With a camel's hair coat wrapped around his belly, a flat checkered cap on his head and a big cigar in his mouth, he looked like something a cartoonist had dreamed up. But in five full years with Boston, he won 113 games (including 3 straight in World Series play) and lost only 49. And in 1919 he hit the longest home run on record—587 feet —in an exhibition game, knocked out 29 more during the season and was purchased by the New York Yankees for $125,000.

The Yankees switched him to the outfield where he could play every day, and for the next ten years he was the biggest star in baseball. The home runs rolled in: 54 in 1920; 59 in 1921; and finally his record 60 in 1927. The money rolled in, too. His salary of thirty thousand dollars was boosted to the unheard-of total of fifty-two thousand a year (for playing baseball!) and finally to a breath-taking eighty thousand—in a day when taxes were low and the value of the dollar was high. In a baseball career that lasted twenty years, Ruth earned at least two million dollars and hit 729 home runs, including 15 in World Series play.

The orphan from Baltimore was rich now, but no less rough. It was as if a twelve-year-old tough kid from the slums had been turned loose on Broadway with his pockets full of money. He lived high in low places. He was a big shot and he let everybody know it. Training rules weren't made for the King of Swat. Ruth broke them all. He was a glutton. All of the privations of his bleak childhood seemed to be driving him into greater and greater excesses—big automobiles, big cigars, girls, liquor, incredible meals at which he consumed enough to keep a boy alive for a week at St. Mary's Industrial School. Nothing was too good, and very few things were good enough for the Babe. Manager Miller Huggins suspended him for breaking rules—but soon took him back.

One day, en route to training camp, he jumped off the train at a Southern railroad station and began consuming hot dogs and soda pop. Twelve hot dogs, they said later, and eight bottles of soda pop, and some people said that he sampled something stronger than soda pop. Within a few hours, his stomach-ache made headlines from coast to coast. Within a few more hours, he was in a New York hospital and very nearly dead. On the sidewalk outside, an enterprising newspaper photographer rounded up a little group of dirty-faced boys, thrust bunches of flowers into their fists and told them to gaze sorrowfully up toward the Babe's hospital window—or anyway toward somebody's hospital window. He got one of the best pictures of the year and the doctors eventually got Ruth on the road to recovery.

On another occasion, James J. Walker, then a New York state senator, in a speech to a group of baseball stars and sports writers, pleaded with Ruth to reform—to keep faith with the kids who looked up to him. Walker was a ham, but a good ham. When he finished, Ruth was weeping. Like a child who had never thought of that angle before, he got to his feet and in a deep voice choked with emotion he promised: never again! More or less, he kept his promise. "No matter how phony or drippingly sentimental the situation," Paul Gallico, sports editor of the *Daily News*, wrote later, "Ruth was always . . . honest and sincere. He, if no one else, believed in it . . . not ever for his own personal glory or to build up an elaborate false character . . . but because he believed that that was the kind of person he was."

Once, perhaps at the behest of a press agent, the Babe went to a hospital where a small boy who worshiped him was sinking after an operation. He sat on the kid's bed and talked baseball. And he said: "Son, I'm going to hit a home run for you this afternoon." Then he went out to the ball park and hit a home run. The boy, for some reason, recovered.

Nineteen twenty-nine was a year the Yankees didn't win the pennant but Ruth hit 46 home runs and batted .345. He had perhaps passed the peak. His legs were beginning to give way. But he wouldn't go down easily. In 1930, he hit 49 home runs and batted .359. In 1932, he was in his last World Series—the Yankees against the Chicago Cubs, a tough club that knew Ruth was slipping and decided to add to his troubles by "riding" him unmercifully. The Chicago crowd joined in, booing and jeering when he came to bat, screaming disdainfully when Pitcher Charley Root hurled the ball over the plate and the Babe swung mightily but missed.

Root threw a second time. Ruth's big hands swung the bat with incredible power, his big, awkward body turning gracefully with the swing, whirling him completely around and twisting his thin legs into a knot as the bat swished viciously— through the empty air. Strike two! The boos mounted to a roar of contempt as the mob figuratively closed in for the kill. Then Ruth rubbed a little dirt on his hands, raised one arm and pointed toward the flagpole in center field. Later, there would be an argument among sports writers as to what the gesture meant, but to the crowd there was only one meaning: the Babe was boasting that he'd knock the next pitch over that flagpole. The jeers rose to a crescendo. Root threw the ball and Ruth swung. The motion seemed easy, almost effortless—but there was the ball, a blur of white, sailing up and up and past the flagpole and out of the park. The Babe was a rough guy to put down.

When, in 1934, the Yankees cast him off by selling him to Boston, the management showed that it was not without a sentimental soft spot for the man, now thirty-nine years old, who had been the biggest drawing card in baseball history. The Yankees announced that Ruth's No. 3 uniform was being retired permanently and would be displayed in baseball's Hall of Fame museum at Cooperstown, New York.

Sport . . . still keeps the flag of idealism flying.
—JOHN GALSWORTHY

College football is one of the last great strongholds of genuine old-fashioned hypocrisy.
—PAUL GALLICO

SEPTEMBER, 1929

the world of sports

The Golden Decade of Sports might be said, rather inaccurately, perhaps, to have ended one breezy day in January of 1929 when a long line of men and women filed through the doors of Madison Square Garden in an eerie silence such as seldom graced that famous arena of champions. They shuffled—thirty-five thousand of them—past soft-voiced police guards, past solemn-faced men in frock coats, past a half-acre of flowers and came at last to a fifteen-thousand-dollar bronze and glass coffin in which lay the body of a baldish, thin-lipped, paunchy Texan named George L. Rickard. He had been better known as Tex Rickard, the man who made prize fighting respectable at a million dollars a fight.

"They must have him tied down in there so he can't turn," mused a sports writer who stood apart from the throng filing past the bier. "Otherwise, Tex would be spinning in that box if he could see all this crowd coming into the Garden for free."

Yet the harsh wisecrack covered a sincere regret that the famous sports promoter had been struck down by a gangrenous appendix when he was at the peak of his career and at a time when vast numbers of Americans were still eager and financially able to support the boxing racket in a style that its stars never dreamed of until the Roaring Twenties. The sports writers and the public were not likely to see again an array as exciting as the giants—some real, some papier-mâché—that Rickard had paraded through the headlines, skillfully, dramatically, tastefully and profitably. The incomparable Jack Dempsey, who could punch lethally in the role of either villain or hero; the handsome Georges Carpentier, who couldn't punch at all but was honored in ignominious defeat; the bull-like Luis Angel Firpo, who couldn't box but knocked Dempsey from the ring; the erudite Gene Tunney, who could box and punch; the popular Jack Sharkey, who won't be remembered as much of a fighter. Of these, perhaps only Dempsey and Tunney were of championship caliber but by the time Rickard got them into the boxing ring they drew more than eleven million dollars in six fights, climaxed by a record $2,658,000 gate for the second Dempsey-Tunney match.

What the New York *Herald Tribune*'s W. O. McGeehan liked to refer to as "the manly art of modified murder" had come a long way under the guidance of Tex Rickard. Boxing had moved out of the back alley and become a spectacle that, for the first time, was staged with regard for the comfort of customers and in surroundings suitable for women fans. Wrestling, too, had become respectable during the 1920's and such stars of the "grunt-and-groan" profession as Jim Londos, Stanislaus Zbyszko, Joe Stecher, Strangler Lewis and Gus Sonnenberg were putting on colorful and exciting contests on tours that carried them all over the nation. There may have been on some occasions a suspicion that the wrestlers knew in advance who was going to win, but at least customers were assured of topnotch exhibitions of the art of wrestling in contrast to faked matches of later years when inane posing, gesturing, phony fist fighting, grimacing, kicking, and hair pulling would hold tens of thousands of old ladies entranced before their television sets in towns and cities all over the nation.

With Tunney retired and Rickard dead in 1929, the boxing

business went into a coma from which it was slow to recover. About the best the heavyweight division could produce that year was Sharkey, who was booed when he won a decision from K. O. Christner, a stubby nonentity; who was boring when he won a decision from W. L. Stribling at Miami Beach before a crowd of socialites and celebrities and One-Eye Connolly, a famous gate-crasher of the day who wormed his way in free wearing a dinner jacket and a monocle. Sharkey also managed to defeat Light Heavyweight Champion Tommy Loughran, but as a candidate for the title he was a flop.

As for the other contenders: Max Schmeling, who looked like Dempsey but didn't pack the same punch, came out of Germany to defeat a character named Johnny Risko of Cleveland, and later got $72,000 for a decision over awkward Paulino Uzcudun, a Basque woodchopper. Fainting Phil Scott of Britain also was trying to get into the money. He managed to defeat a gigantic Argentinian named Victorio Mario Campolo, and later won on a foul from Norwegian Otto von Porat in Madison Square Garden, but it was hard to take him seriously.

Strangely enough, the most remarkable figure in the heavyweight world in 1929 was a wrestler from Italy. His name was Primera Carnera and he was still bigger than Campolo, bigger in fact than anybody who ever made a name in the boxing ring. It is also probable that he was dumber; and it is certain that he was one of the weirdest, most pitiable figures that ever climbed through the ropes. Happy, good-natured and harmless, Carnera stood six feet, eleven and one-half inches, weighed 280 pounds, wore a size twenty-four collar and size twenty-one shoes. He had wrestled professionally in Italy but was billed—falsely, most experts agreed—as a pugilist in the United States, under a management that became involved with some of the least reputable characters in the fight racket. It was a period, in fact, in which mobsters were moving in on the boxing business, determined to cut themselves in on the rich gate receipts even if it wrecked—as it almost did—the so-called sport.

The build-up for Carnera demonstrated the depths to which

boxing plunged. He was exhibited against a number of push-
overs in Europe, where he also fought twice with Stribling,
winning one on a foul and losing the next one on a foul. Even
an amateur could see that he was no boxer, but his freakish
size made him a good drawing card and he was later brought to
the United States to participate in a series of smelly matches.
Carnera didn't know that most of his opponents had been paid
or otherwise "persuaded" by mobsters to "take a dive" and he
tried hard. He was so clumsy and inexperienced, however, that
in an early bout in America his opponent had an extremely difficult time making it appear that he had been hit hard enough
for a "knockout" and some sports writers reported that the
vanquished warrior had, in fact, hit himself on the chin during
a mild flurry of pushing and pulling in order to live up to his
agreement to lose the bout.

But so sad was the state of boxing that in 1933 the gangsters
made Carnera champion of the world with a knockout of Jack
Sharkey, which few experts viewed with anything but suspicion.
Then, innocently believing himself a great fighter, Carnera was
forced to face challengers for the championship who couldn't
be intimidated by the mobsters. Max Baer, the first one he met,
knocked him down thirteen times in less than eleven rounds,
wrestled and rolled with him all over the ring, jeered at him
and easily relieved him of his championship belt.

2

Baseball players in 1929 wore their pants tighter and shorter
than they would a quarter-century later and they expected a
good pitcher to go nine innings—or else! "I'd hate to pitch now-
adays," Dazzy Vance, who won fourteen and lost thirteen for
Brooklyn in 1929, said after being elected to the Hall of Fame
in 1955. "What used to be a pitchers' world has been made
into a hitters' world. That lonely-looking fellow standing out
there on the little pile of dirt is not much more than a glorified
ball server now, stationed there for the convenience of a bunch

of guys gritting their teeth, waving wagon tongues, protected by a postage-stamp strike zone, wearing polo helmets and hitting for the fences to please a crowd that came to see home runs. . . . The public doesn't pay to see a two-to-one pitchers' battle any more. They pay to see the home run—the long ball, I should say, to keep in step with the new lingo—and the people who run the game are making it easier and easier for the guy who swings the bat to get his homer. . . . It sort of makes me sick. I'm glad I pitched when I did."

There must have been something in Vance's complaint. In 1929, he played in thirty-one games, faced almost a thousand batters and allowed a hundred earned runs. In thirteen games played in Brooklyn he held the opposition to three runs or less on all but five occasions. Yet in that year Vance was rated fifteenth among National League pitchers. And in that year only 754 home runs were hit in the League as compared to a total of 1,214 in 1954, an increase of about 60 per cent.

Baseball statistics, however, are something for fans to argue about, and prove practically nothing about the pitching ability of Burleigh Grimes, Charley Root, Carl Hubbell, Freddy Fitzsimmons, Lefty Grove, Eddie Rommel, Howard Ehmke and Urban Faber in 1929 as compared to later stars such as Bob Feller, Sandy Consuegra, Bobby Shantz, Eddie Lopat, Robin Roberts, Warren Spahn and Curt Simmons. In 1929, for example, the batters weren't trying to knock the ball out of the park every time they came to the plate, and as a result they hit the ball safely more often, even if they didn't knock in as many runs. Frank O'Doul, of the fifth-place Philadelphians, won the National League batting championship with a .398 average for 154 games, followed by Babe Herman of Brooklyn with .381, Rogers Hornsby of Chicago with .380 and half a dozen others who topped .350—as compared to Willie Mays's winning mark of .345 in 1954. In the American League, five players—Lew Fonseca of Cleveland, Al Simmons of Philadelphia, Henry Manush of St. Louis, Jimmy Foxx of Philadelphia and Tony

Lazzeri of New York—batted above .350 in 1929, whereas the 1954 title was won by Cleveland's Bobby Avila with a puny .341.

In 1929, however, the influence of Babe Ruth was strong and the sluggers were coming to the fore, aided by introduction of the "lively" baseball. Officials of A. G. Spalding and Brothers, makers of the baseball, insisted that the official standard had not been changed since 1920 when, apparently, a layer of rubber had been added. Most players and sports writers, however, were convinced that the ball was a "rabbit" that gave batters greater power. They pointed out that back in 1913 the famous slugger, Home Run Baker, had been able to hit only twelve balls out of the park as compared to Babe Ruth's sixty in 1927. Whatever the facts, the fans were showing increasing enthusiasm for the long ball hitters and in the future the sluggers would become more and more important to the box office.

Such famous players as Walter Johnson, Ty Cobb, Tris Speaker, and Eddie Collins reached the end of their playing days in 1929 and others—George Sisler and Grover Cleveland Alexander—would soon be through, but a flock of youngsters whose names were just beginning to be familiar were coming up: Catcher Bill Dickey and First Baseman Lou Gehrig had joined Babe Ruth in the Yankee's "murderers' row"; young Mel Ott managed to break into the Giant line-up that year; a pugnacious Yankee shortstop, Leo Durocher, was struggling to boost his batting average above .246; Chuck Klein hit forty-three home runs for Philadelphia; Ted Lyons won fourteen but lost twenty games for Chicago; and Mel Harder managed to win a single game for Cleveland.

As usual, however, it was the veteran players who stood up best when the going got rough. The Philadelphia Athletics, managed by Connie Mack, won the American League pennant with such stars as Mickey Cochrane, Lefty Grove, Jimmy Foxx and Al Simmons. In the World Series they met the Chicago Cubs—Rogers Hornsby, Hack Wilson, Kiki Cuyler—under the direction of Joe McCarthy. On a mild, sunny day in Chicago,

Howard Ehmke set a record of thirteen strike-outs and won the first game, 3 to 1, for Philadelphia. In two other games of the series, the Athletics spectacularly came from behind in the ninth inning to score ten runs on one occasion and three runs in the final game. They took the series, four games to one, and Connie Mack had tears in his eyes as he waved his score card to the cheering Philadelphia crowd at the end of the fifth game.

3

College football got away to an odd start in 1929. In the Rose Bowl at Pasadena on New Year's Day, the Golden Bears of the University of California were hosts to the Golden Tornado of Georgia Tech in a game that held the attention of fans all over the nation. The teams were evenly matched and neither could score in the opening quarter, but in the next period the Californians got a break—or so it seemed for a moment—when Tech fumbled and the ball rolled free near the Southerners' thirty-five-yard line. Roy Riegels, the center and captain-elect of the Bears, came roaring out of the scrambled mass of players, scooped up the ball and started twisting and turning to elude Tech's tacklers. On one attempt to dodge the enemy, he turned completely around and then took off at full speed toward the wrong goal line.

Tens of thousands of voices groaned, shouted warnings but the dazed Riegels merely hugged the ball closer and ran harder. Benny Lom, a speedy California halfback, gave chase, fell upon his teammate on the three-yard line after a sixty-yard run and turned him around. But it was too late. Half a dozen Tech tacklers crashed into them, driving the ball back to the one-yard marker. On the next play, Lom's attempt to punt was blocked and the ball hit a California player before rolling out of the end zone. Georgia Tech scored a two-point safety and won the game, 8 to 7.

Riegels' wrong-way run was the most talked about football incident of the year but, in the opinion of not a few old-time fans, it was merely indicative of a trend. Modern football, they

complained, was changing rapidly—and in the wrong direction.
There was too much emphasis on specialization by players.
Nobody had yet heard of the two-platoon system, but coaches
sent in substitutes so often that a man sitting in the stands,
swathed in a raccoon coat and nursing a whisky flask, couldn't
tell who was playing what position half of the time. Too many
players were softies, unable to last an entire game. Why, in the
old days a substitute never got a chance to play unless somebody broke a leg, but in 1929 it was headline news when eleven
Army players went the entire sixty minutes without a substitu-
tion against Notre Dame.

The character of the game was changing, too. It wasn't just
that forward passing had opened up play, adding new thrills
and higher scores to delight bigger crowds. But the boys also
were tossing the ball around behind the line of scrimmage in an
effort to surprise and deceive the enemy team. There were a
lot of protests from the old-timers when the rules were changed
in 1929 to encourage this revolutionary procedure by declaring
the ball dead at the point of recovery if it was fumbled to the
ground during such maneuvers. This reduced the hazards of
lateral passing by preventing a defensive player from picking
up a fumbled ball and going for a touchdown, and it opened
the way for a razzle-dazzle era of wild offensive play in which
forward, lateral and backward passing would become standard
operating procedure.

The greatest change, however, was to be found in the way
college football had become Big Business—a fifty-million-dollar-
a-year business—in America. All over the country, colleges and
universities had awakened to the realization that there was
money in the football racket; lots of money. Naturally, this fact
was not openly admitted in academic circles. College football
was an amateur sport open to undergraduates who maintained
a specified scholastic standing. Football helped build character.
The money it brought in was incidental—but interesting. All
over the country colleges were busy building big stadia in order
to cash in on the foolishness of customers who would pay four

dollars each to sit, jammed together on a narrow wooden slab, in pale sunshine, in rain, in snow and sleet to watch for a few hours the antics of twenty-two young men with a football. Some schools, according to a survey made by Francis Wallace, realized a profit of as much as half a million dollars on football in 1929.

There were, of course, certain problems. You had to have a big stadium to accommodate fifty or one hundred thousand customers and, after you had built it, you had to pay for it. To pay for it, you had to have a winning football team. By 1929 there weren't enough good football players in the normal registration at any college to constitute a winning big-time team and coaches who wanted to keep their jobs were secretly scouring the country for "amateurs" who could be persuaded— by suitable rewards—to enroll in their colleges. The scholastic ability of many of these recruits was highly doubtful, but it was usually possible to persuade the faculty that it would be better to permit the players to coast through their examinations than to have the college go bankrupt because of failure to meet payments due on the stadium bonds. As a result, a young man with strong muscles and powerful legs could make a short career of college football, meet the best people and, if he had the inclination, even acquire an education if it didn't interfere with regular practice sessions.

"The recruiting and subsidizing of American college athletes has been the darkest blot upon college sport," said a report by the Carnegie Foundation for the Advancement of Teaching in 1929, after a three year study of the problem.

Only 26 of more than one hundred universities and colleges studied were without trace of recruiting and only 29 without subsidizing. . . . Subsidies take the form of scholarships, loans, nominal or disproportionately paid jobs, tuition allowances, favors of various kinds and arrangements whereby athletes are "taken care of." It is estimated that at least one college athlete in seven is subsidized. . . . College athletics as they are conducted today definitely fail in many cases to . . . strengthen such desirable social traits as honesty and the sense of fair play because of the deceit and chicanery with which sports are surrounded.

As might have been expected, nothing much came of this condemnation, although the University of Iowa was suspended that year from the Big Ten Conference on charges of professionalism. This threatened momentarily to touch off an exposé of conditions in other colleges but the idea was so repellent to all concerned that Iowa was later returned to the brotherhood in good standing and the whole issue was forgotten. Coaches who wanted to keep their jobs went right on recruiting and subsidizing players.

The best-known coaches in 1929 were Knute Rockne of Notre Dame, Robert Zuppke of Illinois, Bill Roper of Princeton, Amos Alonzo Stagg of Chicago, Glenn S. Warner of Stanford, and Dr. J. B. Sutherland of Pittsburgh, but only Rockne and Sutherland had top-notch teams. Rockne's attitude toward the rules of intercollegiate football was interesting. He had agreed to a no-scouting arrangement prior to Notre Dame's game with Georgia Tech, but two scouts from South Bend turned up to witness an early contest involving the Georgia team. Informed of this flagrant violation of the agreement, Rockne cleared up everything by saying that he would forget all that the scouts had told him about Tech's team. Notre Dame then knocked off the Southerners by a score of 26 to 6, with lightning-fast Jack Elder, Fullback Joe Savoldi and triple-threat Frank Carideo leading the attack.

In the Ivy League, fleet, little Albie Booth led Yale to a good year until Harvard beat them, 10 to 6, and in the Middle West big, bruising Bronco Nagurski ended his career with two winning touchdowns for Minnesota against Wisconsin. In the Far West, there was a four-way tie for the championship of the Pacific Coast Conference. But in the view of most sports writers, Notre Dame, Pittsburgh and Purdue, which took the Big Ten title, were the strongest teams in the country, and the late November meeting of Rockne's team with Army in Yankee Stadium was probably the outstanding encounter of the year.

Army had not had a good year and had not played Navy because of a dispute over eligibility rules that was raging bitterly
between the high brass hats of both services in Washington.
But when the Cadets took the field before eighty-three thousand spectators in New York they were in top form for Notre
Dame. Throughout the first period they pushed the Irish back
and, early in the second quarter, their star, Chris Cagle,
cocked his arm and tossed a pass to the goal line. At the last
second, Notre Dame's Jack Elder intercepted on the two-yard
line and ran ninety-eight yards for the only touchdown of the
game. This was a crushing blow to Army fans and especially
to Sportswriter Grantland Rice of the New York *Herald
Tribune*, whose story of the game—in the florid style of the day
—began: "The better team lost. The olive wreath that might
have gone to the Army at Yankee Stadium Saturday was turned
into a crown of poisoned thorns by Jack Elder, Notre Dame
halfback." Anyway, the record books would show that on a
bitterly cold day in November, Notre Dame defeated Army,
7 to 0, and ended the season without a loss. Rockne was a fellow
who liked to win.

4

By 1929 the experts were inclined to believe that men had
about reached a permanent peak in demonstrations of human
speed, agility, strength and endurance. Charles W. Paddock,
the "fastest human," had run a hundred yards in nine and six-
tenths seconds on six different occasions and, while the record
had been tied, it seemed unlikely that it would ever be broken
after Paddock retired in 1927. J. E. Meredith's mark of forty-
seven and four-tenths seconds for a quarter-mile had been on
the books for a dozen years and Dr. Otto Peltzer of Germany
had run a half mile in the amazing time of one minute, fifty-one
and six-tenths seconds in 1926. But the most remarkable record-
breaker of the Twenties may have been the Finnish runner,
Paavo Nurmi, who carried a stop watch in his hand in order to
maintain a steady pace through each quarter and who ran all

competitors into the ground with clocklike efficiency when he toured the United States. Nurmi lowered the record for a mile to four minutes, ten and four-tenths seconds.

It seemed unlikely that men could ever do much, if any, better. One sports writer, discussing the possibility of still better marks in the future, daringly predicted that in the next fifty years somebody might run a mile in four minutes and three seconds but he acknowledged that track coaches probably would laugh at his prediction as a "physical and technical impossibility." In the next twenty-five years, however, every world record for track and field events was broken and no less than three men ran the mile in under four minutes.

Improved techniques, bigger and stronger athletes, better methods of training, and better equipment all helped wash out the records that in 1929 had seemed close to superhuman achievements on the field of sport. A few comparative records illustrate the story:

1929 Records		1954 Records	
100 Yards—Paddock and others	9.6	Melvin Patton	9.3
440 Yards—J. E. Meredith	47.4	Herb McKenley	46.
880 Yards—Otto Peltzer	1.51.6	Mal Whitfield	1.48.6
Mile—Paavo Nurmi	4.10.4	John Landy	3.58
5,000 Meters—Paavo Nurmi	14.28.2	Emil Zatopek	13.57.2
High Jump—H. M. Osborn	6 ft., 8¼ in.	Walt Davis	6 ft., 11½ in.
Broad Jump—DeHart Hubbard	25 ft., 10⅞ in.	Jesse Owens	26 ft., 8¼ in.
Pole Vault—Sabin Carr	14 ft.	C. Warmerdam	15 ft., 7¾ in.
Shot Put—John Kuck	52 ft., ¾ in.	Parry O'Brien	59 ft., 2¼ in.

5

The most important development in the sports field at the end of the 1920's may have been the growth of interest in golf and tennis, with increasing participation by women players. Americans had more leisure time than ever before and in the future they would have even greater leisure and the boom in participation sports would become phenomenal. Gray-haired Gar Wood was creating new interest in speed boating and some four hundred thousand persons, including a lot of potential customers, lined the banks of the Detroit River to watch his new *Miss America VIII* set a record of seventy-five miles an hour in winning the Harmsworth Trophy. In Michigan, Chris Smith and his four sons were turning out Chris-Craft boats by the carload for fishermen and water speedsters and a quarter-century later the roar of little speedboats—usually piloted by teen-agers—would make many popular lake and river resorts as noisy as Times Square at the height of a traffic jam.

In tennis, popular interest was intensified by two famous stars of the court, Big Bill Tilden and Helen Wills. Tilden had passed the peak of his career after having won the national singles title half a dozen times but he managed to stagger through to his last triumph in 1929, probably due to the fact that the French stars, René LaCoste and Henri Cochet, who had defeated him previously, were not entered again. G. M. Lott, Jr., and John H. Doeg won the doubles title. Doeg, a young left-hander, had given Tilden a scare in the singles semi-finals, taking two sets of three before the veteran rallied to win. At Wimbledon that year, Tilden lost to Cochet, who won the title, and England's Bunny Austin was defeated by Jean Borotra of France.

Miss Wills, who had come from California as a pig-tailed, poker-faced teen-ager in the early Twenties, lost the final match of the 1922 tournament to Mrs. F. I. Mallory, who had long reigned as women's singles champion. But the next year Miss Wills came back to take the title, which she held except for one year until 1930. In all, Miss Wills won the national title seven times, the English title six times and the French title four times, without losing a set until the final round at Wimbledon in 1933. Miss Wills, who hit a tennis ball almost as hard as a man, made the white eyeshade a national fad for women tennis players, convinced most sports writers that she was a spoiled young lady, convinced most women tennis players that they didn't belong on the same court with the champion, was presented to the Queen of England and retired while still near the top of her game. There was almost nothing that Miss Wills couldn't achieve on the tennis court—except the defeat of Suzanne

Lenglen of France. The great Lenglen, fortified with a little cognac and sugar, took two sets from the American champion in a special match in 1926 and then, undefeated as an amateur, turned professional.

Golf was steadily gaining in popularity throughout the Twenties and Maureen Orcutt, Glenna Collett and young Helen Hicks were as well known on the links as was Miss Wills on the tennis court. Gene Sarazen, Francis Ouimet, Tommy Armour, Al Espinosa and Walter Hagen, who gave the Prince of Wales a couple of lessons during a visit to England, were outstanding players, but they usually had to take off their caps to a rugged Georgian named Robert Tyre Jones. Bobby Jones had twice won the National Open and four times had taken the National Amateur, but he had a rough year in 1929. In the final round of the National Open at Mamaroneck, New York, he needed only a routine 80 to beat the 294 already scored by leader Al Espinosa. But he took seven strokes on each of two par-four holes and managed to gain a tie only by sinking a long putt on the eighteenth green. In the play-off he easily defeated Espinosa but a jinx seemed to be hovering over him from time to time. At Mamaroneck, his blue golf bag containing thirteen clubs was stolen and for a while he thought his famous putter —a smooth-faced, goose-necked blade that he called Calamity Jane—was gone forever. The clubs eventually were recovered from three young boys but the next time Jones played a round in Atlanta a storm forced him to run for the clubhouse, where lightning hit the chimney and showered him with bricks that pierced his blue plaid umbrella and bruised his shoulder. Then, in September, the worst blow of all. A kid from Nebraska, John Goodman, who often bummed his way to tournaments by riding freight cars, knocked Jones out of the National Amateur tournament in the first round. Another youngster, Lawson Little, Jr., defeated Goodman the next day but the title was won by Jimmy Johnston, a St. Paul broker.

Jones, however, wasn't seriously discouraged. The next year

he shook off the jinx and became the only player ever to make a "grand slam" by winning the four major golf championships— the American Amateur and Open tournaments and the British Amateur and Open tournaments—in a single year.

...*am I drunk, Doc, or do I hear music in the air?*...

Nineteen twenty-nine was a wondrous year for Americans . . . for Lee De Forest, a rugged, balding man with shaggy eyebrows, who had been busy trying to do the impossible ever since he designed a perpetual motion machine at the age of thirteen. Son of a Congregational minister and descendant of Pilgrim John Alden, De Forest was born in Council Bluffs, Iowa, in 1873 but grew up in Alabama, where his father became head of Talladega College, a Negro institution.

Young Lee wrote poetry, read the Bible and the classics and exercised his imagination in a manner that kept him in a muddle of controversy for most of his life. "Sketched my airship invention and wired magnet for my induction coil," he noted in his diary in 1891 after going to Massachusetts to attend prep school. "I stick to a thing like a seed-tick." At Sheffield School of Engineering at Yale, he waited on tables. He also invented an improved type-bar movement for his typewriter, a puzzle game and a boiler-condenser device that reused exhaust steam instead of cold water. This was promptly declared impossible by Professor Charles Hastings, who had Lee barred from making further experiments in the Yale laboratory, but later the method became universal practice. Lee's essay on "Aerial Navigation" was thrown out of a Yale contest, but forty years later it was published in the *Yale Scientific Magazine.*

Young De Forest had trouble finding the right job after graduation, but he kept busy. He invented a chainless bicycle and began work on a telephone relay that was later successful. Finally, the Chicago laboratory of Western Electric Company offered him a job at ten dollars a week. Wireless was a great new field and it fascinated De Forest, whose imagination easily leaped ahead into the Electronic Age. He moved from job to job, from laboratory to laboratory, learning all there was to know about wireless. In 1901 from a high tower at Chicago, a year after Marconi had sent a wireless signal across the English Channel, De Forest communicated by wireless with a moving yacht as it disappeared over the horizon. Abraham White helped him organize the American De Forest Wireless Telegraph Company with a broadcasting station on Staten Island, but the inventor was still earning only thirty dollars a week. In 1902, he exchanged messages at forty words a minute (Marconi's system did only fifteen words a minute) with the S.S. *Deutschland,* a hundred miles from New York, but by then Marconi had demonstrated that signals could be sent across the Atlantic from England to Newfoundland.

In 1906, De Forest developed the audion, a small instrument of glass and bent wire which—avoiding technicalities—was a better wireless detector than anything previously invented and which became basic in radio broadcasting, television, long-distance telephony, talking motion pictures, aerial navigation and many other electronic fields. In other words, the audion was to revolutionize modern communications. But revolutions are seldom completed overnight. De Forest's company, looted by stock gamblers behind his back, went broke. He lost virtually everything except a small laboratory and a broadcasting station in New York where he continued his experiments in broadcasting music, using a carbon arc generator. A Navy Yard wireless operator in Brooklyn heard music through his earphones one day and excitedly called in his Chief. The Chief heard it, too, and telephoned De Forest.

"Am I drunk, Doc, or do I hear music in the air?" he demanded. "Are you sending out talk and music over that wireless of yours?"

Doc De Forest assured him that he was hearing music.

The vast industries that would one day grow up from electronics experiments such as De Forest was making were little more than a dream in the first decade of the century. Furthermore, De Forest was no businessman. The field was one of intense rivalries, of controversy, of charges and countercharges, of slick financial deals as different companies struggled for control. In 1908, De Forest's laboratory burned and he suffered a great loss of records and equipment. He set up the De Forest Radio Telephone Company, which prospered briefly and then went forty thousand dollars in the red. The company was reorganized but in 1911, De Forest was arrested on charges of fraudulent company statements in regard to the audion tube, which the prosecution described as a useless gadget. The inventor also was charged with making false claims that people would soon be able to talk across the Atlantic Ocean. Yale classmates raised money for the defense and De Forest was acquitted.

Broke, he took a job with the Federal Telegraph Company in California, where he developed a magnetized steel wire recorder which could be slowed up for transcribing by a stenographer. Trying to raise money he sold seven inventions for fifty thousand dollars to a man who, it developed later, was an agent for the American Telephone and Telegraph Company. De Forest claimed he was "shamefully tricked" and that the rights later earned the company more than three billion dollars. In 1920 he was broadcasting again in New York—there were few receiving sets in existence then—but was closed down on a technicality by a federal inspector who said that "there is no room on the ether for entertainment." He started up again in California, making radio tubes. A year later his factory burned.

In July of 1921, he wrote in his diary: "Today made my first talking movie—of myself." Two years later he showed a talking picture (sound on film) at the Rivoli Theater in New York, with Eddie Cantor doing a monologue and a song, and Lillian Powell doing a bubble dance. Hollywood wasn't interested in such "crackpot ideas." De Forest turned out a number of talking shorts for thirty-four theaters that were wired for sound in 1925 but when he tried to sell stock in his company to the public, New York state officials charged him with fraud. "The public," one official announced, "doesn't want talking films."

In 1929, when the public was clamoring for talking films, De Forest was fifty-six years old. Behind him were enough inventions, controversies, fortunes made and lost for half a dozen careers, but he was only well warmed up. He was producing three types of audion tubes which manufacturers of radio receiving sets were buying in huge quantities. Sales were more than eight million dollars that year and the U.S. Navy gave him a million-dollar contract for tube transmitters. He won a three-million-dollar damage suit against R.C.A. (which later bought his company) on charges that they were illegally trying to squeeze him out of business by monopolistic practices. He was working on television. He patented half a dozen new processes for talking movies and sold the Wurlitzer Corporation an audion application to musical instruments—the forerunner of the "juke box."

And now the Electronic Era was wide-open: radar, light-controlled proximity fuses for bombs, self-directed missiles, aircraft speed and course indicators and the great television industry. De Forest's method for electronic scanning with cathode beam tube was patented in 1949 as a tremendous forward step in television, and in the 1950's he was still beating a path to the door of the U.S. Patent Office with new ideas and refinements of old ideas. On his eighty-second birthday he was working part time for the Bell Telephone laboratories at Los Angeles and part time for the American Television laboratories in Chicago—and nonchalantly predicting that men would soon send rocket ships to the moon.

In thousands of years, there has been no advance in public morals, in philosophy, religion or politics, but the advance in business has been the greatest miracle the world has ever known.

—ED HOWE

The business of America is business.

—CALVIN COOLIDGE

OCTOBER, 1929

big business

The American market place was never so busy, never so exuberant as in 1929 and men who were interested in Big Business were never more confident—with a few exceptions. Two of the exceptions were Chicagoans. One was a seventy-year-old English-born financier named Samuel Insull, a coldly arrogant man with white hair and a neatly clipped white mustache, an admirer of opera singer Mary Garden, the builder of a twenty-million-dollar opera house and office building and the czar of a public utilities empire that stretched from Lake Michigan to Texas. The other was a tall, shaggy college professor named Paul Howard Douglas, a Quaker from the state of Maine, who knew practically everything about the economy of the United States but, unlike Insull, owned only one pair of good pants.

The only link between Insull and Douglas was that both were experts, in theory at least, on a complex corporate structure known as the "holding company" system, which was an important factor in American business in 1929. The holding company system apparently began about 1890 in New Jersey, when the state fattened its treasury by passing a law that permitted companies incorporated there to buy and hold stock of other corporations. The idea quickly spread to other states. Thus "a new era of American capitalism began," Frederick Lewis Allen noted in *The Big Change.*

For now a group of competing companies no longer needed to form a trust in order to combine themselves into a giant concern which would command the market and choke off competition. They could organize a new corporation, a holding company, which would buy the stock of their various companies—or, more strictly, exchange its shares for theirs—and this holding company would thereupon control the operations of all of them.

In the 1920's, the holding company system was flourishing and there had grown up an intricate system of interlocking directorates that sometimes enabled corporation executives to do some remarkable juggling of funds behind the scenes. To take a simple but rather unusual example, the Continental Trading Company had been organized by Oilman Harry Sinclair, James O'Neil, president of the Prairie Gas and Oil Company (a Rockefeller concern) and Colonel Robert W. Stewart, chairman of Standard Oil of Indiana (also a Rockefeller concern). The Continental Company made a deal with Colonel A. E. Humphrey of the Mexia Texas oil fields, to buy 33,333,-333⅓ barrels of oil at $1.50 a barrel. This oil was then resold to Standard Oil and to the Sinclair Consolidated Oil Company at $1.75 a barrel, with the organizers of Continental set to realize a profit of about eight million dollars. As a matter of fact, they made only about three million profit and, in the end, didn't keep much of that because some of the profits were turned over by Sinclair to Albert B. Fall, the Secretary of Interior, and became involved in the Teapot Dome Oil scandal. Thus it was a United States Senate investigation that made the Continental deal public.[1]

---

[1] After a Senate committee had disclosed the deal, John D. Rockefeller, Jr., suggested in 1929 that Colonel Stewart resign the chairmanship of Standard Oil of Indiana, but the Colonel declined the suggestion. Stewart and Rockefeller then engaged in a battle for proxies prior to the next meeting of the fifty-

Samuel Insull had been twenty-one years old when he came from England to the United States and became secretary to Thomas A. Edison. He rose rapidly in the great utilities industry that grew out of Edison's discoveries and by 1904 Insull's Chicago Edison Company was unrivaled in the city. Soon afterward, he gained control of the Chicago transit system. He merged Commonwealth Edison with Chicago Edison. He created Middle West Utilities. He brought in the People's Gas and Coke Company. Other mergers extended his utilities control throughout the state and then expanded it into a Middle Western network of interlocking concerns. He even bought textile mills in New England. By 1929, he was sitting at the top of a corporate pyramid that included more than three hundred steam plants and some two hundred hydroelectric generating plants, which served almost two million customers. Several hundred thousand persons had invested money—often the savings of a lifetime—in his enterprises, confident that an Insull company was no less solid than bonds of the United States. His corporation's assets totaled two and a half billion dollars.

Insull himself was an unusual figure. He isolated himself from the public, spending much of his time in a handsome penthouse overlooking the Chicago river front or on an estate of forty-two hundred acres, valued at close to a million dollars. On the farm, incidentally, everything was done by electricity— the feeding, the watering of stock, the milking of his prize herd of cows, the shearing of his prize flock of sheep. The farm buildings were heated by electricity so that the animals enjoyed an unchanging temperature in all seasons. In some ways,

---

eight thousand stockholders of Standard of Indiana. "If the Rockefellers want a fight," Stewart, a burly 240-pounder standing six feet tall, said, "I'll show them how to fight." As it turned out, Rockefeller, standing five feet ten inches in his stocking feet and weighing 170 pounds, was ready for a fight. Although he was a minority stockholder in Standard of Indiana and actually departed on a trip to Egypt while Stewart was busy trying to line up votes, his representatives gathered two proxy votes for every one that Stewart could capture and in March the annual stockholders convention elected a new chairman. Stewart, whose salary had been $125,000 a year, was obliged to retire on a life pension of $75,000 a year.

Insull represented the backbone of Big Business in the farming states and his word carried more weight at many banks than the word of anybody except the Secretary of Treasury.

But in 1929, Insull was in trouble. There were hidden weaknesses in his complex empire. He had overexpanded. He was hard and often merciless in business deals and had many enemies. And now they had begun striking back at him by buying up large blocks of stock in his corporations, wresting control from his hands and forcing him to buy back at exorbitant prices. For many reasons he had to manipulate his finances and shift his funds from corporation to corporation to hold the line. His reserves were depleted, but he needed still more money. He drained it from Chicago banks. He turned thirty thousand employees into stock salesmen who urged Middle Westerners to pour more and more of their savings into Insull concerns. Many of them did, and Insull stayed atop his rotted empire.

About this time the Insull operations attracted the attention of thirty-seven-year-old Professor Douglas, a rugged extrovert who liked to swim a few miles along the coast of Lake Michigan whenever he could get away from the rarefied atmosphere of his economics classes at Chicago University. Douglas had won academic fame by writing scholarly books with titles such as *Real Wages in the United States, 1890–1926*. His idea of relaxation was to spend an evening curled up with a copy of the Federal Budget, which he could read and absorb at lightning speed. One book reviewer remarked that in his writings on economics Douglas was so high up in the academic stratosphere that he gave "a feeling of the calm detachment of one making an aerial survey of a piece of ground that was once a battlefield."

But in the late Twenties, the Cook County Real Estate Board had become interested in the affairs of Samuel Insull and now the board asked Douglas to descend from the clouds and take a look at what was going on in the workaday world of utilities financing. Douglas accepted the invitation to investigate the Insull empire. It is doubtful that anybody could have been more blissfully ignorant of what he was getting into; that anybody could have known less about the ramifications of the Chicago political, gangster and financial alliance into which he was sticking his nose. When, as his study progressed, he began suggesting that there was something wrong with the Insull corporate structure, he was abused by almost everybody. Businessmen complained that he was a radical. Politicians tried to get him fired from the University. Gangsters muttered that the "perfesser" was talking too much about the political-racketeer alliance that held Chicago in its grip. Stockholders in Insull companies screamed that he was trying to rock the boat. State and city officials ignored his proposals for official action.

One day when Douglas had to make a trip to the state capital to argue against a new Insull bond issue, he discovered that his only good pair of pants was at the cleaner's shop and that the shop was closed. Hurriedly, he searched the neighborhood until he found the cleaner's home, persuaded him to open his shop and finally climbed into his good pants in time to catch the train to Springfield, where—as usual—his argument against Insull was impatiently turned aside. But the train ride gave him a chance for reflection. "Oh, what a fool you are, Douglas," he said to himself. "Only one good pair of pants to your name and here you are trying to fight the whole Insull empire!"

Yet the duel between the professor and the old utilities czar was significant. Insull represented the old order at its worst when he sat at the top of the corporate pyramid. Douglas spoke for reform in the interest of investors and of the public, and it would not be long before Congress acted to outlaw such corporate monstrosities as grew out of the holding company system. Douglas' fight, futile as it seemed at the time, was a symbol of the beginning of the end of many financial shenanigans carried on in the name of Big Business. Soon the Insull empire would come tumbling down in a wild flutter of worthless stock certificates, wrecking banks, wiping out the savings of thousands of persons and bringing some remarkable changes in the lives of both Insull and Douglas.

The utilities magnate fled to Europe, was indicted and returned in 1932 for trial. But he had not lost his cunning. In the hands of an astute press agent, the coldly arrogant financier was transformed into an old white-haired man who had spent his life and his fortune trying to benefit the Midwest, who was practically penniless, who rode the public busses instead of being driven in a limousine, who smiled sweetly at children and photographers and who, when it came to a showdown in the courtroom, easily won vindication by a jury of his peers.

Still more remarkable was the change in the professor. Having once rubbed elbows with public officeholders, racketeers and ward heelers, Douglas never went back to his ivory tower. He ran for a job on the City Council, was elected and loved it. When World War II came along he had enough political pull to be admitted to the United States Marine Corps as a private at the age of fifty. Severely wounded in battle in the South Pacific, he came home to recover and to be elected in 1948 to a seat in the United States Senate.

2

In 1929, Big Business was getting bigger in all parts of the United States, and spreading out to areas where there had been little or no industry in the past. In Los Angeles, for instance, civic boosters counted 125 new factories in the city and near-by areas. California's output of manufactured goods that year rose above three billion dollars, an increase of 51 per cent in ten years as compared to 13.5 per cent for the nation as a whole. Industrial construction throughout the nation mounted more than 18 per cent over 1928 and was at a near-record total of almost a billion dollars for the year.

Furthermore, mass production was bringing prices down for not a few manufactured products. In the spread-eagled automobile field, for example, there were so many companies competing for sales that the buyer had a hard time making up his mind no matter how much or how little he was prepared to pay. In the lowest price field, a snappy little Whippet runabout cost $595, a Ford cost $625, a Plymouth $655, a Chevrolet $675 and a Durant $695. Going up a step, the Dodge sold for $845, the Pontiac $745, the DeSoto $845, the Olds $925, the Erskine $945, the Jordan $1,395, the Reo $1,395, the Buick $1,320, the Moon $1,345—and there were a dozen other six-cylinder automobiles in the same price range, some of them roadsters with an uncomfortable contrivance called a "rumble seat" stuck on behind. Of fifteen other models in a somewhat higher price category, the sporty Marmon could be bought for $1,465, the Elcar for $2,465, the Gardner for $2,395 and the Franklin for $2,980. But if the buyer could find nothing to his taste among these, he could wander on into a still loftier price range where he could choose from thirty-four different offerings. These included the Kissel at $3,785, the racy Stutz at $3,570, the Chrysler Imperial at $2,875, the LaSalle at $2,420, the Cadillac at $3,295, the Lincoln at $4,800, the Stearns-Knight at $5,500, the Pierce Arrow at $5,875 and that remarkable machine known as a Locomobile at $12,500—to name a few.

The automobile industry, with its many rival companies, was just beginning to conform with the general trend of business and banking toward mergers and consolidations that meant bigger and bigger corporations. Economists preached "the advantages of administered prices, controlled by wise business-men," Thurman Arnold, later in charge of the Anti-Trust Division of the Department of Justice, wrote.

The idea that industry must be planned by a hierarchy of corporate executives was accepted by the American people. They cheerfully bought stock in bigger and bigger mergers, and happily watched that stock rise. Men began to dream of a new world order in which both panics and wars could be eliminated. Panics would be impossible because all industry was regulated by sound banking houses, which would come to the rescue when danger threatened. Wars would be impossible because international business, which had everything to lose and nothing to gain by war, would prevent any powerful and civilized nation from aggression. Uncivilized nations which bankers did not dominate were too weak to count.

In the first eight months of 1929, investors put up more than seventeen million dollars a day to finance the birth and growth of industry in the United States—or over six billion dollars a year. Security corporations, better known as "investment trusts," absorbed the largest slice of this money—$1,494,000,000 —but public utilities came in for $777,191,000, oil for $220,599,-000 and aviation plants for $158,741,000. One so-called "investor" was Cyrus S. Eaton, a native of Pugwash, Nova Scotia, and a resident of Cleveland, Ohio. Eaton united the Republic Iron and Steel Company, Central Alloy Steel Corporation, Donner Steel Company, Inc., Bourne-Fuller Company, Trumbull Cliffs Furnace Company and their subsidiaries to form the Republic Steel Company, with assets of $350,000,000 and an ingot capacity of five million tons. Only United States Steel with twenty million tons and Bethlehem with eight million tons were larger. Eaton, who had started out to be a minister but got sidetracked into public utilities, remarked that he knew nothing about steel and that he was "only an investor." The nation's steel production that year topped 56,400,000 tons, which was more than the combined production of the rest of the world and a highly respectable figure in comparison to the American peak of 105,199,000 tons in 1951.

An indication of the "bigness" of American corporations was provided by figures released in 1929 on earnings for the past year. General Motors reported earnings of $276,468,000; American Telephone and Telegraph $143,170,000; U.S. Steel $113,-999,000. And for the first half of 1929 almost all of these corporations were earning still more—U.S. Steel, for example, was more than five million ahead of its 1928 record. Kroger Grocery and Baking Company, which controlled the Piggly Wiggly Corporation, reported a net profit for the first six months of 1929 of $4,015,000 as compared to $2,538,000 in 1928; Westinghouse

Electric and Manufacturing Company was up from $7,792,000 to $13,131,000.

The nation's banks were merging and expanding, too, and the shares of Manhattan's First National Bank shot up twelve hundred points in two days to $7,300 a share. Experts figured that the rise meant a gain of more than two million dollars to George F. Baker, chairman of the board, who was believed to hold some two thousand shares. The New York Corn Exchange Bank and Trust Company and the National City Bank announced plans for a merger that would give this nation the biggest bank in the world with total resources of $2,386 million —surpassing the $2,303 million resources of the Midland Bank, Ltd., of England. But due to unforeseen circumstances the deal was later canceled. In California, Amadeo Peter Giannini had secured control of Bank of America and was busy forming the $400-million Bankitaly Company of America. William Henry Crocker, only son of a founder of the Southern Pacific Railway, attempted to merge his First National Bank, his First Federal Trust Company and the American Trust Company into a $400-million institution rivaling Giannini, but had to abandon the plan. In Detroit, merger of the People's Wayne County Bank, the First National Bank of Detroit, the Peninsular State Bank, the Detroit Security and Trust Company and the Bank of Michigan formed the largest institution between New York and Chicago, with resources of $725 million. (In 1933 this merger was dissolved.) In Minnesota, North and South Dakota and Montana, thirty-seven banks were united in a chain headed by the First National Banks of St. Paul and Minneapolis, and given the name of First Bank Stock Corporation.

Some experts viewed the nation's "merger mania" with misgivings [2] and others were critical of the trend toward branch

---

[2] In the industrial field alone, there were some twelve hundred mergers in 1929. The number of mergers was greatly reduced in the 1930's but rose again to more than four hundred in 1946. Mergers in 1954 totaled 387. Foremost Dairies, Inc., for example, acquired no less than forty-eight other corporations between 1948 and 1954.

banking. When the American Bankers Association met in convention, the speech of John W. Pole, Comptroller of the Currency, was tensely awaited as an indication of the views of the administration and particularly of Secretary of Treasury Andrew Mellon. But Pole had nothing unfavorable to say about the trend, asserting that 20 per cent of all banking offices were branch banks and that the thing for Congress to take up was not whether but how far banking houses should be permitted to go in this direction. The merger mania was unchecked.

3

One day late in September of 1929, a pugnacious little man in a leather jacket climbed into a two-seater Consolidated biplane at Mitchel Field on Long Island and pulled a voluminous opaque cloth over his head. He was in an angry mood, having just lost an argument with Henry F. Guggenheim, an aviation enthusiast and president of the Guggenheim Fund. The little man was thirty-three-year-old Lieutenant James H. Doolittle, who was probably the Army Air Corp's best flier and who literally flew the wings off a plane diving at two hundred miles an hour at the Cleveland Air Show and had to take to his parachute. Doolittle's irritation arose from the fact that Guggenheim had refused to let him take the biplane aloft without a copilot. This might have seemed like quibbling on the part of Guggenheim except for one thing—Doolittle was undertaking the first "blind" flight ever made. Under his opaque cloth he couldn't see anything except the instrument panel in the cockpit, but the copilot that Guggenheim made him take along could see everything and, if necessary, he could take over the dual controls to avoid a crash.

As it turned out, the copilot sat with folded arms throughout the flight. Flying blind, Doolittle lifted the plane from the runway, flew for fourteen miles in a big cricle and then brought the little craft back to a perfect three-point landing on Mitchell Field without ever getting a glimpse of the sky or the earth.

It was one of the most important flights in aviation history for a number of reasons. For one thing, it preserved the life of James H. Doolittle, who would go onward and upward to be one of the inspirational figures of World War II—a daring general in Europe and North Africa and a resourceful leader in the historic and supposedly impossible first American aerial attack on Tokyo. But most important, of course, Doolittle's blind flight demonstrated that aviation had come of age. Until that day aviators could not cope with fog or darkness. A pilot who could not see the horizon was likely to be lost. Radar was still a long way off, but Doolittle's plane carried three new instruments—a visual radio direction finder that permitted him to keep on a direct path toward a radio beacon at Mitchell Field, an artificial horizon that showed whether his craft was flying level or tilted and a barometric altimeter that showed how high he was above the ground. Lindbergh's flight to Paris had made the nation air-minded and the manufacture of airplanes in the United States jumped from two thousand in 1927 to more than five thousand in 1929. Now Doolittle had demonstrated that airplanes of the future could fly on schedule, at night, through fog or rain, under almost any weather conditions. Another giant industry was being added to the American economy and it gave impetus to the business boom.

Aviation news was in the headlines almost every day during the year. The Guggenheims, the Rockefellers, Dwight W. Morrow, Harold S. Vanderbilt, Otto H. Kahn, Jacob Schiff and others showed their confidence in the future of flying machines by devoting large sums to finance research in commercial flying. A fleet of new seaplanes opened an aerial route to Buenos Aires, with a government subsidy for mail. The ships were made of the new light duraluminum metal, had hundred-foot "parasol" wings and carried forty-eight passengers in luxurious lounges and compartments decorated in "modernistic style."

General Motors and E. I. du Pont de Nemours and Company put up three-quarters of a million dollars as the first step in building an experimental "steel island" midway between the United States and Bermuda as the first of a series of seadromes on which airplanes could land en route across the Atlantic. The plan, later abandoned, was to build floating islands with runways twelve hundred feet long, hangars, storage facilities and a hotel with restaurant and bar for weary travelers.

From Lake Constance, in Switzerland, the twelve-motored German airplane Dornier DO-X lifted a record load of 170 passengers and flew above the lake for a hundred miles. From Little America in the Antarctic, Commander Richard E. Byrd and Pilot Bernt Balchen flew sixteen hundred miles to the South Pole, where they dropped the American flag, and returned to their base. At St. Louis, Dale Jackson and Forest O'Brine landed their airplane after setting an endurance record of 420 hours, 21 minutes and 30 seconds in the air, winning a prize of $31,225 and gifts of $2,756. Flying over the Mexican territory of Quintana Roo, Charles A. Lindbergh made Ameriica's first archaeological discovery from the air—a Mayan temple which had been hidden for centuries in the jungle. In New York, a special airplane service offered to fly football enthusiasts to New Haven in forty-five minutes for the Harvard–Yale game at a fare of twenty-five dollars each.

A hint of the future importance of regular aviation schedules came from California's Transamerica Corporation, the big Giannini holding company which had just declared a stock dividend. It was customary on the New York Stock Exchange at that time to allow the seller of a stock seven days to deliver the certificates, which was time enough to send certificates by train from the West Coast to New York. This was known as the "Seller Seven" formula and it was important because it meant a seven-day allowance for payment for the stock. But the holders of the new Transamerica certificates were in a hurry to add to the flames of speculation on the New York Exchange and the securities were jammed into thirty mail bags, turned over to the U.S. Postal Service and sent by airmail from San Francisco to New York in less than three days. Thus the transaction could be completed more quickly and "Seller Seven" was changed to

"Seller Three" in keeping with the times. In Mexico fresh shrimp were loaded into a refrigerated airplane for the first time for shipment to Los Angeles.

But in 1929 the speed of air travel was just beginning to be realized. Over the English Channel, before the eyes of a million spectators, including the Prince of Wales, a lanky Englishman named R. L. R. Atcherley crouched over the controls of a little supermarine Rolls-Royce seaplane that flew a mile in 10.83 seconds—a record-smashing 332.49 miles per hour. In view of the fact that at that time even under the most favorable circumstances the fastest automobile required 15.56 seconds to go a mile, the fastest motorcycle 32.53 seconds, the fastest racing boat 38.07 seconds and the fastest horse (Roamer in 1918) 1 minute and 34.80 seconds, it was easy to see that in the future anybody in a hurry was likely to travel by airplane. But it took a great deal of imagination in 1929 to believe that within twenty-five years regularly scheduled airplanes carrying passengers would greatly exceed Atcherley's record over long distances and that men would fly rocket-like planes at approximately fifteen hundred miles an hour or about a mile every two and one-half seconds.

There were, of course, some men with a great deal of imagination. One of them was young Fritz von Opel of Germany, whose family had just sold its automobile plants to General Motors, which was fighting Henry Ford for supremacy in foreign markets. Von Opel had been experimenting for several years with rocket-driven automobiles but in 1929 he shifted to rocket airplanes and blasted off from an airfield near Hamburg. Spurting fire, the craft rose to an altitude of fifty feet, flew for seventy-five seconds and made a crash landing from which Von Opel emerged, smiling and excited.

"I can scarcely grasp my joy!" he exclaimed. "The time will soon come when planes will travel five thousand miles an hour and circle the earth in five hours. That will amalgamate all the peoples of the globe into one."

4

Two key figures in the business boom of 1929 were the Advertising Expert and the High Pressure Salesman. The whole concept of advertising had changed during the Twenties and by the end of the decade there seemed to be less emphasis on the quality of a product and much more emphasis on the contention that a product would make the buyer more popular or more efficient or more healthy or more wealthy.

"Overpaid at $100 a week . . . yet he should be earning $10,000," was the headline over an advertisement for the Alexander Hamilton Institute, which provided executive training for businessmen by correspondence. The North American Institute, which offered correspondence courses in public speaking, featured the heading: "They snickered when I got up to speak —but from the first word I held them spellbound." Ipana tooth paste advertisements warned against "pink tooth brush—an SOS from your gums." A cigarette company advised everybody that the way to overcome an embarrassing moment was to "be nonchalant—light a Murad." General Motors Corporation advertised "Body by Fisher" with paintings of exquisite and desirable women rather than paintings of the automobiles designed by Fisher. Full-page advertisements for Listerine introduced a new and repugnant word to the public by advising unpopular young men and women that their trouble might be halitosis or bad breath, and Life Buoy soap advised the same unhappy young men and women that they might be suffering from B.O., which was short for "body odor."

But perhaps the most popular advertising device of the day was the "society leader" or "famous personage" testimonial in which the name and photograph of a notable figure was linked, often vaguely, with a product to convey the message that if it's good enough for Mrs. Vandergilt it's good enough for you. The Simmons mattress company in 1929 ran a series of advertisements in which appeared an imposing array of many world-famous persons, including George Bernard Shaw, H. G. Wells,

Guglielmo Marconi, Henry Ford and others. Presumably, these personages were urging the public to buy Simmons mattresses, but when and if you read the quotations under the photographs you got something like this:

"I believe in sleep," said Guglielmo Marconi when interviewed by the Princess Carlos de Rohan. "It inspires me."

"I go to bed about nine o'clock every night," says Henry Ford.

". . . sleep. I cannot do without it," says H. G. Wells.

The Simmons advertisements led to an unusual development in London where the famed Harrods department store, shopping place for royalty, asked Shaw, Wells and Arnold Bennett to "lend the influence of their pens to the cause of Business" by writing an advertisement for Harrods. The three writers declined in letters to the management explaining why such a thing was impossible. "Our only paymaster ought to be the reader," Wells wrote. "The writer classes himself with the teachers and the priests and the prophets." Shaw was just as shocked by the idea: "Its acceptance would be the last depravity of corruption in literature . . . like offering the Archbishop of Canterbury a handsome cheque for dropping a recommendation of somebody's shoes or soap into his next sermon." Bennett said that "public opinion in Britain is not yet ripe to approve the . . . scheme." But all three writers gave Harrods permission to publish their letters and the communications, with pictures, appeared in a series of department store advertisements that aroused such admiration among American hucksters that the series was posted on the bulletin board in the New York offices of the J. Walter Thompson Company.

American advertising during the year included a couple of spectacular cigarette campaigns. Old Gold cigarettes introduced the "blindfold test." Week after week, company representatives selected certain groups such as factory workers, club-women, bankers, office workers or newspapermen and asked hundreds of them to participate. Each contestant was blindfolded and then offered four different brands of cigarette, with a sip of coffee in between each one. He was then asked to choose the one he preferred. Such results as appeared in full-page magazine and newspaper advertisements suggested that Old Gold easily led all the rest.

Even greater turmoil was caused in the advertising industry by a Lucky Strike campaign in 1929. George Washington Hill, the irrepressible president of American Tobacco Company and perhaps the most flamboyant of the country's advertisers, originated a new slogan intended to appeal to women and especially women who were worried about gaining weight: "Reach for a Lucky instead of a sweet!" The reaction of pleasantly plump women to this slogan was never accurately ascertained, but the reaction of the sugar and candy industries as well as various church organizations was prompt and vigorous. Although smoking was common among younger women, it had previously been considered "not quite cricket" to admit it in advertisements. Hill's direct appeal to women, including pictures of a girl reaching for a cigarette, not only distressed the sugar producers but provoked the Methodist Board of Morals into a cry of outrage that the tobacco trust was ruining the health of young mothers and "coining the blood of babies into dividends." "Womanhood," added Dr. Daniel Poling, head of the International Society of Christian Endeavor, "is being exploited for trade."

George Washington Hill's company made no acknowledgment of these attacks but apparently the pressure was too great for comfort, and the "Reach for a Lucky instead of a sweet" slogan was permitted to fade out of its advertising. Women, however, smoked more and more in public and in 1929 even the railroads—which had been stubborn about the conduct of female passengers—were forced to drop their rule against women smoking in the dining cars. Everybody, as a matter of fact, seemed to be smoking more cigarettes that year and production increased over 12 per cent to 122,800 million. (A quarter-century later annual production would be quadrupled.) Competition was keen among cigarette sellers and at various times during the year the regular price of fifteen cents a package was slashed to two packages for a quarter and, later, two packages for twenty-three cents in many stores. In New York, Macy's department store, which could afford to give away cigarettes in order to draw customers, went a step further and sold a carton of ten packages for $1.09 or about eleven cents a package.

5

Advertising was currently designed to create the desire to own an electric refrigerator or to learn how to be the life of the party by playing popular songs on the piano, but salesmanship was essential to get the customer signed on the dotted line— even if he could pay only 10 per cent down and $2.98 a week thereafter. Businessmen in 1929 were not forgetful of the fact that there had been a recession in business in 1921 when production was high but when manufactured goods had piled up as inventories to a disastrous point. Since that time production had continued to increase, with the value of finished products and construction materials mounting 50 per cent to thirty-eight billion dollars in 1929. Yet in the last year of the Twenties business was at a new peak of prosperity and businessmen generally were confident of the future.

There were various reasons why new high levels in production did not cause fear of a repetition of the 1921 recession, but one important factor was the high development of the art of salesmanship which kept the goods moving out to customers. By 1929 the era of the high pressure salesman was in full flower. The door-to-door salesman was trained in the art of forcing his way through a half-opened door, of talking fast and furiously and of using ingenuity and subterfuge to make a sale. The sales manager was often looked upon as a slave driver who kept boosting each salesman's "quota" over the record of the previous quarter and making it clear that failure to reach the goal set would jeopardize a salesman's job. Often salesmen gave up part of their commissions or sold vacuum cleaners or electric toasters at a loss in some instances in order to make their "quotas."

James L. Kraft, president of Kraft Cheese Company, wrote an article describing the heartbreaks and disappointments of his early store-to-store sales experiences but pointing out that in less than a generation Kraft salesmen had become a great force in the business world. "I do not suppose anyone else ever planned a cheese business to live through the ages," he concluded, turning a confident eye toward the future. "[But] after we are gone, there will be Kraft salesmen trekking the veldt of Africa, braving the snows of Siberia and battling the superstitions of Mongolia—all earnestly striving to increase Sales."

As a result of pressure selling a large part of the output of manufactured goods was purchased on the installment plan. In 1929, the personal income of the nation—wages, salaries, rentals, dividends, etc.—was about eighty-five billion dollars and manufacturers' sales totaled almost six billion dollars. In the same year, installment credit rose just over three billion dollars. This represented a credit trend that would be intensified a quarter-century later. In 1954, personal income before taxes had increased approximately three and one-half times the 1929 total and manufacturers' sales had increased by four times. But installment credit had leaped up no less than seven times the 1929 total and almost equaled the total of manufacturers' sales.

The attitude of the Republican administration in 1929 was reflected in an official report that suggested there was no limit to the capacity of the consumer to consume. The report was made, after long delay, by an Unemployment Committee which had been appointed in 1921 by President Harding, with the then Secretary of Commerce, Mr. Hoover, as chairman. But instead of reporting on unemployment, as originally intended, the committee reported on the growth of prosperity between 1922 and 1929. Primary production was found to have increased about 17 per cent while manufacturing and transportation had grown 28 per cent. The committee remarked on the nation's

"almost insatiable appetite for goods and services" and emphasized that much of the current buying was Optional Consumption—purchases made from choice rather than from necessity
—or Leisure Consumption, which was money spent as a result
of shortened working hours. The committee also took a whirl
at explaining the United States' "economic balance." Once, it
said, the economy was regulated in jerky fashion by periods of
overproduction followed by a "pause for consumption to catch
up," but now there "is a more even flow from producer to
consumer. . . . In many cases, the rate of production-con-
sumption seems to be fairly well under control. . . . Unemployment due to the business cycle has not been marked."

6

When the gross national product of the United States topped
the hundred billion dollar mark in 1929—$103,800 million in
fact—it looked as if prosperity were here to stay.[3] President
Hoover pointed out that it was within the power of the nation
to abolish poverty and suggested a program that he believed
would lead in that direction.

"Everybody can get rich," declared Democratic National
Chairman John J. Raskob, who was an executive in the great
Du Point and General Motors industrial empires.

"That's rich!" scoffed the Arkansas *Gazette.*

But Raskob found an attentive audience of Americans when
he later explained what became known as the "15X theory."
In the past, it had been customary to estimate that a stock
earning ten dollars a share should sell for about a hundred dollars or ten times its earnings. (This had nothing to do with
dividends paid.) Raskob now seemed to feel that such estimates were out of date and that stocks might reasonably sell at
fifteen times their earnings-per-share. More people were inclined to listen to Raskob than to the Arkansas *Gazette* and a
good many corporation issues were boosted well above their
theoretical worth even on the basis of formula 15X. Mont-

[3] A quarter-century later the national output would be up to $380 billion.

gomery Ward, for example, had earned $14.26 per share, but at one time shot up to 439 which was about thirty times its earnings.

During the Twenties there had been many mergers of corporations that—as *Fortune* magazine said later—had "water in their veins and a gleam of monopoly in their eye." But even corporations overloaded with debt piled up during the 1921–22 recession seemed to be able to pay off fantastic obligations and still make a profit in the first half of 1929. "No slackening of the industrial pace need be anticipated," said Banker J. G. Royale. "Steady continuation of prosperity," echoed *Trade Winds*, the organ of the Union Trust Company in Cleveland. Business, added Lionel D. Edie of the Investment Research Corporation of Detroit, was being run better than ever before and the "new era" guaranteed stability, expansion and unbroken progress. Thanks to improved distribution and plentiful production, a "hand-to-mouth" buying of inventories was being practiced, Edie said, and the current low existing inventories (this was disputed in some quarters and by the end of the year inventories actually amounted to almost thirteen billion dollars) assured that production schedules were being "held in balance with a conception of rationalization of output."

But without regard for such gobbledygook of financial and business experts, it was true that, in addition to aviation, numerous new business horizons were being opened up. Radium offered many possibilities—a new X-ray stethoscope, for example, to detect internal flaws in steel. A marvelous new metal called molybdenum and used to harden steel was coming into use as a result of the success of the Climax Molybdenum Company, which controlled 80 per cent of the world's production. Aluminum production jumped to a quarter-billion pounds in 1929 and new alloys, such as duraluminum were making it possible to build more efficient machines. Big news in the automotive field was the "perfecting" of new pistons with light steel alloy used to replace the heavy iron previously used and with special struts controlling expansion and contraction of the

metal. Synthetic dyes, a new shatterproof glass, quick-drying
paints and a dozen new chemicals from the Du Pont laboratories were helping to transform everyday life in America. In
New York, Harden F. Taylor, vice-president of Atlantic Coast
Fishery, amazed guests by serving lamp chops that had been
prepared by the butcher a year earlier. They were succulent
and juicy, having been frozen for twelve months. The meal
served to dramatize Taylor's new method of freezing fish in
forty minutes as compared to older methods that required from
a couple of hours to a day and a half. The Taylor, Birdseye and
other methods of quick-freezing had made it possible for the
fishing industry, which was in dire straits in the early Twenties,
to make a comeback to the tune of more than a hundred million
dollars in 1929.

As industry expanded and corporations grew larger, the skyscrapers towering over America's big cities grew taller. The
tallest building in the world had been the Woolworth tower
rising sixty stories and 792 feet above lower Broadway, but in
1929 several taller spires were being planned or built. Of these,
the Bank of the Manhattan Company building, 927 feet high,
attracted little attention as compared to the new Chrysler tower
and the Empire State Building in mid-Manhattan. The Chrysler
Building was originally scheduled to be sixty-eight stories and
about eight hundred feet high but its spire was made taller so
that it would be higher than the new Bank of the Manhattan
Company structure. Then along came Alfred E. Smith, who
announced that he had become president of the Empire State
Building Corporation which would erect an eighty-story, sixty-
million-dollar office building rising to a height of a thousand
feet.

The Chrysler Building architects promptly began revising
their blueprints, again increased the height of their spire and
ended up with a building 1,046 feet tall—the tallest in the
world. It held the record only until the Empire State architects
could make a few changes of their own, including a slender
dirigible mast on the roof. When their building was completed

it was 1,472 feet tall and had 102 stories as well as a clear title to the world's record. The dirigible mast proved impractical and the corporation turned down the offer of a cigarette company to transform it into a gigantic replica of a lighted cigarette, which would easily have been the greatest advertising triumph of the century. Eventually the mast was converted into a television broadcasting tower.

The construction of such tall buildings prompted many persons to ask whether there was any limit to the height of skyscrapers and the American Institute of Steel Construction, after two years of study, decided in 1929 that there wasn't. The Institute's experts said to go right ahead and build them higher as far as construction was concerned, but that it might be a good idea to stop at one hundred and fifty stories because of such problems as elevators and increasing costs of the upper stories. They decided, in fact, that buildings of sixty-three to seventy-five stories—depending on the cost of the land—offered the best money-making possibilities. Beyond such heights, the margin of profit on rentals began to diminish and would turn into a loss after the hundred and thirtieth story.

7

Two lively old men put on a lively celebration in 1929 to symbolize the progress of American business over half a century. On his eighty-second birthday, Thomas A. Edison, discoverer of the incandescent electric light bulb, was the guest at Dearborn, Michigan, of Henry Ford, originator of the "tin lizzie" automobile. As a special honor, President Hoover dropped by to congratulate Edison and was himself greeted by a shrill cry from the famous inventor: "Hello, fisherman!"

Deaf but still full of life, Edison re-enacted, step by step, his discovery fifty years before of the electric light at his laboratory in Menlo Park, New Jersey. He attended the dedication of the Edison Institute of Technology and the Museum of American Industries, which Ford had endowed with five million dollars and in which were preserved in good working order many of

Edison's tools and contrivances. En route to the ceremony, the old inventor carelessly walked across a sheet of freshly laid concrete near the entrance, making a pattern of footsteps which Ford delightedly ordered preserved for posterity. He also persuaded Edison to take off his concrete-splattered shoes and add them to the museum's exhibits.

Edison cut a big green and yellow birthday cake and talked to reporters about his latest interest—growing rubber in the Gulf of Mexico area of the United States. With the President and Ford, he rode on an ancient train of three cars, drawn by a still more ancient engine which the automobile manufacturer had had restored. Recalling the days of his youth, Edison acted the role of a "news butcher" on the train, selling newspapers and fruit. Mr. Hoover bought a peach.

It was a memorable and jovial day. But when the man who brought electric light to the world was asked by reporters for some philosophical comment on his life and times, he said: "I am not acquainted with anyone who is happy."

Two other men who had made unusual contributions to the progress of business were in the news in 1929, but only because their careers had come to an end. One was slight, gray-haired Asa Griggs Candler, descendant of a notable family in Carroll County, Georgia; great-grandson of a regimental commander in the Revolutionary War and son of a family whose property lay in the path of Sherman's march through Georgia. When Asa was born, the family was in poor circumstances. As a boy, he studied pharmacy and worked in various drugstores in Atlanta. But he was interested in business and in 1889 he scraped together five hundred dollars to make an investment in the operations of one J. S. Pemberton, who for several years had been peddling locally a syrup to be used in making soft dranks.

Candler, who had observed the sale of the syrupy drinks in drugstores, had an idea that something might be done with the little business and by 1900 he had control of the company. His idea turned out well. By 1929, after he had sold the company for twenty-five million dollars, thirsty customers in the United

States and seventy-five foreign countries were drinking eight million glasses of Coca-Cola every day at five cents a drink. Candler donated more than ten million dollars to Methodist Church organizations, offered to lend thirty million to cotton growers who were cut off from the European market during World War I, advanced almost four hundred thousand to the city of Atlanta when it ran out of funds in 1918 and gave each of his five children five million. He wrote his own funeral notice, with the dates blank, and left precise instructions for burial in full dress clothes.

David Buick, former partner in a Detroit plumbing concern, also died in 1929. At the time Candler was getting control of Coca-Cola, Buick was interested in experiments of Henry Ford and R. E. Olds with the horseless carriage. He sold out his partnership, sold his rights to a bathtub enameling process, raised a hundred thousand dollars and started an automobile factory in a barn with his son as his first employee. Three years later, the first Buick automobile started a sixty-mile trip to Flint, Michigan. It broke down and was towed home by a team of horses but later made the trip successfully. In Flint, Buick raised more money to finance his company. The automobile that he turned out was a good one, but the field was highly competitive and the company struggled along until William C. Durant, head of a carriage concern, became its financial genius and raised a million dollars to launch a campaign that would put Buick across with the public. By 1910 they were making progress but there were quarrels, arguments and misunderstandings, too. David Buick pulled out of the company, taking a block of stock which he soon lost in unsuccessful oil operations in California. He went into Florida real estate and when the Florida boom collapsed, he was broke. At sixty-nine, Buick went back to Detroit and got a job at the information desk in the Detroit School of Trades.

In March of 1929 he was taken to Harper Hospital, suffering from cancer. "I'm not feeling sorry for myself," he said. "It was the breaks of the game. Money means nothing. . . ." When he died, the company that he founded had produced more than two million Buick automobiles and was advertising to the world that "when better automobiles are built Buick will build them."

8

The confident spirit of business did not mean that there were no dark clouds in the sky during the summer of 1929. There were, in fact, a number of unhappy developments in the business and financial world. New England was one of the trouble spots because textiles were the blood stream of New England manufacturing, and textiles were moving out or losing ground. Take just one example. In 1927, the world's largest cotton maker was believed to be the Amoskeag Manufacturing Company on the Merrimac River in New Hampshire. It produced cottons, wools and rayons, boasted eight hundred thousand spindles and twenty-five thousand looms. But in 1929 Amoskeag's annual report showed a loss of almost a million dollars, described local taxes as "a great handicap in such difficult times" and said that the management could only promise to keep the mills running as long as possible.

Wall Street was more concerned by another development in New England, an indication that not everybody there believed the booming stock market was on firm ground. This skepticism was evidenced by the Massachusetts Department of Public Utilities when it refused the request of Boston Edison to split its stock four to one. The company had asked approval on the grounds that everybody was doing it and Boston Edison had to keep up with the times. Mere refusal of permission might have been overlooked but the Department began an investigation of the company's rates because it suspected that speculators had pushed the price of stock up to a level where it was a very poor buy on the basis of earnings. This was an attitude akin to heresy.

The oil industry also had a headache due to overproduction. *The Lamp*, published by Standard Oil of New Jersey, reported that crude oil production in the first six months of 1929 was

forty-five million barrels over the amount that could be marketed and that refiners had produced eight million barrels of
gasoline more than could be sold in the same period. The result
was a price war. Royal Dutch Shell, the great Anglo-Dutch
company headed by Sir Henri Deterding, added to the trouble
by spending forty million dollars to build service stations
throughout many Eastern states, bidding for territory previously
dominated by Socony, the Standard Oil Company of New York.
Both companies began cutting prices, forcing smaller concerns
to do the same, and by September the cost of a gallon of gasoline to the automobile owner was down to sixteen cents, plus
tax.

Late in the summer, the Federal Reserve index of industrial
production was declining. It had been at 126 in June but by
October it was down to 117, and freight car loadings were
sharply off. In addition, there had been a series of bank failures
during the year. In February, the City Trust Company bank of
New York, with deposits of seven million dollars, had gone
under and in July the banking firm of Clarke Brothers closed its
doors on three thousand depositors who had entrusted the firm
with some four million dollars. In the same month, no less than
twenty-five Florida banks closed their doors, partly due to crop
losses caused by the Mediterranean fruit fly, partly as an aftermath of the earlier land boom collapse and partly as a result of
rumors that caused runs on sound banks. The Federal Reserve
System rushed a million dollars by airplane to Tampa to reassure depositors and another four million was sent in by rail
and plane to prevent further failures.

In Minneapolis, W. B. Foshay, once a budding artist from
Ossining, New York, but later known throughout the Middle
West as a skilled financier, had built up a chain of companies
that included utilities, retail drugs, hotels, textiles and flour mills
in thirty states and five foreign countries. The Foshay Building,
modeled after Washington's Monument, was one of the show
places of Minneapolis. But in 1929 Foshay had overextended his
operations and the W. B. Foshay Company, a holding company

with an estimated value of twenty million dollars, went into the hands of a receiver. It was the largest failure in the history of the Northwestern states.

Nor was it just the big operators who were occasionally encountering soft spots in the national prosperity. Down in Louisiana, the editor of the Leonardtown *St. Mary's Beacon* took a long look around the countryside and decided that business wasn't so booming as some people seemed to believe. "Despite the constant reports of prosperity and good business in old St. Mary's county," he wrote editorially,

businessmen find it hard to make collections. Automobile salesmen are over-anxious to make sales. They are compelled by the makers to sell so many cars a month and they exert every known effort to dispose of their quota. Consequently, they sell to people whom they positively know will never be able to pay for their cars. Garage owners today who have put their last dollar into the auto business find that all they have to show for their money is a few automobiles, a tremendous large pile of junk, a book of uncollectible accounts and a book balance looking like the North Pole.

These haphazard examples of clouds in the business sky were not in themselves, of course, indicative of weakness in the American economy as the summer of 1929 faded into autumn. What was really important was a sudden change in the temperature of Wall Street. The soaring stock market suddenly ceased to soar. Blue chip stocks began to sink. There was trouble in the air.

...*two and two make four....*

Nineteen twenty-nine was a year of speculation by Americans . . . but not by Bernard Mannes Baruch, a tall, square-faced, handsome man who had the spirit of a gambler and the common sense of a bookkeeper, who had learned in youth how to cope with a crooked crap shooter and became known in old age as an Adviser to Presidents. "Certainly I have given advice to Presidents," he once told a reporter, "but that doesn't necessarily mean that they took it."

Baruch was born in South Carolina in 1870. His father, an immigrant from Prussia, was a physician who had served with the Confederate Army. Young Bernie was privately tutored, learned German, Hebrew, Greek, Latin and French before the family moved to New York, where he entered City College in 1884. He played baseball, once started a riot by bowling over the opposition catcher trying to stretch a triple into a home run, was struck with a baseball bat and permanently deafened in one ear. He loved to gamble on anything—poker, horse races, cock fights. He took a look at the Colorado mining camps after college, learned how to spot a crooked gambling table and, on one occasion, profited by betting "with the house" until the management caught on and threw him out.

Back in New York, he got a five-dollar-a-week job as messenger for a stockbroker and graduated into selling bonds. When he got his wages up to twenty-five dollars a week he began speculating in the market, gave his father advice on how to invest savings of eight thousand dollars—and the whole sum was lost. Later young Baruch got an eighth interest in the brokerage firm in lieu of a raise, business suddenly boomed and he made a profit of six thousand dollars. By 1897, he had picked up sixty thousand in sugar speculation and bought a seat on the Stock Exchange for nineteen thousand dollars. Then he backed his brother in a theater enterprise that went broke.

Baruch was taking a Fourth of July holiday on Long Island in the summer of 1898 when he heard news of the destruction of the Spanish fleet off Cuba and knew that it meant victory for the United States in the Spanish-American War. It was Sunday and there were no trains running but he hired a locomotive to rush him and his small brother to New York—frightening many drivers of carriages en route as the locomotive roared past unguarded crossings. He rushed to his office, discovered that he had forgotten his keys, lifted his brother up through the transom to unlock the door and then sent off cables to London to buy stocks. The New York Stock Exchange was closed the following day, July 4, but Baruch, his firm and some of his friends made a handsome profit in London.

He made $150,000 in a deal with Thomas Fortune Ryan, lost his shirt plunging in stocks of a liquor concern and had to give up his cabriolet and two grooms. He bought copper and made sixty thousand dollars in 1899. He sold copper short and made seven hundred thousand in 1900. In 1903 he had his own office but no customers and sat at his desk looking out over lower Broadway, reciting Gray's "Elegy in a Country Churchyard." Later, Daniel Guggenheim engaged him to negotiate for certain smelting mills that were also wanted by the Rockefeller interests. Baruch worked out a deal. When Guggenheim asked him what fee he expected, he said a million dollars. The copper king shrugged and paid. Baruch split the fee with two friends who had helped him without expectation of reward. Later, when

Guggenheim was in need of ready cash Baruch walked into his office and handed him half a million dollars.

In 1907, Baruch lost heavily speculating in coffee but he was soon cleaning up on sulfur in Texas and a company in Africa that was formed to produce rubber but found diamonds. He went into the Juneau mine in Alaska when the stock was worthless. It eventually became a bonanza. He was always in the market and he always had at least a million dollars on hand to take advantage of any sudden opportunities. He didn't hesitate to fight the elder J. P. Morgan, but he knew how to make friends, too. He bought Hobcaw Barony in South Carolina, twenty-three thousand acres that included plenty of hunting swamps and woods and the cabins of many Negro squatters who were never asked to move. Many political figures were his guests there. One U.S. senator pompously asked a Negro guide if he knew that the party he was escorting made the laws of the land.

"Yessah," the guide replied, "and if you all don't know more about law than you do about whisky and ducks, Washington is sure in a bad way."

Admiral Carey Grayson was a frequent hunting guest, but he seldom hit anything. One day he finally brought down a bird and, upon picking it up, discovered a tag clamped to its leg on which was printed: "Compliments of B. Baruch."

Baruch's contribution of fifty thousand dollars to the Democratic campaign fund in 1914 led to a close friendship with William McAdoo and Woodrow Wilson, started his reputation as Adviser to Presidents. His nod could get a friend a job in Washington with no questions asked. He was put in charge of wartime purchasing, headed the War Industries Board with wide powers. His threats of government intervention forced the steel industry to lower the wartime price of steel tank plates from an outrageous $22.00 to $3.25. Shortly before the armistice, he was said to have cleaned up half a million dollars in one day by selling short but denied that he had received any inside information from government sources. Brought before a Senate investigating committee and asked his occupation, he replied: "Speculator." There wasn't much left for the committee to prove. Later, he testified that his income was more than two million dollars in the year before the United States entered the war but dropped to six hundred thousand dollars in 1917 because he had sold his holdings at a loss to be eligible for his government job.

In 1929, almost everybody was gambling on the stock market except Baruch, the gambler. He was confident of the future of the country and of business in general. But when he looked at prices on the board and compared them with earnings he didn't need a bookkeeper to tell him that prices were too high. He began unloading stocks and investing in bonds. When in doubt about any investment, he told his friends, the wise thing "is to sell to the sleeping point—the point where you can sleep without worrying." Baruch had no trouble with insomnia in the autumn of 1929.

In later years, he was a distinguished figure in Wall Street and Washington, a kind of "elder statesman" whose career was capped by presentation of the controversial Baruch Plan for control of nuclear weapons at the United Nations after World War II. Frequently, he was a White House caller. Sometimes the President was a guest at Hobcaw. Often Baruch sat on a bench in LaFayette Park opposite the White House, basking in the sun, feeding peanuts to the squirrels and discussing vital issues of the day with political leaders. But, as he grew older, he was often out of step with unorthodox ideas that emanated from the White House.

"Why are you so stubborn when you see the President?" a friend asked.

Baruch looked surprised. "Do you expect me, just for the sake of being pleasant, to say that two and two make six if the government insists on it?" he asked. "I say two and two make four. I'm *very* stubborn about that."

A flyer, a flicker
A twelve o'clock ticker.
What wiped you out so soon?
I should have sold at ten o'clock
I stalled around till noon.

—*The Sucker's Mother Goose*

If we understand the financial situation, the American
business structure is absolutely sound except on certain
weekdays between ten and three.

—HOWARD BRUBAKER

Everything nailed down is comin' loose.
—Gabriel to De Lawd in *Green Pastures*

NOVEMBER, 1929

wall street

If 1929 was a pivotal year, a year of transition, then Wall Street was the pivot on which it swung from one extreme to another between January and November. The stock market was regarded as a kind of barometer measuring economic pressures and as it climbed to record heights—heights that would not be touched again for twenty-five years—optimism mounted. Calvin Coolidge in his last message to Congress had declared that there was never "a more pleasing prospect than that which appears at the present time" and President Hoover had told Americans that there was no good reason why there should not be two chickens in every pot and two cars in every garage. Secretary of Treasury Andrew Mellon asserted as the year started that business was going forward on an even keel and that all was well. The public attitude was expressed in a jingle in the *Saturday Evening Post:*

> Oh, hush thee, my babe, granny's bought some more shares
> Daddy's gone out to play with the bulls and the bears,
> Mother's buying on tips, and she simply can't lose,
> And baby shall have some expensive new shoes!

The rise of the stock market, if not the rise of a "get-rich-quick" fervor among Americans, had begun in 1924 and continued steadily for three years, except for a slight break in 1926. Gains were made slowly but solidly. For example, the prices of twenty-five leading industrial stocks in 1924 were at an average of 106, as reported by the *New York Times.* By the end of 1927, the average was up to 245. This seemed reasonable to most investors because of increasing corporation earnings and the prospect of still greater earnings in the future. It was not until 1928, according to the analysis by Professor John Kenneth Galbraith, that things really began to get out of hand. "The nature of the boom changed. The mass escape into make-believe, so much a part of the true speculative orgy, started in earnest. . . . Men sought not to be persuaded of the reality of things but to find excuses for escaping into the new world of fantasy."

In the past, the stock market had been largely the domain of men supposedly well trained in the intricacies of finance and investment, but 1928 saw hundreds of thousands of amateurs—shoe clerks, taxicab drivers, housewives and chorus girls—rushing to buy a few stocks on margin and hoping that they could double or triple their savings on a rising market. The Exchange ceased to be a market place where quotations supposedly represented the business situation in the nation. For tens of thousands of speculators, it became a device for gambling, for betting on whether prices would go up or down in a comparatively short period. No race track plunger ignored the form charts as recklessly or listened to the tipsters as credulously as did the little speculators. The words of famous financiers and of government officials were studied and interpreted by the newspaper financial writers for the benefit of countless investors who wouldn't and quite probably couldn't read an annual corporation report. The political situation was reviewed by news correspondents in the light of its effect on the stock market.

On one occasion, John J. Raskob's words of optimism about the automobile industry, in which he was a high executive, sent General Motors stock up twelve points in two days and encouraged a general market rise. An announcement that the New York Stock Exchange was investigating trading in Radio Corporation of America caused that issue to lose twenty points in a day, after which it regained fifteen points, lost nine points and then shot up another eighteen points in the next few days. Stock market news was on the front pages of most big afternoon newspapers day after day, and often the closing quotations competed for headline space with the baseball scores in the final street sales editions.

President Hoover, when he was Secretary of Commerce, had been quietly interested in taking some kind of action to dampen down the flames of speculation, but such efforts as he had made (without success) were unknown to the public generally and his election was followed by a new wave of buying stocks. By the beginning of 1929, the *New York Times* industrial average had gone up 86 points to 331 and some experts were beginning to worry—usually in private—about where it would all end. The *Times* financial writer pointed out some strong factors behind the bull market, but added that there were also "distinctly disquieting" developments such as the rash abuse of credit, the abnormal money stringency (call money was at 12 per cent),[1] a "fantastic illusion" regarding the economic future of the nation and a public appetite for "the most reckless stock speculation."

[1] Call money usually was borrowed for very short periods—a week or a month —to finance stock deals, and the high rate did not represent a heavy drain on the speculator. For example, if a speculator borrowed at twelve per cent to buy a stock that stood at one hundred and the stock rose one point during the month his gain would be enough to pay the interest on his loan. Long-term borrowers, on the other hand, were paying only about six per cent.

Such warnings, however, were usually lost in a wave of optimistic statements in the newspapers. The speculators kept right on speculating and the big transatlantic liners such as *Leviathan* established stock quotations boards and brokerage offices on shipboard so that travelers could continue to trade by radio while en route to Europe. The Western Union Telegraph Company announced that it was spending about four million dollars to speed up its stock market ticker service from three hundred characters a minute to five hundred characters a minute. In 1929, speculators would thus be able to get the results of their gambles almost twice as fast as in previous years.

2

Among the various philosophical and religious movements groping for a new approach to man's problems in 1929 was one called New Thought. In a discussion of New Thought at the time, writer Gilbert Seldes noted that the movement had a sound business side because it "advised stockbrokers to become one with God so they might put over big deals." This was one of the few suggestions put forward during the Twenties for any kind of outside influence over operations of the Stock Exchange, a private and self-governing institution that could and did thumb its nose at high government officials. The idea of Congress seriously discussing anything comparable to the Securities Exchange Act of 1934 or the idea of permitting a government agency to say how much margin should be required for purchase of stocks was so outlandish that it never even occurred to the stockbroker of 1929. And if it had occurred to him that by 1954 the government would require a margin of 60 per cent he would have been convinced that the Russian "Reds" had taken over Washington.

The stock market, everybody kept saying in 1929, was not a gamble; it was an investment in the future of America as well as a wonderful way to make money without working. "Now suppose you buy 100 shares of ABC common at par, paying down the full price of $10,000 ($100 a share)," Will Payne wrote in *The Saturday Evening Post.*

When it goes to 200 you have a profit of $10,000. But suppose an accommodating broker lets you trade on a uniform margin of twenty dollars a share and pyramid your profits. Then your original $10,000 buys 500 shares instead of only 100. When ABC reaches 120 you have a profit of $10,000 and buy another 500 shares with that as margin. At 140 you have a profit of $30,000, so you buy an additional 1000 shares. . . . In short your line of stock doubles at every twenty point advance and when ABC common gets to 200 your profit is $310,000 instead of the beggarly $10,000 that you would have made by purchasing 100 shares outright.

Payne, whose article actually was an argument for a conservative approach to investments, pointed out that such a deal as he had outlined in ABC common was virtually impossible in practice and that anybody who tried it was reasonably sure to be wiped out. But the idea fascinated many persons.

And the loquacious John J. Raskob argued in an article in the *Ladies' Home Journal* that practically anybody could make money even if he could save only fifteen dollars a month to invest in good common stocks. In twenty years, he pointed out, such an investor could make around eighty thousand dollars, presumably on the basis of current stock market conditions. Or if that was too slow, it should be possible to speed up the process by creating investment trusts for the small investor, who could then have experts supervising the job of increasing his capital at a rapid pace just as the big experienced investor was already doing with the aid of the rising market.

There were some five hundred investment trusts or investment companies in existence at the time and, although they didn't operate exactly as the poor man's friend along the lines suggested by Raskob, they were estimated to have sold about three billion dollars' worth of securities in 1929. A trust might hold securities in many different companies and thus spread the risk taken by each investor over a wide range, depending on the judgment of its management. Some investment trusts were fly-by-night ventures such as one in Boston that sold twenty-five million dollars' worth of securities to the public and then went into bankruptcy. Some were as respectable as the House of Morgan and, in fact, J. P. Morgan and Company in 1929 sponsored an investment trust whose stock rose from seventy-five to ninety-nine dollars in four days.

The most remarkable trust may have been the Goldman, Sachs Trading Corporation, launched at the end of 1928 by one of New York's most respected investment banking and brokerage partnerships. The Trading Corporation issued one hundred million dollars' worth of stock at a hundred dollars a share, all of which was bought by the parent concern of Goldman, Sachs and Company, which then sold 90 per cent of it to the public at $104. Within a month the stock was up to $222.50 or about twice the assets of the Trading Corporation. In the next six months the Trading Corporation was busy merging with other investment trusts and launching new and larger trusts of its own, with a kind of incredible confidence that the public would continue to buy, which it did. In one month, the concern sold more than a quarter-billion dollars' worth of securities to Americans who wanted to become "partners" in Big Business.[2]

3

Wall Street in 1929 was feuding with the Board of Governors of the Federal Reserve System. Some financial experts believed that the Federal Reserve Board should exert its influence against unbridled speculation by raising its rediscount rate from 5 to 6 per cent and thus reducing the money available for loans to speculators. Wall Street speculators believed the Board should keep its hands off.

The way it worked was this: A speculator buying on margin

---

[2] In 1932, the original stock of Goldman, Sachs Trading Corporation, which sold for $104, was worth $1.75.

had to have, in effect, a loan of money to cover the amount of his investment that he could not put up in cash. Banks lent money to brokers and brokers to customers, with the securities purchased as collateral. Such loans are known as broker's loans or call loans and by 1929 they had increased from about one billion dollars in the early 1920's to almost six billion. And the rate of interest on such loans had gone up from a normal 5 per cent to 12 per cent, a handsome profit to the lenders that attracted money from all over the world to New York. The Federal Reserve System entered into this situation because it lent money to New York banks at 5 per cent interest and the banks could relend the money in the call market at 12 per cent. In view of the high rate in the call market there might legitimately be some question as to whether a moderate increase in the Federal Reserve rate would have any noticeable effect on speculation, but it was a psychological factor that alarmed Wall Street because even at 12 per cent there was a shortage of credit available for the market.

In February there were ominous rumors from Washington, where the Federal Reserve Board had been meeting regularly, that the rate might be raised. It wasn't, but the Board issued a couple of vague warnings that it had "a grave responsibility whenever there is evidence that member banks are maintaining speculative security loans with the aid of Federal Reserve credit." This meant virtually nothing, but it was enough to cause a sharp decline in the market in February and—as the Board continued to meet without making any announcements— a heavy break late in March. The March break, which wiped out many small investors and temporarily sent the rate for call money up to 20 per cent, seemed to demonstrate that a firm stand by the administration might halt the orgy of speculation. But it also demonstrated something else: the possibility of panic. Washington remained hesitant and silent.

In Wall Street, however, there were powerful men who were neither hesitant nor silent. One of them was Charles E. Mitchell, head of the National City Bank, a believer in the boom market and a man who had taken about six million dollars in nine years as personal profits from his bank's participation in stock pools. With a dramatic flourish, Mitchell announced that to combat the market drop the National City Bank would put twenty-five million dollars into the call money market and, in defiance of Washington, would borrow from the New York Federal Reserve Bank to do so. His action virtually checkmated the administration's cautious moves. Senator Carter Glass of Virginia cried out that Mitchell had "slapped the Federal Reserve Board squarely in the face" and demanded, vainly, that he resign as a director of the New York Federal Reserve Bank. Mitchell, however, had made his point. Most commentators of the day praised him for acting boldly to halt the market decline and criticized the administration for meddling in the affairs of Wall Street. The market promptly rallied and advanced into a summer of unprecedented boom.

Everybody was trying to get into the act. Newspapers and periodicals were crammed with explanations and forecasts of the market trend. Books were written on how to beat the stock market. Publisher Bernarr Macfadden launched a new ten-cent stock market newspaper to serve the tens of thousands of speculators who couldn't understand the technical language of the *Wall Street Journal.* Methodist Bishop James Cannon, Jr., who had been speculating through a bucket-shop concern that was later closed, announced that "there is no reason to call a man a gambler because he sells his stock at a profit. If the trading in stocks . . . is immoral, then the church should eliminate from her membership the heads of the stock exchange houses, clerks, bookkeepers, men and women who buy and sell stocks." Financier Bernard Baruch asserted that the economic condition of the world appeared to be "on the verge of a great forward movement" and Professor Irving Fisher of Yale declared that stock prices have reached "what looks like a permanently high plateau." The *Saturday Review of Literature* awarded a prize for poetry to Oscar O'Kelleigh of Pittsburg, Kansas.

The ticker? Yes, is beautiful—lacquer
  does hide the sullen steel.
The tape flows like soft May days that pass
  to summer. . . .
One thing more I'd like to know:
  does time still buy
On margin?

4

Out in Chicago, a slim, silver-haired man was talking about retiring. That was news because the man was Arthur W. Cutten, who had won fame as a Bull in the market, a man who rode the boom and made a fortune doing it. After insisting that he didn't want to talk about his affairs, Cutten pointed out to newspaperman John Gunther of the Chicago *Daily News* that he was almost sixty years old and that he was getting a little tired of market operations. "I've never played at all, never had a chance to do anything but work." Perhaps he would pull out and go to Europe for a while.

His attitude, he hastened to add, was not due to any belief that stocks had been overvalued as a result of five years of rising quotations. "The stock market today is a fair game," he said. "Everybody has a chance. That is, everybody who isn't a fool. But a man can't expect to make money on a stock if he buys without any notion of what the stock is—as so many fools do."

There were a number of experts in 1929 who were ready to agree that there were a great many fools in the market, but when they spoke out against unrestrained speculation they seemed to arouse only scorn and abuse. "When a state of excitement long continued passes into a state of delirium, prices cease to have any relation whatever to values," Garet Garrett pointed out in a mildly worded protest in *The Saturday Evening Post.*

From there on what causes the price line to rise is the power of suggestion acting on the imagination. . . . Is the American ideal of continuous, orderly progress in the production and exchange of wealth [being] promoted or hindered? The answer is not arguable.

Any use of credit that tends inevitably to bring to pass a credit crisis is a liability to the whole economic structure. And ultimately . . . it is the consumer who pays the final bill of loss.

Paul M. Warburg, who had helped formulate the Federal Reserve System, was widely abused when he criticized the Federal Reserve Board for losing control of the money situation, denounced investment trusts as "incorporated stock pools" and said that failure to restrain speculation would eventually lead to a general economic crash. Roger W. Babson, publisher of business and financial statistics, warned the National Business Conference that sooner or later a crash was coming and that it would probably result in "a serious business depression." He was denounced by financial writers as "a chronic bear always predicting disaster" and "always wrong."

In September, the market was bobbing up and down but was at or near a new high at the start of the month. The unevenness was partly blamed on the operation of stock pools in which a group of traders pooled resources to push up the price of a particular stock. The group would start active trading in the stock, thus attracting the interest of speculators all over the country. Rumors would arise that something big was in prospect. If the plan worked out well, the public would begin to buy and the price would shoot upward. Then the pool would sell out and split the profits. A Senate committee later found that thirty-three commercial banks had made some seventy-six million dollars available to stock pools and had themselves participated directly in 454 pools. In 1929, no less than 105 separate stock issues were subject to pool manipulation.

As an example of the gains made by leading stocks, General Electric was up from 128 in March of 1928 to 396 in September of 1929; United States Steel was up from 138 to 261; Westinghouse was up from 91 to 289; American Telephone and Telegraph was up from 179 to 304. But, according to Professor Galbraith's calculations, "the great bull market of the nineteen-twenties came to an end" on September 3. "On some days that followed—only a few—some averages were actually higher. However, never again did the market manifest its old confidence."

5

Americans tend to think back on the Great Bull Market of 1929 as a wild and steady wave of buying orders building up on the shores of Wall Street until it topped the spires of lower Manhattan—and which then collapsed in an instant on Black Thursday, October 24, to inaugurate the Great Depression. Actually, it was neither that swift nor that simple. The house of cards began to give way in September, the day of greatest disaster was October 29 and it was not until November that the market ended—temporarily, at least—its historic nose dive.

There had been a definite if moderate downturn in the national economy in September, with factory production slightly off and steel output declining. Home building was depressed and foreign trade had decreased over a period of several months. The French and other governments were selling United States securities. In England, a huge empire of investment trusts and other enterprises built up by a financier named Clarence Hatry collapsed when Hatry was arrested on charges of issuing unauthorized stock and forging stock certificates. Many British investors were so hard-hit they were forced to sell their holdings in New York.

None of these or other adverse developments at the time was regarded as particularly grave, although some economists would later cite them as warning signals. The fact remains that in September—perhaps merely because tens of thousands of investors began to wonder whether it was time to get out—the stock market lost ground, regained the ground it had lost and then lost a bit more as October rolled around. The second and third weeks of October witnessed a severe decline in prices and, for the first time in six months, the ticker fell behind on selling orders on Monday, October 21. By closing hour, however, there had been some recovery and Professor Irving Fisher made it clear that the net result was beneficial because the drop in stock values had been "merely a shaking out of the lunatic fringe" of speculators. The New York *Sun* remarked that "only the speculators" were hurt and the Troy, New York, *Times* said that the break was "only a local disturbance." Newspaper readers were interested in a report from Chicago that gangsters, who had been called on for additional margin, replied by dynamiting the home of the manager of a brokerage credit department and tossing stench bombs into the offices of three brokerage houses. "A new kind of wolf has invaded LaSalle Street," said a deputy police commissioner. "The racketeer who replies with a bomb when called on for more margin."

The Philadelphia *Inquirer* published an amusing if rather unkind cartoon showing a sneaky little Speculator grabbing for his hat amid a whirlwind of falling stocks, while big, silk-hatted Mr. Business walked undisturbed through the gale with a smug smile on his face—his coattails not even ruffled. "It will take more than this," said the caption, "to blow his hat off!"

On Tuesday, Charles E. Mitchell, who had been on a trip to Europe, returned to New York and again took a bold position by telling reporters that the market was fundamentally sound and would correct itself. The next day the market dropped so rapidly that the *New York Times* industrial average lost 29 points and stood at 384, back where it had been in June.

The next morning—Thursday—the market opened unspectacularly but trading soon became very heavy and prices began sliding. The ticker could not keep up with transactions but, as each new quotation was belatedly printed on the tape, it was evident that the trend was downward. Traders could only guess how far downward because of the delay on the ticker, but some stocks were losing ten points between reported sales. Gradually, as the confusion increased, a kind of hysteria seemed to grip Wall Street and broker's offices all over the country. United States Steel sank from 205 to 190. Montgomery Ward, which had touched a 1929 high of 156, opened at 83 and dropped to 50. Everywhere across the nation the wires carried the message: sell, sell, sell! Little speculators who had saved and borrowed and borrowed again to get in on the free ride to riches were sold out when they could not raise still more cash to cover their margins. Brokers who had urged clerks and housewives and garage mechanics to invest their savings and become partners in American industry were frantically trying to dump stocks at any price. The many thousands of shares thus tossed suddenly into the whirlpool intensified the downward price spiral and at times there were no bids at all for stocks offered for sale.

By eleven o'clock hysteria had turned to panic. In brokerage offices everywhere men and women stared at the quotation boards or the ticker tape screens with horror and fascination. A crowd gathered in the street outside the New York Exchange and stood in silence, waiting for nobody knew what unless it was a sign from the heavens. In Seattle, the secretary of a finance company shot himself. The New York Exchange closed its visitors' gallery to the public, presumably to hide the shrill shouts and frantic scurrying on the floor below. Experts estimated that by one o'clock stock valuations had shrunk some eleven billion dollars.

The story of Black Thursday, however, was not ended. Late in the morning a secret emergency meeting had convened in the offices of J. P. Morgan and Company at 23 Wall Street. The head of the House of Morgan was in Europe but partner Thomas W. Lamont met with Charles E. Mitchell, chairman of the board of the National City Bank; Albert H. Wiggin, chairman of the Chase National Bank; William C. Potter, president of the Guaranty Trust Company; and Seward Prosser, chairman of the Bankers Trust Company. The purpose of the meeting was to get some "organized support" behind the market—the traditional role of Big Banking stepping in to stop a panic.

These men controlled resources estimated at six billion dollars and could influence still greater resources. They were regarded as pillars of the financial community. If any men could save the market, they were the ones to do it and when word of their meeting spread there was a stir of hope along Wall Street. The five bankers, later joined by George F. Baker, Jr., of the First National Bank, decided to form a pool that, without trying to set any firm price level, would seek to steady outstanding securities in a manner that would restore trading on the Exchange to an orderly basis. The amount of money they agreed to put up has been estimated at sums ranging all the way from thirty million to a quarter-billion dollars. But the actual amount perhaps was not of greatest importance. The thing that they were counting on was a bold move that would be of sufficient psychological force to end the atmosphere of panic.

Obviously, this required publicity and by the time the meeting broke up reporters had been tipped off and were waiting at Lamont's door. He set the tone for the rescue attempt by quietly pointing out to the newspapermen, who had been frantically covering the greatest disaster of their careers, that there had been "a little distress selling on the Stock Exchange." But, he added, it had been found that "there are no houses in difficulty and reports from brokers indicate that margins are being maintained satisfactorily." In brief, his remarks conveyed the idea that there was nothing fundamentally wrong and that the bankers were ready to help steady the market.

The main act of the rescue drama then shifted to the Stock Exchange floor. At about half-past one o'clock, Richard F. Whitney, vice-president of the Exchange and well known as a floor trader for the House of Morgan, shouldered his way through the milling crowd of traders until he stood at Post No. 2, where steel shares were traded. In a confident voice, he proposed to buy ten thousand shares of United States Steel at 205, well above the last previous bid. He got only two hundred shares but jauntily left his order for the rest and proceeded on across the floor as the tickers flashed the news of his bid. Within a few minutes, Whitney placed almost a score of similar orders for the purchase of other leading securities representing an investment of probably twenty million dollars.

The effect was electric. Nobody could longer doubt that the bankers had moved in to get things back under control. By the time Whitney left the floor, hysteria was subsiding. Prices began to recover. Steel went up to 206, an over-all gain of almost 2 points for the day. Montgomery Ward climbed from a low of 50 back to 74 and the *New York Times* industrial average for the day showed a decline of only 12 points, representing a tremendous comeback from the midday lows. Montgomery Ward, which had been down as much as 33 points, closed with a loss of only 9 points. J. I. Case actually made a net gain of 7 points. Panic had been halted before it brought complete disaster.

Black Thursday had been quite a day for everybody, and a long one, too. Almost thirteen million shares had changed hands for a new Stock Exchange record. A great many thousands of persons who had been "in the market" were out before sundown. But the forces of darkness had been held at bay by the six determined bankers who threw the weight of their expert financial knowledge, their high positions, their reputations for integrity and their money into the balance at a critical moment. It was, too, as *Time* magazine pointed out, a "financially historic moment for Hero Richard Whitney." [3]

[3] Of the seven heroes of Black Thursday, three were destined to be in the newspaper headlines at later dates for quite different reasons. As disclosed later at congressional hearings in Washington, Banker Wiggin had half a dozen private holding companies, three of which were incorporated in Canada for tax reasons. One company, sentimentally named Shermar Corporation for his daughter, dealt in the stock of the Chase National Bank of which Wiggin was chairman at $275,000 a year. This corporation sold short 42,500 shares of Chase stock between late September and early November of 1929, during which time Wiggin was "participating" in the bankers' rescue pool. The profits on the operation were more than four million dollars. In 1933, Charles E. Mitchell was arrested by U.S. District Attorney Thomas E. Dewey on charges of income tax evasion. Mitchell's income for the first six months of 1929 had been well over a million dollars, but due to some unhappy banking deals and the stock market break he was heavily in debt to J. P. Morgan and Company. He sold 18,300 shares of National City Bank stock to his wife at a loss of $2,872,000, thus wiping out all tax liability for the year. He was acquitted after a sensational trial in New York. Richard Whitney became involved in some disastrous investments in the 1930's and, heavily in debt, posted securities belonging to other persons as collateral for new loans. His company, a bond house, was sus-

6

*Any newspaperman knew in the last week of October that the
stock market was the big news of the day. Financial writers who
had never known anything but the obscurity of the last pages of the
last section of the newspaper were suddenly shifted to page one,
with instructions to explain what was happening in words of one
syllable. The words of famous financiers, however incomprehen-
sible, blossomed into headlines. Reporters haunted the doorsteps
of Big Businessmen in hope of getting a few words that would
clarify the confusion that had enveloped Wall Street.*

*In the midst of this crisis, an enterprising executive of the United
Press Associations remembered his friend, Frank Vanderlip, who
knew the newspaper business from his youth but had become an
important personage in the financial world. In response to a telephone call, Vanderlip agreed to talk to a reporter about what was
going on in Wall Street. But no sooner had an interview been
arranged than a crisis arose in the United Press office. All of the
experienced reporters were on other assignments. Casting a sour
eye around the city room, the editor finally spotted a thin-faced
young man who had just arrived in New York from Indiana and
Colorado and who needed a compass to find his way from Times
Square to the Brooklyn Bridge. He beckoned him to the city desk,
gave him Vanderlip's address and told him to get a move on.*

"But what should I ask him?" the reporter exclaimed.

"Good lord, man! Ask him what all this means!"

*With a heavy heart and a dry tongue, the bewildered reporter
made his way to Wall Street and was ushered into the big, paneled
private office of Vanderlip, an imposing figure who was teetering
back in a chair behind a large desk. In the presence of a man who
stood so close to the center of the frenzied news of the day, the
reporter could only gulp.*

---

pended from the Stock Exchange for insolvency, and the busy Dewey arrested
him on charges of grand larceny. Whitney was sent to prison.

"*Well,*" *Vanderlip said at last, the flicker of a grin beginning to play around his mouth, "what can I do for you?"*

Another gulp. Then the words of the ctiy editor came back.
"*Mr. Vanderlip, what does all this* mean?"

Vanderlip's eyes were twinkling now. "What does all what *mean?" he responded.*

"*Well,*" *the reporter said with a quivering wave of his hand, "all* this. *What does it* mean?"

"*Young man,*" *Vanderlip said, "I'm going to tell you what I think it means, but first I want you to tell me what* you *think it means."*

Trapped, the reporter decided to resort to frankness. "Mr. Vanderlip," he said, "I've only just arrived in New York and I've got only ten bucks to my name as of this moment. I not only don't know what it means—I don't even know what it is! I supposed New York was like this all *the time."*

Vanderlip chuckled. "The fact of the matter is," he said at last, "that I don't know what it means either. My friends don't know what it means and probably nobody knows just what it means. But I told your boss I'd give you a statement, so get your paper and pencil ready."

When the statement was finished, the reporter expressed his thanks and started to leave but Vanderlip stopped him.

"*Young man,*" *he said, "what did you say your name is?"*

"*Smith,*" *the reporter replied. "H. Allen Smith.*[4] *And thank you, Mr. Vanderlip."*

7

On Friday after Black Thursday and during the short Saturday morning session, the stock market was reasonably steady. All over the nation, business leaders competed in issuing statements designed to sooth frayed nerves and President Hoover

---

[4] Smith later wrote many books, starting with *Low Man on a Totem Pole,* in which Wall Street and the stock market were never mentioned.

chipped in with a declaration that "the fundamental business of the country . . . is on a sound and prosperous basis." In Chicago, Eugene M. Stevens, president of the Continental Illinois Bank, said there was nothing in the business situation to "justify any nervousness." Charles M. Schwab said about the same thing in regard to the steel industry and the *New York Times* pointed out that Wall Street was now "secure in the knowledge that the most powerful banks in the country" were prepared to prevent a panic. "Nearly every stock [is] at bargain prices by any modern economic standard," *Time* magazine asserted.

Yet, on Monday, things were worse instead of better. Selling orders had accumulated over the week end as people all over the country decided that the time had come to get out of the market regardless of what the most powerful bankers in the country might do. The price trend was rapidly downward. U.S. Steel dropped to 186 and there was no Whitney to bid it up again. A.T. & T. lost 24 points; General Electric lost 47. The decline was too much for the bankers' rescue pool and, at another meeting, they decided that the best they could do was try to make the downward trend an orderly one.

Tuesday, October 29, was the climax, repeating and intensifying all that had gone before. Sales—often in large blocks of stock—were tremendous from the opening. Prices dropped spasmodically and the bankers' pool fell apart at the seams. Often there were no buyers at all for issues that were offered for whatever they would bring. A messenger boy at the Exchange, according to Frederick Lewis Allen, put in an order to buy White Sewing Machine Company stock (which had been at 11) for one dollar a share, and because there were no other bids, ended up as a stockholder. The ticker lagged far behind sales throughout the morning. At noon the forty governors of the Exchange were secretly asked to gather by twos and threes in the office of the president of the Stock Clearing Corporation. At a nervous, jittery session in the smoke-filled office they discussed closing the Exchange, but finally decided against such action for the time being.

By closing hour, the demoralization of prices seemed to be complete. Steel was down to 167 at one time, but closed at 174. Westinghouse which had once touched 286 was selling at 100. The big investment trusts were dropping just as rapidly. Blue Ridge Investment Trust, an offspring of Goldman, Sachs Trading Corporation, had been at 24 in September but was down to 3 by the close of trading on October 29. Other investment trusts were in still greater trouble and there were no bids at all for their stock. Volume of trading was unprecedented and, when the ticker finally caught up hours after closing time, no less than 16,410,000 shares had changed hands. It was a record that had not been broken or even approached a quarter-century later. When the debris was finally cleared away, the *Times* industrial averages were down 43 points. In effect, all of the gains of 1929 were wiped out in what Professor Galbraith would later describe as "the most devastating day in the history of the New York stock market, and it may have been the most devastating day in the history of markets."

The theatrical publication *Variety* summed up what had happened even more succinctly in its celebrated headline:

WALL ST. LAYS AN EGG!

8

The first weeks of November were notable for a number of gestures intended to serve as psychological shots in the arm for the nation's economy. U.S. Steel declared an extra dividend, as did American Can Company, which also raised the regular dividend. American Tobacco Company declared two-dollar dividends on both common and common "B" shares. Praise was showered on Julius Rosenwald, chairman of Sears, Roebuck, who had offered to cover the margin accounts of his employees; and on Standard Oil of New Jersey, which had announced that it would lend forty-three dollars a share or eleven dollars above the market at the time to employees who had borrowed on their holdings.

John D. Rockefeller declared that "fundamental conditions" were sound—a phrase that was already well shopworn—but he created news by adding that "my son and I have for some days been purchasing sound common stocks." New York bankers boldly increased their loans by about a billion dollars in order to make up in part, at least, for some two billion that had been called in by banks elsewhere in the country during the worst phase of the crash. The Federal Reserve Board, which had belatedly increased the rediscount rate to 6 per cent during the summer, reinstituted the 5 per cent rate. The administration disclosed that taxes would be reduced immediately and President Hoover said he was calling a conference of representatives of industry, agriculture and labor to "organize and co-ordinate a forward movement of business." The Ford Motor Company knocked fifteen to twenty-five dollars off the price of its automobiles.

All of these developments, *Time* magazine noted, "meant Prosperity was expected to remain, meant bigger corporate earnings and dividends, more spending and employing by the rich." On various days, the market struggled to respond to such encouraging prospects but it was a losing struggle. By mid-November the *New York Times* industrial averages, which had once stood at 469, were down to 220. Radio Corporation of America was off from 101 to 28; Montgomery Ward from 137 to 49; Westinghouse from 286 to 102; A.T. & T. from 304 to 197; General Motors from 72 to 36; and U.S. Steel from a September high of 261 to 150. Here was the American dream of easy riches in collapse and, for many, it was stone cold dead in the market place that had held such shining promise of plenty. No statesman, no broker, no banker could utter words that would bring it easily back to life, although not a few would try.

It was more or less correct to say in November of 1929 that Americans didn't know just what had hit them, and it might be added that even a quarter-century later the economists would still be arguing over just what *had* hit them. Immediately after the crash, such experts as Professor Fisher said that the whole disaster was due to "mob psychology" and that "the market went down because it went down." A little later, there arose in some quarters a suspicion that perhaps the mass of small speculators had been taken for a ride; that the market had been manipulated by big operators who made a killing. There definitely were big operators and big pools which executed many coups during the course of the Big Bull Market, but the years have disclosed nothing to support the theory that sinister forces brought about the crash. Too many big operators went down along with the shoe clerks and the housewives. Still another question was whether the stock market collapse started the Great Depression of the 1930's or whether the economic downturn was already on the way, with the crash as a kind of by-product. Looking back over the years, Professor Galbraith wrote in 1955 in *The Great Crash* that the high production of the 1920's had not outrun the wants of the people. But, he added,

business in 1929 was . . . exceedingly fragile. It was vulnerable to the kind of blow it received from Wall Street. Those who have emphasized this vulnerability are obviously on strong ground. Yet when a greenhouse succumbs to a hailstorm something more than a purely passive role is normally attributed to the storm. One must accord similar significance to the typhoon which blew out of lower Manhattan in October 1929.

In any event, the rustle of worthless securities descending on Wall Street during the drab days of November was like a blanket of snow covering the boisterous, roaring Twenties. It was the end of an era. Eleven years after the First World War, America had come to a turning point not just in its economic history but in its way of life. Americans would not soon forget "the crash of '29" because things were going to get worse before they could get better. There would be bitterness but there would also be a drastic change in the public attitude toward government regulation of the securities market. In the dark days ahead, people would say that it must never happen again —and for quite a while, at least, they would mean every word of it.

...all I do is belabor the obvious....

Nineteen twenty-nine was an educational year for Americans . . . for Dwight David Eisenhower, an intense, round-faced man who wanted to join the Navy but ended up at West Point, who felt "conceited" when he dreamed of commanding an armored regiment but ended up as chief of history's greatest armed forces, who hoped that he would never hear the word "politics" again but ended up in the White House. "All I do," he said many times when discussing the reasons for his success, "is belabor the obvious."

In Abilene, Kansas, in 1890 there was nothing obvious about the future of an infant who would be known as Ike Eisenhower. His family had moved west from Pennsylvania with a sect called the River Brethren, dedicated to piety and pacifism. Abilene was hardly more than a raw, dusty frontier town and the Eisenhowers were poor, lived on the wrong side of the railroad tracks, depended in large part on their garden for survival. Yet it would be years before Ike, looking back on his childhood, realized with not a little surprise that he had actually been a "poor boy." He went to the public schools where his quick, broad smile and his athletic prowess won easy popularity. He was the star halfback on the football team and a top-notch baseball player who earned a few dollars playing with semiprofessional teams. "I might have tried to make a career of baseball," he said later, "but professional players in those days were a tough bunch—too rough for me. And there was another reason—I had trouble hitting a curve."

He got a job in the Belle Springs Creamery, working nights, and he took the competitive examinations for an appointment to the Naval Academy at Annapolis. He made the highest score but the senator who had sponsored his candidacy perversely decided to appoint him to the Military Academy instead because he could enter at an earlier date. It was a "cruel blow" but Ike accepted. At West Point, he was a good football player until he injured his knee in a game against Carlisle but he was a rule-breaker and an erratic student who finished a hundred and twenty-fifth in the class of 1915, which included Omar N. Bradley, James Van Fleet, Joseph T. McNarney and George Stratemeyer. It was generally acknowledged, however, that Ike was the best stud poker player in the class.

When the United States went to war in 1917, Captain Eisenhower was married and an instructor in an officers' training camp and, later, the commander of the nation's only Tank Corps training camp. He had six thousand men and one tank, a French model. There just weren't any more of those newfangled weapons available. But by the time the war ended (just as he was being ordered overseas) he had made a reputation as an organizer for which he received the Distinguished Service Medal. The next decade was discouraging for young Army officers. The service was whittled down to a handful of soldiers; promotions were slow and assignments (the Eisenhowers spent three years in Panama) not always pleasant. But for Ike it was a period of hard, continuous study. By 1927 he had been graduated at the head of his class at both the Command and General Staff School and the Army War College.

The boy who grew up on the wrong side of the tracks had learned a great deal more than just military theory. He now knew how to dig quickly to the core of a complicated problem;

how to concentrate on fundamentals. He knew how to control his quick temper. He wasn't hesitant to argue with his superiors, but he knew how to take the edge off impatient words by turning on the broad, boyish grin that was a rare mixture of warm friendliness and impishness. Ike's brain worked fast and to the point, but in a pinch that incredible grin was a secret weapon that could sway a man or a multitude—and often did.

Eisenhower kept on learning. In 1929 General Pershing sent him to France to study the World War I battlefields for the Battle Monuments Commission, and he learned more about what had happened in 1917 and 1918 than the men who had fought there. He returned to join the staff of the Secretary of War and, in the mid-1930's, went to the Philippines where he "studied dramatics" for four years under General Douglas Mac-Arthur. Eisenhower seldom saw eye to eye with MacArthur but he respected the General's military acumen. And in the long, hopeless struggle to build a Philippine national army he learned a great deal about diplomacy, about political chicanery, about the heartbreaks of trying to create a defense force with very little equipment and still less money.

When he returned to the United States at the beginning of 1940, Lieutenant Colonel Eisenhower was well known to service leaders but utterly unknown to the public. The war in Europe had started and the Army was expanding, but Ike was tied to desk work at Fort Lewis at a time when he wanted to be helping General George Patton organize one of the new tank divisions. He might be called a "conceited individual," he wrote to a friend, but he had set his sights high in the hope of commanding an armored regiment. He was offered a job on the War Department General Staff but talked his way out of it in the hope of getting duty in the field, and finally in 1941 he was made Chief of Staff, Third Army, for the big war games in Louisiana. On September 29 he was made a temporary brigadier general and the newspapers misspelled his name as "Ersenbeing." On December 7 the Japanese attacked Pearl Harbor and on December 14, Eisenhower was ordered by telephone to report in Washington to General George C. Marshall.

The Chief of Staff spent twenty minutes describing the situation in the Pacific and then turned to Eisenhower. "What should be our general line of action?" he asked, but what he meant was: have you got what it takes to handle a big job? A big grin would buy you nothing here. This was it. Eisenhower's reply was concise, but covered a lot of ground. He was mindful of our need for allies in what would be a long struggle, of the necessity for single, responsible commands rather than the First World War concept of co-ordinated command, of the vast mechanized forces that would have to be assembled to strike back. "Our base must be Australia," he said, "and we must start at once to expand it and secure our communications to it. In this we dare not fail."

Marshall nodded his satisfaction; he had found his man. Eisenhower began to dream that "when I finally get back to the troops I'll get a division!!!" He never got back. In June of 1942 Marshall instructed him to plan the setup for a joint Allied operation in Europe and, three days after it was completed, ordered him to London as Commanding General, European Theater of Operations. He was fifty-one years old, and still had a lot to learn. "It is a rather lonely life I lead . . . a sense of strain develops entirely aside from the job itself." He argued against Winston Churchill's politically inspired plans to invade the Balkans. "Once this war is won, I hope never again to hear the word 'politics.'" He laughed uproariously when, during the African invasion, he took over operational command of Gibraltar—the Rock, "the symbol of the solidity of the British Empire," commanded by a boy from Kansas! He learned that paper plans didn't always work on the battlefield. "You must be tough." He learned to be tough, and when his anger rose his incredibly blue eyes could turn as cold as polar ice. And when, at last, it was over he foolishly believed his job was finished, too. He wanted no part of politics. He did not even know whether he was a Democrat or a Republican.

But it wasn't that easy. His sense of duty was strongly ingrained. "There is no question in my mind that Nathan Hale accepted the order to serve as a spy with extreme reluctance and distaste. Nevertheless, he did so serve." When the time came, Eisenhower, too, would serve.

*Thus ends this year of publick wonder and mischief
to this nation, and therefore, generally wished by all
people to have an end.*

—SAMUEL PEPYS, 1666

DECEMBER, 1929

end of a decade

The Roaring Twenties didn't end with a bang, but neither did they end with a whimper. In retrospect, it might seem that when bleak December brought a close to that fabulous decade the American people would have been justified in feeling that the end of their world had arrived. But it was not that way at all.

America was not only a powerful industrial nation; it was a young industrial nation. The factories were still there. The coal and iron were still there; the food and the people were still there. What had happened was that big and foolish America had been on a year-long binge; a real, hell-raising binge like Saturday night at the county fair. It had listened happily to the deceptive pitch of the barkers in fancy vests at the entrances to the sideshow tents and had been lured onto the roller coaster by an enticing dame called Lady Luck. Naturally, in the cold gray dawn of December, America woke up with a supercolossal hangover that was all wool and a yard wide. It was painful and it made a guy feel foolish. There wasn't any use reaching for your pocketbook because you knew it was gone. But this was another day. It was time to mutter "Never again!" and to get back on the job. The headache would go away. The shaking hand would steady. Boy! Will you mix me a bicarb, please?—and say! just put it on the tab until payday, will you? Yeah, I'm a little rocky this morning. But come to think of it—we had a helluva time while it lasted!

After the first shock had worn off, most Americans were able to enjoy the many jokes and wisecracks that grew out of the market collapse and the confusion attending it. Eddie Cantor, who had been planning to live on his investments, wrote a book called *Caught Short! A Saga of Wailing Wall Street* that had everybody in stitches. He described himself as a comedian, author, statistician and victim, and dated his tome 1929 A.C., meaning "After the Crash." Almost everybody got a good laugh out of the story of one speculator whose margin account was exhausted and who was sold out twice in one day by his rattled broker.

Groucho Marx, according to a tale related by Margaret Case Harriman, had invested in a number of stocks on the advice of friends. When the crash came, he seized his list of investments and rushed to the office of his attorney, Morris Ernst, for advice. Ernst checked the list over and discovered that most of Groucho's stocks had taken a nose dive.

"Where did you get this recommendation?" he asked Groucho, pointing to a stock that had dropped fifty points or so.

"That one was suggested by my friend, Bernard Baruch."

"What about this one—down from 122 to 58?" Ernst continued.

"Well, that was on the recommendation of Gerard Swope."

At last Ernst found one item on the list that had not suffered disaster. It was a stock that had lost only one point in the crash.

"Where on earth," he exclaimed, "did you get *that* tip?"

"Oh, *that*," Groucho replied. "I got that one from a wardrobe woman in the Shubert Theater in Chicago."

There also were some unusual tales drifting back from foreign lands, especially from France where many American artists, writers and loafers had more or less settled down to live on their paper profits. A large percentage of these expatriates suddenly found themselves broke after the crash and unable to buy even a third-class passage back to the United States. Some of them went to work and others sold their furniture and clothes. One enterprising group of Americans who had been living high in Paris organized a parade of their sports automobiles down the Champs Elysées, each car marked with a "for sale" sign and a price that the owner intended to use to pay his way back home. In a dispatch from Constantinople, an American correspondent reported what Turkish newspapers were saying about the aftermath of the crash in New York. One Constantinople newspaper informed the Turks that New Yorkers were in grave distress and living mainly on bread, cheese and cabbage, being unable to afford anything else. They had no table linen, the story added, although it failed to make clear whether the linen had been seized by creditors or was being held by the laundries pending payment of overdue bills. As a result, most New Yorkers were said to be eating off old newspapers and not a few, presumably evicted from apartments, were living on the roofs of skyscrapers. This was so amusing that the *New York Times* printed the story on its front page.

A few gags and exaggerations were also dreamed up by New Yorkers for their own amusement, including some rather grim ones. There was, for example, the story of the midtown hotel clerk who asked each new arrival whether he wanted a room "for sleeping or for jumping." Another concerned the two men wiped out in the market, who had leaped hand-in-hand from a high roof. They had held a joint stock account.

An ability to laugh, however, did not mean that all was lightness and fun. Many thousands of men and women who had happily retired to live—some meagerly, some in great comfort—on their investments now discovered that they had to go back to work. Some of them never were able to find jobs. Some of them made new fortunes. In Indiana, a prominent manufacturer who had retired in order to complete his interrupted college education saw his investments so depleted by the Wall Street collapse that he had to return to business. Two years later he had restored his finances, again returned to school and later became a college president, which had been his goal for years.

Alexander Woollcott's biographer estimated that the New York critic had about a hundred thousand dollars spread thinly on margin in September, but found himself seven thousand in debt in December. Woollcott audaciously raised his prices for contributions to magazines, became perhaps the highest-priced book reviewer in history and was soon back on his financial feet. "In the empty, silly, noisy years which immediately preceded the Wall Street crash," he wrote later, "I used to get hot tips on the market from big shots. I suppose they rather fancied themselves in the role of Maecenas, giving a financial lift to someone more literate (and therefore more incompetent and idiotic) than themselves. No good ever accrued from these tips except the potential benefit which anyone can experience by merely losing money."

A wealthy man who lived on a large estate near New York told his neighbors in November that he had lost four million dollars in the market crash. He fired three gardeners, five stablemen, the first and second butlers, the assistant chauffeur and various other employees, including the pastry cook. Then he gave his neighbors the impression that he was looking earnestly for a high window, suitable for jumping. While putting his affairs in order, however, he discovered that he had carelessly overlooked some three million dollars that was in safe investments. This prompted him to cease worrying about a high window, but he cautiously refused to rehire the discharged servants except for his beagle trainer.

Few were so lucky or so absent-minded. News dispatches from all over the country told of suicides which were—often inaccurately—blamed on the crash. Two brokers in Philadelphia, a grain dealer in Chicago, a utilities president in Rochester, New York, a civil engineer in Scranton, Pennsylvania. And not a few in New York, including James J. Riordan, a man of considerable political influence and president of the County Trust Company, which, incidentally, was in sound condition. The fact that newspaper reporters naturally checked into all suicides to determine whether they could be linked in any way to the market tended at times to give the impression that Wall Street was a dangerous place to walk because of falling bodies. This false impression was exploded later by statistics showing that there were only forty-four suicides in all of Manhattan between mid-October and mid-November as compared to fifty-three in the same period of 1928. The same was generally true for the United States as a whole. There were, for instance, more suicides during the summer months of 1929 when the market was booming than during the months of the big crash.

2

The first snow of the season had hardly covered the White House grounds when President Hoover began a series of conferences with industrial, financial, agricultural and labor leaders, designed to reassure the public as to the economic future of the nation. "Words are not of any great importance in times of economic disturbance," the President said. "It is action that counts." Sitting behind his big desk, smoking a cigar, Mr. Hoover took the position that there had been no business recession but that there was a threat of one. As to the market collapse, he believed that: "The long upward trend of fundamental progress gave rise to overoptimism as to profits, which translated itself into a wave of uncontrolled speculation in securities, resulting in the diversion of capital from business to the stock market, and the inevitable crash." By the first week in December he believed that "we have re-established confidence."

Most of the leaders who attended the White House conferences seemed to agree with him. Henry Ford snapped out the opinion that the market collapse was due to "a serious withdrawal of brains from business" and recommended "reducing prices to the level of actual value" as well as increasing wages.

He told the President that he was going to boost wages. In general, the industrial leaders told the President that they would not cut wages if the unions would take a co-operative attitude. Other conferees promised the President to help in stabilizing economic conditions and devising means for increasing the nation's purchasing power. Thirty-five public utility officials, led by Owen D. Young, pledged almost two billion dollars to the President's program for stimulating industrial activity, particularly in regard to expansion and new construction.

Mr. Hoover also sent telegrams to the governors of all states urging them to inaugurate "energetic, yet prudent" public works programs to relieve unemployment. As Christmas approached, the President was hard at work and appeared to be making progress. The only sour note came one afternoon when a group of thirty-five young men and women appeared on Pennsylvania Avenue and began marching back and forth in front of the White House, carrying big placards that said:

DOWN WITH HOOVER

THE HOOVER BUSINESS

CONFERENCE IS A DECLARATION

OF WAR ON THE WORKING MASSES

They hadn't marched very long, however, before White House and city police appeared and arrested them on charges of parading without a permit. The paraders jeered and sang the Communist "Internationale" as they were led off to the police station. As soon as Mr. Hoover heard about the arrests he ordered the demonstrators released, saying that "the President considers that the misguided youths calling themselves Communists . . . should be released and sent to their parents. He does not believe any such discourtesy seriously injures the Republic and a night in jail is only doing them the favor of giving them a cheap martyrdom." To most Americans, this seemed a sensible way of dealing with such crackpot demonstrations.

3

The year 1929 was "the year of Mighty Change" in the opinion of Joseph V. Stalin, the Communist dictator of Soviet Russia. Stalin had been ill for some weeks but censorship concealed all details of his illness. There were frequent rumors that he was dying and at public ceremonies the people occasionally cried out for government officials to say whether the Man of Steel was sick or well. They got no replies, but at last Stalin himself appeared unexpectedly at a celebration in Moscow and was greeted by thunderous cheers. He was thin but his smile was benign. The dictator could well afford to smile. In 1929, he had succeeded in expelling from Russia his ancient enemy, Leon Trotsky. And then had come the gratifying news that the capitalistic nations had been shaken to the core by the Wall Street crash. Hailing "the year of Mighty Change," Stalin declared that "we are attacking capitalism all along the line and defeating it. Without foreign capital we are accomplishing the unprecedented feat of building up heavy industry in a backward country. . . . When we have industrialized the Soviet Union and set the peasants to driving tractors . . . we shall see which country can be called backward and which the vanguard of human progress."

As viewed from the towers of the Kremlin there seemed, indeed, to be a mighty change in the face of America in December of 1929. Yet the change was not easy to see if you were walking on Main Street in Sauk Center, Minnesota, on Bourbon Street in New Orleans, on Grant Street in Pittsburgh or on Fifth Avenue in New York. At the newly opened Fifth Avenue jewelry store of Black, Starr and Frost-Gorham, Inc., where the interior was sixteenth-century Italian Gothic, an exquisitely matched pearl necklace was confidently offered to Christmas shoppers for seven hundred thousand dollars.

Christmas shopping in general was at a brisk pace and in volume exceeded the sales records of 1928, although it was noted that the greatest increases in buying were in chain stores featuring low-priced goods. In the Middle West retail sales were "considerably" higher than in the previous holiday season and one Chicago department store sold more than a million dollars' worth of goods in a single day despite a snowstorm. "Prosperity," said the New York *Herald Tribune*, "is still with us, though it is not hysterical prosperity." The *Herald Tribune's* chart of a hundred stocks, which had shown an average of only 155 on November 14, was back up to 177 in early December as the market made a slight recovery. U.S. Steel, which had fallen to 150, was back to 171 by the end of the year; A.T. & T. was up from a low of 193 to 222; General Electric rose from a low of 168 to 243 and General Motors from 33 to 40.

"A general price rise ends 1929 stock trading, with Wall Street moderately bullish for 1930," the *New York Times* reported.

In Chicago, talk about the market collapse had given way to sharp argument over how to play bridge. There were two basic theories of contract bridge. One was known as the Vanderbilt convention, a bid of one club to oblige your partner to declare strength or weakness; the other was the new forcing system, in which the initial bidder, seeking a stronger indication of his partner's strength, bid two in any suit. In a big room on the mezzanine floor of the Drake Hotel, some three hundred leading American bridge players battled morning, afternoon and night for four days to decide who were the bridge champions of the nation. Prominent among half a dozen prize winners were Ely Culbertson and his wife, Josephine, proponents of the "forcing" system and perhaps the best-known bridge team in the United States.

In Philadelphia, the economic situation had failed to make any impression on the artistic temperament of the famed conductor of the Symphony Orchestra. Interrupting an audience that was applauding him, Leopold Stokowski declared: "This strange habit of beating the hands together is meaningless and, to me, very disturbing. We try to make sounds like music. Then you make this strange sound called clapping. I don't know where it originated but it must have been back in some dark forest in medieval times." He turned abruptly back to the orchestra and the audience delightedly clapped hands again.

In Hollywood, financial disaster was completely ignored by Warner Brothers who released a new motion picture called *Is Everybody Happy?* starring one of "jazz's first jazzbos," Ted Lewis. In New York, a five-foot rattlesnake was discovered crawling unhappily around a subway station and was killed by a policeman, who threw it in an ash can. At the University of Chicago, Dr. Sydney I. Falk announced discovery of *polymorphous streptococcus*, the germ that causes influenza. It looked like "a microscopic chain of unmatched beads which a child had strung." In New York, the American Birth Control League held its first general conference in five years under sponsorship of such well-known citizens as Mrs. Thomas Lamont, Mrs. Eleanor Roosevelt, Norman Thomas and Harry Emerson Fosdick. Mrs. Margaret Sanger, who had resigned as president in 1928, was replaced by Mrs. Frederick R. Jones, wife of an insurance economist. The League was informed that there were only twenty-nine centers in the United States, most of them under disguised names, where birth control information was made available. In the New York *Journal*, readers were urged to join in a new circulation-building stunt by writing a letter on "Why I want to go to Paris"—the winner, whether a man or a woman, to be taken to Paris personally by the star of a current motion picture, voluptuous Irene Bordoni.

One of the most remarkable results of the big crash, however, may have been the fact that John Davison Rockefeller, Jr., was left "holding the bag" in a huge New York real estate deal. Rockefeller, a violinist of some skill in his youth, and a number of other wealthy men had been interested for some time in efforts to build a new home for the Metropolitan Opera Company. They agreed that a real estate development with the opera house as its center would not only enhance the beauty of Fifth Avenue in the lower Fifties, but that the development could make the opera company self-supporting in the future

As the first step in this agreement, Rockefeller leased a run-down area bounded by Fifth Avenue, Forty-eighth Street, Sixth Avenue (later the Avenue of the Americas) and Fifty-first Street, paying a rental of over three million dollars a year under a lease which, with options, runs until 2015.

The lease was no sooner signed, however, than the Wall Street collapse frightened the sponsors of the development plan and they hastily took cover, leaving Rockefeller clutching a bag that contained some of the most expensive rock and 229 of the most dilapidated old brownstone houses—many of them harboring speakeasies—in New York City. Rockefeller made no attempt to get out from under a deal that would lose approximately four million dollars a year, including taxes of one million. But there was only one alternative open to him and that was to defy the Wall Street disaster by constructing a commercial office building development on the site. Ten years and $125 million later, Rockefeller Center's fourteen towering office buildings were a vast commercial center, one of the nation's most spectacular attractions for sight-seers and an impressive monument to the builder's faith in the future.

4

For better or for worse, Americans who died in 1929 had never heard of jet airplanes, the "sound barrier," brain washing, the Iron Curtain, split-level or ranch-type houses, Marilyn Monroe, polaroid cameras, deep freezers, guided missiles, plastic toys, radar, Dave Garroway, the Bloody Mary cocktail, Dacron, Gina Lollobrigida, jive, bulldozers, the Works Progress Administration, scrabble, Senator Joseph R. McCarthy, naphtha fire bombs, V-8 automobile engines, the Kaiser automobile, Kleenex, Grandma Moses, contour furniture, electric typewriters, color television, Frank Sinatra, technocrats, picture windows, chlorophyll tooth paste, Mary Martin, Cellophane, economic royalists, eggheads, foam rubber, guilt by association, the Duke of Edinburgh, the withholding tax, drive-in movie theaters, bobby-soxers, toreador *pants for women, Joe DiMaggio, the $64,000 question, indirect lighting for the living room, Fiberglas, automatic transmissions for the family car, Richard M. Nixon, a vaccine for infantile paralysis, Cinerama, gobbledygook, Fala, sulfanilamide as a germ-killer, Katharine Hepburn, antihistamine, the escape from Dunkirk, the New Look in fashions, Mrs. Wallis Simpson, electric razors, the United Nations, frozen vegetables, the four-minute mile, formica, Nashua, bubble gum or the atom bomb.*

5

Anybody who looks back to 1929, the eleventh year after the First World War, cannot easily avoid the temptation to compare what happened then to the state of the nation in 1956, the eleventh year after the Second World War. The idea that "history repeats itself" was a hoary proverb in Plutarch's time and doubtless no more respected by historians then than it is today. The changes that have taken place in American life in the last quarter-century have been tremendous and will tremendously influence the future. Yet, there is a certain fascination in the similarities to be found in a study of events on the eve of 1929 and on the eve of 1956.

Economically, the United States was moving toward new peaks in 1929 after a fairly steady rise since 1918. Almost the same thing occurred between 1945 and the beginning of 1956: production of industrial goods went up 30 per cent; employment rose by over 20 per cent; over-all consumer credit more than tripled and reached an unprecedented peak of more than thirty-four billion dollars; personal income in the nation increased 75 per cent to more than three hundred billion dollars. Furthermore, the Stock Exchange was booming in 1955, and the number of investors had increased to around eight million or five times as many as in 1929. The earnings of many corporations broke all past records and General Motors profits rose above one billion dollars.

At the same time, home building showed signs of tapering off in 1955 as it had done in 1928 and 1929 following a postwar boom. And the position of the farm population was strikingly reminiscent of 1929 as net farm income per capita decreased from more than seven hundred dollars in 1948 to approximately six hundred dollars in 1955. There were signs of discontent with the Republican administration in some agricultural areas—also reminiscent of 1929—and the Democrats were making efforts to capitalize on the situation.

The similarities did not end there. As in 1929, the great problem in international affairs was disarmament and again the experts were saying—perhaps more accurately this time—that another world war would mean the end of our civilization and possibly the utter destruction of the great population centers around the globe. At the end of the first decade of the Atomic Age in 1955, an article in *Harper's Magazine* asserted that "we can be quite certain that a major unrestricted war would begin with a disaster for us, as well as for [the Russians], of absolutely unprecedented and therefore unimaginable proportions. . . . A future war resulting in mutual annihilation is far from being impossible." Along the same line, Dr. Albert Einstein had remarked: "I don't know what weapons will be used in World War III but I can predict what weapons will be used in World War IV—stones."

And in 1956, the two powers that had emerged in the decade after the First World War were dominant in international councils. Soviet Russia again had survived a great war and a series of internal conflicts within the ruling Communist party, and had achieved a position of greater influence than ever before in world affairs. The United States again had thrown its weight into the balance to sway the outcome of a world war and had emerged far more powerful and far more willing to accept the burden of international leadership. And, incidentally, Admiral Byrd was again heading an expedition to the Antarctic.

These parallels and many others—traffic jams, for example!— could be regarded with interest as 1956 rolled around without necessarily offering any clues to the future. The differences between 1929 and 1956 were important, too—possibly more important than the similarities. In the last quarter of a century, the government's power to deal with economic perils had been vastly strengthened and government in general had become more alert to the necessity for drastic action in an emergency. In October of 1955, just after the stock market had suffered the sharpest one-day decline since 1929, the chairman of the President's Council of Economic Advisers, Arthur F. Burns, said that the nation's business was "poised on a high plateau with neither the threat of inflation nor of recession . . . ever very distant. We must be alert. . . . The only rigidity that we can afford is the principle that the best way to fight a recession is to prevent it."

By 1956, the machinery for maintaining economic stability had been greatly strengthened. The powers of the Federal Reserve Board had been increased. Purchase of stocks on margin could be prohibited and the Securities and Exchange Commission could enforce important controls on market manipulation and on conditions that encourage speculation. Furthermore, the distribution of national income was more equitable than in 1929, the working man's living standard had been raised by a substantial margin and the social security system had become an accepted part of the economic fabric, as had some form of government support for farm prices.

Nobody could know how well or how poorly these changes would serve to protect the nation's economic balance until the next great emergency arose, whatever or whenever that might be. It had not been easy in 1929 to foresee what lay ahead, to guess whether the country would move into an era of unparalleled prosperity or into the most desperate depression in its history—not any easier than it would be in 1956 to forecast the future. But it would always be true that a great many Americans were willing to try.